Vol. XC

Bible Expo
and Illuminator

FALL QUARTER September, October, November 2018

Beginnings

UNIT I: The Beginning of the World

UNIT II: The Beginning of Human History

UNIT III: Cataclysm and a New Beginning

Editor in Chief: Todd Williams

"CHRISTIAN LIFE SERIES"
UGP
UNION GOSPEL PRESS

Edited and published quarterly by
THE INCORPORATED TRUSTEES OF THE
GOSPEL WORKER SOCIETY
UNION GOSPEL PRESS DIVISION

Rev. W. B. Musselman, Founder

Price: $4.65 per quarter*
$18.60 per year*
*shipping and handling extra

ISBN 978-1-59843-679-2

LOOKING AHEAD

Critics often begin their attacks on the Bible with the book of Genesis. In their minds, if this book can be discredited, the rest of the Bible is undermined. This quarter's studies are in Genesis and are important to us because of this attitude. We begin at the beginning of the world in the first unit. Lesson 1 describes the first three days of Creation. This includes light, day and night, the firmament, the appearance of dry land, and vegetation.

Lesson 2 covers the creation of sun, moon, and stars; fish and fowl; and land creatures on days four through six. Lesson 3 is a study of the creation of people and the establishment of the seventh day as a day of rest. Lesson 4 is the first lesson in the second unit, which details the beginning of human history. This lesson focuses on the preparation of the Garden of Eden as Adam's dwelling place. Lesson 5 describes Adam's placement in that garden and the creation of Eve to be his helper. It also establishes the beginning of marriage.

A major turning point in mankind's history is studied in lesson 6, where the tempter shows up and Eve listens to him and follows his tempting thoughts. Adam follows her lead, and both of them disobey God's command about the tree of knowledge of good and evil. In lesson 7, we learn the severe consequences of their disobedience, with the serpent, Eve, and Adam being addressed by God and thoroughly chastened. This introduction of sin into God's creation leads to the murder of Abel by Cain in lesson 8.

The third unit takes us to a cataclysmic climax of the growth of the sinfulness that followed, but it leads to a new beginning with Noah. This unit reveals to us the greatness of God in His dealings with mankind. Lesson 9 is a description of the sinfulness that spread throughout the entire creation, along with an introduction to Noah, who remained righteous in a wicked world. In lesson 10, we see how God prepared a special way of preserving Noah in the coming judgment.

Lesson 11 details the entrance of Noah, his sons, his wife, his sons' wives, and the animals into the ark he had built. The Flood occurs in lesson 12 and is described as the means of the destruction of every living thing on earth. This was not the end, however, and lesson 13 is a study of the new beginning after Noah exited the ark.

—*Keith E. Eggert.*

A Simple Explanation

JOE FALKNER

"Dad, where did I come from?"

It was a simple question but one for which the father thought he had a few more years to prepare an intelligent and age-appropriate answer. The room seemed suddenly void of oxygen as he tried to speak. His face turned red; sweat formed on his brow. The words that managed to escape his lips made no sense to the son who was convinced his dad knew the answer to all questions foreign and domestic.

As his dad took a deep breath, the boy continued, "You know, Dad, Billy came from Ohio. Where did I come from?"

The question of our origin and purpose in existence has perplexed mankind from the beginning, yet the One who created us simply and definitively answered the question without blushing. He stated the facts and gave no explanation. "In the beginning God created the heaven and the earth" (Gen. 1:1). However, His answer enrages scientists and skeptics who deny His existence. So, instead of accepting a simple answer to the question, scientific journals spew forth theories of big bangs, spontaneous generations, biopoiesis, and panspermia. (Do not be alarmed if you do not know the meaning of those theories, for those who propose them do not seem to understand them, either.)

The Apostle Paul blasted worldly wisdom with his declaration in I Corinthians 1:27-29: "But God hath chosen the foolish things of the world to confound the wise; and God hath chosen the weak things of the world to confound the things which are mighty; and base things of the world, and things which are despised, hath God chosen, yea, and things which are not, to bring to nought things that are: that no flesh should glory in his presence."

It is understandable that secular scholars without a relationship with the Creator would deny a divine origin to the universe. It makes little sense, however, that Christians would accept such views when the Bible clearly teaches that God created all that exists. Rather than defending the simple biblical account of God's design of the universe and His creation and purpose for man, many Christians today believe the biblical account on Sundays, but they turn to the so-called "scientific" answers Monday through Saturday.

As a high school student, I followed that same belief scenario. I believed the Creation account only when I was in church. At that time, I had no problem with the obvious dichotomy in my mind. I was thrilled with science and planned to major in some branch of it, probably geology. The desire to get ahead in my scientific knowledge led me to seek out answers from the books in the city library.

I wanted to know how to date the many rocks and fossils that were collecting in my room, lining my windowsill, and scattered across my bookshelves. I picked up a book on geology. It had to have the right answers because it was so thick. I still remember reading the answer to my questions. On the left-hand side of the page, I read, "The fossil is dated by the layer that it is in." That

(Editorials continued on page 186)

Scripture Lesson Text

GEN. 1:1 In the beginning God created the heaven and the earth.

2 And the earth was without form, and void; and darkness was upon the face of the deep. And the Spirit of God moved upon the face of the waters.

3 And God said, Let there be light: and there was light.

4 And God saw the light, that it was good: and God divided the light from the darkness.

5 And God called the light Day, and the darkness he called Night. And the evening and the morning were the first day.

6 And God said, Let there be a firmament in the midst of the waters, and let it divide the waters from the waters.

7 And God made the firmament, and divided the waters which were under the firmament from the waters which were above the firmament: and it was so.

8 And God called the firmament Heaven. And the evening and the morning were the second day.

9 And God said, Let the waters under the heaven be gathered together unto one place, and let the dry land appear: and it was so.

10 And God called the dry land Earth; and the gathering together of the waters called he Seas: and God saw that it was good.

11 And God said, Let the earth bring forth grass, the herb yielding seed, and the fruit tree yielding fruit after his kind, whose seed is in itself, upon the earth: and it was so.

12 And the earth brought forth grass, and herb yielding seed after his kind, and the tree yielding fruit, whose seed was in itself, after his kind: and God saw that it was good.

13 And the evening and the morning were the third day.

NOTES

The First Days of Creation

Lesson Text: Genesis 1:1-13

Related Scriptures: Job 38:1-11; John 1:1-10

TIME: unknown   PLACES: Heaven and earth

GOLDEN TEXT—"The earth was without form, and void; and darkness was upon the face of the deep. And the Spirit of God moved upon the face of the waters" (Genesis 1:2).

Introduction

We cannot overestimate the importance of our belief in Creation. Since it is entirely miraculous, this is one of the first areas of biblical teaching that comes into question by those who wish to reject the Word of God. If the account of Creation is credible, the rest of the Bible must also be considered as valid and worthy of being accepted.

For those who accept the literal, historical, grammatical method of biblical interpretation, the account of Creation serves as a solid foundation for accepting all the Scriptures. Any theory or approach that weakens scriptural authority must be rejected.

For example, some view the days of Creation as long eras of time. Theistic evolutionists use this approach to explain the alleged geologic ages, but believing in creation and evolution at the same time produces confusion about God's work. We will accept the days of Creation as the twenty-four-hour solar days that Scripture most naturally appears to describe.

LESSON OUTLINE

I. **DAY ONE OF CREATION—** **Gen. 1:1-5**

II. **DAY TWO OF CREATION—** **Gen. 1:6-8**

III. **DAY THREE OF CREATION—** **Gen.1:9-13**

Exposition: Verse by Verse

DAY ONE OF CREATION

GEN. 1:1 In the beginning God created the heaven and the earth.

2 And the earth was without form, and void; and darkness was upon the face of the deep. And the Spirit of God moved upon the face of the waters.

3 And God said, Let there be light: and there was light.

4 And God saw the light, that it was good: and God divided the light from the darkness.

5 And God called the light Day, and the darkness he called Night. And the evening and the morning were the first day.

A dark beginning (Gen. 1:1-2). Upon reading the first three words of this text, one might be tempted to ask, the beginning of what? The statement takes us back to the first act of Creation, not to a time prior to that. This is the beginning of the cosmos, not the beginning of all things, since God has existed in eternity past and at some point in that past created the angelic world. Verse 1 is, therefore, a summary statement of all that occurred during the six days of Creation.

Genesis 1:1 also sets forth God's existence, but it does not delve into the how or why: "In the beginning God." The biblical view of creation does not have to be seen as in conflict with science, but it does conflict with any worldview that sees creation as apart from God. It was God the Creator who began the universe as we know it. The phrase "the heaven and the earth" is a figure of speech called a merism, in which two extremes are mentioned but the intent is to include everything in between.

The initial earth was formless and empty—little more than a dark abyss. God apparently created a mass to which He then gave meaning, order, and productivity. There was a watery covering over this mass, and it was over this that the Holy Spirit was hovering. This indicates that further creative activity was about to begin. Nothing was a product of chance or evolution. It was a definite process originating from God; furthermore, the entire Trinity was involved.

John later wrote about Jesus, God's Son, "In the beginning was the Word, and the Word was with God, and the Word was God. The same was in the beginning with God. All things were made by him; and without him was not any thing made that was made" (John 1:1-3). Paul wrote, "For by him were all things created, that are in heaven, and that are in earth, visible and invisible, whether they be thrones, or dominions, or principalities, or powers: all things were created by him, and for him" (Col. 1:16).

The introduction of light (Gen. 1:3-4). Each day of Creation began with a command from God, as seen in the word "let." The first command was "Let there be light," followed immediately by the result: there was light! This pattern is typical for what happened each day: after every command comes the report that it happened. In most cases this was followed by God's evaluation of it as good.

"God's first creative word produced light. The elegance and majesty of Creation by decree is a refreshing contrast with the bizarre creation stories of the pagans. Here is demonstrated the power of God's word. It was this word that motivated Israel to trust and obey Him. The light was natural, physical light" (Walvoord and Zuck, eds., *The Bible Knowledge Commentary,* Cook). This very first creative word should also be an encouragement to us to accept the trustworthiness of God. What a great beginning this was!

The fact that God's initial act was the creation of light has far-reaching significance. First, light is what God uses to dispel darkness. Its initial use is here, where we see physical light dispelling physical darkness.

Second, Jesus is identified as the Light of the World. John recorded that He said, "I am the light of the world: he that followeth me shall not walk in darkness, but shall have the light of life" (John 8:12). John also wrote, "In him was life; and the life was the light of men" (1:4).

In saying this about Jesus, John also pointed out that "the light shineth in darkness; and the darkness comprehended it not" (vs. 5).

Third, in the book of Revelation, John described "the holy city, new Jerusalem, coming down from God out of heaven" (21:2). Here there is going to be no darkness at all because of Jesus: "And the city had no need of the sun, neither of the moon, to shine in it: for the glory of God did lighten it, and the Lamb is the light thereof" (vs. 23).

John gave further information in other details about this holy city: "And there shall be no more curse: but the throne of God and of the Lamb shall be in it; and his servants shall serve him: and they shall see his face; and his name shall be in their foreheads. And there shall be no night there; and they need no candle, neither light of the sun; for the Lord God giveth them light: and they shall reign for ever and ever" (Rev. 22:3-5).

Day and night (Gen. 1:5). God then named light and darkness by calling them "Day" and "Night." It was God's right to do this naming. Just as a parent has the right to name a child and as an inventor has the right to name an invention, so God the Creator had the right and authority to designate day and night. The phrase "the evening and the morning were the first day" puts a time frame on His activity. It is from this wording that the Jews reckoned each new day as beginning at sunset, with the evening coming before the morning.

The fact that there was an evening and a morning indicates the rotation of the earth. Even though the physical sources of light were not yet created, there was a difference between light and darkness. We are not told the initial source of light, only that it was created.

DAY TWO OF CREATION

6 And God said, Let there be a firmament in the midst of the waters, and let it divide the waters from the waters.

7 And God made the firmament, and divided the waters which were under the firmament from the waters which were above the firmament: and it was so.

8 And God called the firmament Heaven. And the evening and the morning were the second day.

The firmament (Gen. 1:6-7). The next act of creation was a firmament that is said to have been put in the "midst of the waters" to divide the waters. This firmament included the atmospheric heaven, forming a large expanse between lower waters and upper waters. It was apparently what we most commonly call the sky. This mention of lower and upper waters is not clearly described, so a couple of ideas have been proposed.

Some believe the separation was between what would become the seas on earth and the mists above it. Some go further by saying these mists formed a watery blanket above the earth with a space below it. John MacArthur stated that "this could possibly have been a canopy of water vapor which acted to make the earth like a hothouse, provided uniform temperature, inhibited mass air movements, caused mist to fall, and filtered out ultraviolet rays, thus extending life" (*The MacArthur Study Bible,* Nelson).

In his book *The Genesis Record* (Baker), Henry Morris explained how this canopy might have been the source of water that fell from the heavens during the Flood of Noah's lifetime. It would answer the question concerning the massive amounts of water that came upon the earth from above along with the amounts from beneath Noah's ark. Prior to the Flood, there had not been rain on the earth, so this was clearly a new phenomenon for which there needed to be a source of water. Such a canopy would supply it.

He also pointed out that the concept of an antediluvian water canopy over the earth has appeared in many writings, both ancient and modern. Warren Wiersbe commented that, "when separated from the landmass, the lower waters eventually became the ocean and the seas; and the upper waters played a part in the Flood during Noah's day (Gen. 7:11-12; 9:11-15)" (*The Bible Exposition Commentary,* Cook).

Designated as heaven (Gen. 1:8). Once again God took the prerogative of calling something what He wanted it to be known as. We noted earlier that such a right belongs to whoever has the authority over it. There is an example of this in Israel's later history, during the life of King Jehoahaz, who was so evil that God removed him after only three months (II Kings 23:31-33). Pharaoh Necho replaced him and "made Eliakim the son of Josiah king in the room of Josiah his father, and turned his name to Jehoiakim" (vs. 34).

This naming process revealed Pharaoh's sovereignty over those he conquered. In a similar way God's naming of things after He created them shows His sovereignty and lordship. These details are not without significance.

The word "heaven" in Hebrew derives from a root meaning "to be lofty" or "aloft." The English word refers to something that is imposing in its height, elevated, or exalted. It speaks of a certain grandness that sets the object above everything else around it. This naming was certainly appropriate. When we gaze into the sky and look out into the realm of the stars, we cannot help being amazed at the awesomeness of our God.

We should keep in mind that the Bible speaks of three heavens (Paul said in II Corinthians 12:2 that he was caught up to the third one). The first is the atmosphere, the second is the stellar heavens, and the third is the dwelling place of God.

DAY THREE OF CREATION

9 And God said, Let the waters under the heaven be gathered together unto one place, and let the dry land appear: and it was so.

10 And God called the dry land Earth; and the gathering together of the waters called he Seas: and God saw that it was good.

11 And God said, Let the earth bring forth grass, the herb yielding seed, and the fruit tree yielding fruit after his kind, whose seed is in itself, upon the earth: and it was so.

12 And the earth brought forth grass, and herb yielding seed after his kind, and the tree yielding fruit, whose seed was in itself, after his kind: and God saw that it was good.

13 And the evening and the morning were the third day.

The appearance of earth (Gen. 1:9-10). On this day, God dealt with the waters under the firmament by gathering them together in such a way as to make dry land appear. The Hebrew word translated "seas" is a plural word. It refers to a number of bodies of water, not just the oceans. This was a significant step in making order out of the chaos described in verse 2. Without the separation of water and land, it would have been impossible for God's climactic creation, man, to live on and occupy the place.

One of the psalmists described the process this way: "Thou coveredst it with the deep as with a garment: the waters stood above the mountains. At thy rebuke they fled; at the voice of thy thunder they hasted away. They go up by the mountains; they go down by the valleys unto the place which thou hast founded for them. Thou hast set a bound that they may not pass over; that they turn not again to cover the earth" (Ps. 104:6-9).

When God addressed Job after his spiritual struggles over suffering, He said, "Or who shut up the sea with doors, when it brake forth, as if it had issued out of the womb? When I made the cloud the garment thereof, and thick darkness a swaddlingband for it, and brake up for it my decreed place, and set bars and doors, and said, Hitherto shalt thou come, but no further: and here shall thy proud waves be stayed?" (Job 38:8-11).

The tremendous cataclysmic upheaval of the surface of the earth involved in this event is beyond our imagination! Land would have been rising and falling all across the face of the massive ball, and out of it came the dry land that God called earth.

The appearance of vegetation (Gen. 1:11-13). After the earth had appeared, God created the first form of life to grow on it. This included grass, seed-producing herbs, and fruit-bearing trees. Since the next chapter records God instructing Adam about eating from the trees, and since Eve ate fruit from the forbidden tree in chapter 3, it is obvious that the trees were created as mature and already producing. God created some things with the appearance of age, which was necessary for six days of Creation.

God also specified that He made everything to reproduce through seeds that would maintain the unique characteristics of each type of plant. There were fixed boundaries in reproduction, seen also in the animal world (Gen. 1:21, 24-25). This is further proof of God's creative processes and refutes the teachings of evolution that claim reproduction across species lines. The origins of plant life, animal life, and human life are directly related to God's spoken words and creative activity.

Since the Hebrew word translated "kind" is not an exact biological term, the clear indication is that God created different families of plants (and animals) when He brought them forth. There was not just one plant or one animal from which genetic mutations took place. God amazingly created a great variety of plants and creatures for our benefit and enjoyment. The first days of Creation show an almighty, sovereign God bringing into existence a remarkable place for man!

—Keith E. Eggert.

QUESTIONS

1. In the summary statement of Genesis 1:1, what does the "beginning" refer to?

2. What does the initial mention of God teach us about Him?

3. What was the earth like when God first created it?

4. What truths make the creation of light so significant?

5. What did God call the first appearance of light and dark?

6. What was the next act of creation, and what did it divide?

7. What does God's naming of the things in creation show us?

8. What does the word for "heaven" mean, and what does that convey to us?

9. What was significant about the formation of the seas?

10. What important truth do we see in the creation of seed-bearing vegetation?

—Keith E. Eggert.

Preparing to Teach the Lesson

Many are confused about the way our world came to be. The Bible has the answers we need. In the first unit, we will explore how all of creation came to be and how we as human beings fit into God's plan. In this opening unit, it is interesting to see how God had us in mind as He put all of creation into place.

TODAY'S AIM

Facts: to see how God had a master plan for the creation of the world and us as human beings.

Principle: to remember that in the beginning God created the heavens and the earth.

Application: to recognize that God's Spirit was there in creation and is here to help us today.

INTRODUCING THE LESSON

Have you ever wondered what it was like before the world and all creation around us came to be? Scientists have come up with all kinds of theories about that. Some believe in the big bang theory. Others speak of evolution. Most theories exclude the hand of God. But the Bible is consistent: God created this world for us. He had us in mind when He put the world together. It is exciting to learn that God had a master plan for us and the world.

DEVELOPING THE LESSON

1. Darkness and light (Gen. 1:1-5). It is interesting that there was nothing but darkness before the earth was created. The earth was empty and had no form. It is hard to describe emptiness in the context of darkness alone. When God stepped into this chaos, the darkness disappeared as God's light entered in.

God still shows up in our world today in the Person of the Holy Spirit. It is the same Spirit who was there at the very beginning of time. God was there, and He acted.

Genesis 1:1 states that "in the beginning God created the heaven and the earth." After the initial act of creation, God's first task was to take on the darkness. He caused light to come in with the word of His command, for He Himself is light. The result was good. He separated the darkness from the light.

In Genesis 1:5, we read that "God called the light Day, and the darkness he called Night." Then we read that "the evening and the morning were the first day." To us it seems to be in the wrong order, but we must remember that this was written for a Hebrew audience. Their day began at sundown and ended the following day at the same time.

Here are some things to think about today. The Holy Spirit was there at the beginning of time, active in creation. How does He work in our lives today? What is His role in dispelling the darkness of our own world? Emphasize to the students that God creates only what is good.

2. Waters above and below (Gen. 1:6-8). Here we see God bringing further order to the world He had made. He was sorting out His creation and putting everything in its assigned place. The word "firmament" is indicative of the spread of the sky as a curtain above us. It separates the waters above in the clouds from the waters below on the earth. Here we see that our God is a God of order. This was God's work for the second day, evening to morning.

3. Land and seas (Gen. 1:9-13).
God spoke again and gathered the waters on the land into one place. He then called the collected waters "Seas." The dry land was called "Earth." Lead the class to see how systematic God was in His creation of the world. At this stage in His work, God looked at all that He had made so far and voiced His approval. It was all good. When God does something for us, it will always be good. God never does what is evil for His creation.

At God's next command, grass, seed-bearing plants, and seed-bearing fruits followed. Notice the repeated emphasis on seeds here. God put into nature the power of multiplication and self-procreation, all packaged in tiny seeds. Seeds are symbolic of potential and of power to grow. God has invested His creation with the power to grow and reproduce. It does not require another word from Him to bring about each new generation. It happens according to the power He placed within living things at the beginning.

God again said that what He had done on that third day, from evening until morning, was all good. We can almost imagine God smiling in approval at what He had made. His heart rejoiced that He could bless His creation and invest it with His power. God continually invests His creation with His presence through His Spirit. Revelation 4:11 declares, "Thou art worthy, O Lord, to receive glory and honour and power: for thou hast created all things, and for thy pleasure they are and were created." Do not forget to worship the Living God, who created and continues to sustain all of His creation.

ILLUSTRATING THE LESSON

When God's Spirit steps into the darkness of our world, He brings in order and invests it with His power.

GOD'S SPIRIT BRINGS ORDER

Chaos   Order

CONCLUDING THE LESSON

We have already seen how one word from God turned the chaos and the emptiness of our world into order and productivity. When we feel we are working hard and getting nowhere, we should remind ourselves that what we need is a spoken word from our God that allows His Spirit to come in and transform our broken world and turn it into something beautiful and productive. Everything that God creates is good.

It is important to be personally assured that the great God who created the heavens and the earth is our God. He loves us so much. He does all things for our good. It may not happen instantaneously, but when He steps into our lives, He begins to bring order out of our chaos and turns our darkness to light.

ANTICIPATING THE NEXT LESSON

In our lesson next week, we will continue to look at the work of God's creation of our world. Next week we see how our God created special lights for the day and for the night to make our world a habitable place. Then He populated His new world with life on land and sea. We will continue to see His work in the beginning of our world.
—*A.Koshy Muthalaly.*

PRACTICAL POINTS

1. Creation powerfully demonstrates God's intention to be known (Gen. 1:1; cf. Rom. 1:19-20).
2. Only God can create something out of nothing (Gen. 1:1-2).
3. God has not changed—He still brings order into chaos, substance into emptiness, and light into dark places (vss. 3-5).
4. God provides order in nature so that all creation functions effectively (vss. 6-8).
5. We can trust God, our Creator, to provide everything that we need (vss. 9-10).
6. We can trust that God's goodness will be displayed at the proper time (vss. 11-13).

—Cheryl Y. Powell.

RESEARCH AND DISCUSSION

1. What is "general revelation"? Is this "general revelation" sufficient for salvation? Why or why not?
2. How does understanding of God's physical creation help us to know more of His character and mind (cf. Job 38:1-11)? How does that understanding affect our worship?
3. Why is it important that believers understand that everything God created is good?
4. How does God's separation of light from darkness illustrate our salvation (cf. John 1:1-10)?
5. How can Genesis 1:1-13 help us as believers understand God's purpose for our lives? How can we encourage others with this truth?

—Cheryl Y. Powell.

ILLUSTRATED HIGH POINTS

God created

A Christian cosmologist (one who studies the universe) presented the evidence for the universe having been created by an omnipotent God. Afterward, he asked four physics professors what they thought. One said he could not deny the truth of his lecture; however, none of them turned their lives over to Jesus Christ.

One was unwilling to give up sexual immorality. Another claimed deep wounds inflicted by professing Christians.

This is typical. People can know truth but refuse to believe.

God created

Christians should not be overwhelmed by the proliferation of the theory of evolution. Remember, it is still an unproven theory. Evolution can be rejected on biblical grounds, knowing that neither biology, geology, nor paleontology have proved it.

Edwin Conkin, a prominent biologist who gave over one thousand lectures crusading for evolution, stated that "the probability of life originating by accident is comparable to "the probability of the unabridged dictionary resulting from an explosion in a printing shop" (christiancourier.com/articles/1579-five-guestions).

In the beginning

Scientists tend to be pretty smart people. Sometimes it seems that they try to overwhelm the rest of us with their erudition.

We are grateful that God, who is omniscient, knowing far more than any man or all men put together, simply stated, "In the beginning God created the heaven and the earth" (Gen. 1:1).

—David A. Hamburg.

Golden Text Illuminated

"The earth was without form, and void; and darkness was upon the face of the deep. And the Spirit of God moved upon the face of the waters" (Genesis 1:2).

My grandfather was a man who loved working with his hands. He was constantly mending something, working the soil, or caring for his animals.

In his later years, Granddad used his hands for woodworking. He loved to make those black silhouettes. It brought him joy. He was at peace among the tools and materials of his workshop.

What astonished me was how he could imagine and create something out of a slab of wood. He would hold up a sheet of plywood and ask, "Can you see a fellow running? He is on the move to somewhere fast." In a scant amount of time, the figure would emerge. He would set it against the wall, pleased with his creation.

But could we still create if there were no raw materials to make something?

That is exactly what God did. Before this earth and the universe ever existed, they were in the mind and heart of God. When He put the Creation into motion, there were no raw materials. All He had was dark, formless chaos. God saw what would be, and He lovingly brought it about as a perfect, breathtaking masterpiece.

What compelled God to create? After all, He had no need of a universe. God has no lack of anything. Why, then, would He want an earth?

The answer to that question is also the reason why my grandfather made his silhouettes—joy. God found joy in the act of creation, just as my grandfather took pleasure in his woodworking.

Stop a moment and think. At this point in earth's creation, our world was just a blob in the universe. There were no plants, animals, or anything. Yet God was still excited about what was happening. Why would God be ecstatic about a formless void in the darkness?

Like my grandfather, God did not simply see what was there. When He gazed at that formless void, He saw more than that. God saw what it would become— a place with plants, many amazing animals, raging seas—and even us.

When was the last time you marveled at our created world? We can spend hours gazing at fine paintings, detailed sculptures, and even photographs. We put them on prominent display. But what about fallen maple leaves on the sidewalk? Do you always just crunch them under your feet, or do you pick one up once in a while and marvel at its intricacy? Do you consider the thousands of tiny cells in it, each with a purpose?

Creation is so vast and immense that it cannot be understood by our minds. My challenge to you is to spend some time each day reflecting on the world God created for us. Take a moment to stop and consider its beauty, its power, and its vast detail. There is no man-made thing that has even come close. It is truly wonderful and awe-inspiring. Only the Master could have formed such an immensely beautiful world.

Creation humbles me and points me back to the One who formed it all for us. As the psalmist did in Psalm 148, I find myself calling out to all around me to give praise to Him for His glorious gift that He carefully made. Perhaps His marvelous works will do the same for you.

—Jennifer Francis.

Heart of the Lesson

During my senior year of high school, the men's basketball team went to the state tournament. Because this was the first such achievement in the school's history, the principal canceled classes and the entire student body rode buses to the game. I seldom clapped at basketball games, but I yelled and cheered with the other fans at that game until I was hoarse. We were proud of our team.

When God created the world, He too had a cheering section! The morning stars sang, and the angels shouted for joy as they watched (Job. 38:7).

1. The beginning of our world (Gen. 1:1-2). Heaven and earth have a starting point, unlike God, who always has existed. The beginning in Genesis 1 is the beginning of God's creation of our world and everything in it. The heaven and the earth came into being through God's spoken word, not by chance or by an accident. Our world was God's idea and His work.

In its earliest stage, earth lacked a definite form. Our world was a dark, watery mass, devoid of anything living. God's Spirit hovered over the surface of the earth's waters. He was very close to His creation. Several writers compare the Spirit's hovering with a mother bird caring for her young.

2. Light and darkness (Gen. 1:3-5). Light was the first thing God brought into being as He prepared the earth for habitation. God was pleased with the light and said it was good. Light and goodness are part of God's very nature; in Him is no darkness at all. Jesus, the Son of God, who was with God the Father during the Creation, is the Light of the World (John 8:12).

Next, God separated the light from the darkness. Each was to have its place. God named the light "day" and the darkness "night." The light and darkness provided the components that make up a day. Keil and Delitzsch noted that the first three days of Creation were produced by a recurring interchange of light and darkness rather than by the sun rising and setting (*Commentary on the Old Testament,* Eerdmans).

3. Sky (Gen. 1:6-8). God created the firmament—the skies and atmosphere surrounding the earth. Earth's waters now resided either above or below the firmament. God named the firmament "heaven."

4. Seas, land, and vegetation (Gen. 1:9-13). God next gathered the waters under the firmament into seas and caused dry land to appear. He was pleased with this separation and said it was good.

Then God created vegetation—all sorts of grasses, herbs, bushes, and trees. Each of these seed-bearing plants was to reproduce its own kind—its own species. God looked at the vegetation that now covered the earth, and He said it was good.

The biblical account of Creation tells us how our world and everything in it began. Our world is a creation of God, spoken into being by His power and creativity. God made the world, plants, animals, and humanity simply because He wanted to do so.

The Creation account teaches us about God. He is orderly and wise. For example, He created vegetation—things to eat—before He created animals and people. God is powerful. He spoke, and everything came into being. God is creative, as evidenced by the world around us. God was and is involved with His creation. His Spirit was present, and He reflected upon His work and said it was good.

—*Ann Staatz.*

World Missions

Things could not get much darker for Shelly. She had grown up in a Christian home, gone to church, heard the Bible stories, and had a grandmother who prayed for her.

But Shelly wanted excitement, and that could be found with her father. Going to live with him introduced her to life on the edge, and in time, to drugs. Her father sold them. Shelly began doing drugs and was soon entrenched in addiction.

Her family tried to help. More than once, Shelly was sent to Christian camp, where she learned to act as if she had cleaned up her life—but only long enough to get back to the drugs. Things got worse. Shelly turned to prostitution and for twenty long years she lived a life most churchgoing people would shun in horror. She made a lot of money, but it never lasted. She did drugs so much that getting arrested sometimes was a relief because she would sleep for days, recovering from the sleep depriving side effects. Her mug shots show a miserable woman with glassy eyes, unkempt hair, and a face filled with despair.

Things got even darker. Her boss turned to human trafficking and told her she was going to be in charge of the new, young girls he "owned." Shelly did not want to be part of that kind of evil. But after seeing him murder another person who refused, she was convinced that she had no choice. God intervened through an arrest. Though her boss paid off the policeman and got away, Shelly was taken in.

"I just saved your life," the policeman said. Still, Shelly did not turn her life around.

Her grandmother kept praying, year after year, never giving up.

Nevertheless, things got even darker. Shelly was recruited into a drug deal and was arrested in Turkey. The international incident landed her in a horrible Turkish prison.

The news broadcast described what had happened, and a military couple living there saw it. That couple could have watched and said, "There's another bad person doing bad things," and changed the channel. They could have talked about how dark the world was getting or how hopeless modern times were. They could have condemned Shelly for the wrong choices that had brought her to such a low place.

Instead, this couple decided to be light in the darkness. They determined they were going to smuggle Shelly a Bible in prison, and they did. They literally brought light into a dark place, for Shelly had been sentenced to solitary confinement for a year.

Solitary for a year with nothing but a Bible! God's light permeated that dark cell and Shelly's darkened life. It broke through years of rebellion and sin. Shelly's life was completely changed. She turned back to God and was made clean. Shelly has been serving the Lord ever since, her story a powerful reminder that no one is beyond hope.

Sometimes we may be overwhelmed by the darkness of our world or the darkness in certain people, but let us never forget that no darkness in existence can ever prevail against light. Light always wins. This is why we should always be ready to give the Light of the World—Jesus Christ—to those around us. He still changes lives, the Word still does not return void, and light still defeats darkness.

—*Kimberly Rae.*

The Jewish Aspect

Genesis is the book of beginnings. The title, "Genesis," is the Greek word for "beginning." The Hebrew word, berēshith, comes from the Hebrew for the first words of the book, "in the beginning." The Torah (the first five books of the Hebrew Scriptures) teaches that it was God who created the world. Traditional Jewish belief holds that Creation marks the absolute beginning of the temporal and material world. While God has existed eternally, Genesis 1 marks the beginning of the universe in time and space. "Before the mountains were brought forth, or ever thou hadst formed the earth and the world, even from everlasting to everlasting, thou art God" (Ps. 90:2).

God created the original heaven and earth from nothing. By willful act and divine word, He spoke all creation into existence. In the New Testament, John said that God existed before the creation of the world. "In the beginning was the Word, and the Word was with God, and the Word was God" (John 1:1). The reference to Genesis 1, "in the beginning," is striking, as ancient Jews would have quoted from the book of Genesis as berēshith. In this beginning, there already was the Word. This is also found in the Psalms. "By the word of the Lord were the heavens made; and all the host of them by the breath of his mouth" (33:6).

The primary Hebrew word for God, Elohim, is used in Genesis 1. This form of the divine name occurs more than 2,500 times in the Old Testament. According to Jewish belief, the plural ending im indicates a plural of majesty. "Elohim . . . plural in form though commonly construed with a singular verb or adjective. . . is, most probably, to be explained as the plural of majesty or excellence, expressing high dignity or greatness" ("Names of God," www.jewishencyclopedia.com).

The Hebrew word bara means to "create," "shape," or "form" and is used exclusively with God as its subject. It refers to the instantaneous and miraculous act of God by which He brought the universe into existence. It leaves no doubt that God is an eternal being.

The Hebrew phrase translated "without form, and void" (Gen. 1:2) means "unformed and unfilled" and describes the condition of earth after the initial act of Creation. It was the "Spirit of God" who moved upon the face of the waters. This is the Spirit of Elohim, high and mighty, also called Ruah ha-Kodesh, or Holy Spirit.

Elohim completed the universe by separating certain things and naming them. Separating and naming were considered acts of dominion in the ancient world. It was the token of lordship. Reuben changed the names of the cities of the Amorites after he had conquered them (Num. 32:38).

The first chapter of Genesis also emphasizes God's creative act and the quality of the created objects. "And God saw that it was good" appears repeatedly (vss. 10, 12, 18, 21, 25). God ordered the existence of light, firmament, waters and dry land, evening and morning; and He called forth grass, herb-yielding seed, and trees yielding fruit. He created every living creature.

Immediately following each directive was God's observation that His work was good. God looked over everything that He had made and called it "very good" (Gen. 1:31). The word "good" in this context indicates the moral goodness of the creation and the good purposes it was intended to serve. Genesis 1 teaches about the eternal God, the Creator, and all the good things He has made.

—Deborah Markowitz Solan.

Guiding the Superintendent

The earth is the perfect place for humanity to live and thrive. This is no accident. Our universe is the result of God's careful and loving plan; it is a gift for His people.

The first chapter of the Bible (Genesis 1) is the only account we have of how the universe and, more specifically, how our world came to be. The Bible does not try to argue for God's existence. It simply states that God was already there at the beginning. He is responsible for the entire universe as we know it. Genesis 1 is the catalog of God's mighty creative acts.

DEVOTIONAL OUTLINE

1. God created order and light (Gen. 1:1-5).

It can be said that Genesis 1:1 is the most important verse in the Bible. It lays the foundation for all that follows.

In ten words (English text), the reader is told that God was there at the beginning. Before He could shape the universe, it was necessary for God to create the very building blocks for it. The text is simple and yet very profound: "God created the heaven and the earth" (Gen. 1:1).

These building blocks were initially energized by God's Spirit. At first the world was "without form, and void" (Gen. 1:2), and darkness was everywhere; that is, there was no light. God handled the situation, saying, "Let there be light" (vs. 3).

The formlessness was dealt with in Gen. 1:3-13, which records the first three days of Creation. The creative activities of days four through six (1:14-26) dealt with the emptiness.

The statement "and God said" (Gen. 1:3) alludes to and hints at a very important biblical theme—obedience. When God spoke, nature obeyed.

Light was first to be created, and this allowed time to begin. Then day and night were distinguished.

God laid the groundwork in anticipation of future creative activities. All was ready for further shaping and the preparation of the world for mankind.

Each creative day was divinely evaluated the same way. God saw that all was good (Gen. 1:4).

2. God continued His creation (Gen. 1:6-13).

The creative activities for days two (vss. 6-8) and three (vss. 9-13) completed God's dealings to undo the "formless" condition of verse 2.

On day two of Creation, God handled the formlessness that consisted of water and darkness. On the second day of Creation, God divided this large watery mass (called "firmament" in Genesis 1:7) into the lower waters (where the fish would live) and a protective canopy of water above the earth. The space in between is what we would call the atmosphere.

While day two dealt with dividing the water, day three focused on dividing the land. Contrary to modern evolutionary thought, all the land vegetation, plants, and trees came into existence on one day. God was continuing to bring order to His world.

CHILDREN'S CORNER

text: **I Kings 16:29—17:7**
title: **Evil King, Hidden Prophet**

Elijah was God's man of the hour during an evil time for His people. Elijah had to stay hidden in obscurity for a while, but God used this period to prepare him for a great work of making known His truth and holiness.

—*Martin R. Dahlquist.*

Scripture Lesson Text

GEN. 1:14 And God said, Let there be lights in the firmament of the heaven to divide the day from the night; and let them be for signs, and for seasons, and for days, and years:

15 And let them be for lights in the firmament of the heaven to give light upon the earth: and it was so.

16 And God made two great lights; the greater light to rule the day, and the lesser light to rule the night: he made the stars also.

17 And God set them in the firmament of the heaven to give light upon the earth,

18 And to rule over the day and over the night, and to divide the light from the darkness: and God saw that it was good.

19 And the evening and the morning were the fourth day.

20 And God said, Let the waters bring forth abundantly the moving creature that hath life, and fowl that may fly above the earth in the open firmament of heaven.

21 And God created great whales, and every living creature that moveth, which the waters brought forth abundantly, after their kind, and every winged fowl after his kind: and God saw that it was good.

22 And God blessed them, saying, Be fruitful, and multiply, and fill the waters in the seas, and let fowl multiply in the earth.

23 And the evening and the morning were the fifth day.

24 And God said, Let the earth bring forth the living creature after his kind, cattle, and creeping thing, and beast of the earth after his kind: and it was so.

25 And God made the beast of the earth after his kind, and cattle after their kind, and every thing that creepeth upon the earth after his kind: and God saw that it was good.

NOTES

Creations in Sky, Sea, and Land

Lesson Text: Genesis 1:14-25

Related Scriptures: Psalms 19:1-6; 104:24-30

TIME: unknown   PLACES: Heaven and earth

GOLDEN TEXT—"God made two great lights; the greater light to rule the day, and the lesser light to rule the night: he made the stars also" (Genesis 1:16).

Introduction

The Creation story in the Bible is not the only one in existence; some of the ancient pagan nations had their own creation stories. In most of those, however, the material universe is viewed as eternal and the gods were the ones who were brought into existence. The Babylonian story named Enuma Elish begins with a watery, formless universe that produced two gods.

The Enuma Elish was discovered in the middle of the nineteenth century when archaeologists dug into the library of King Ashurbanipal of Nineveh.

Religious texts were found that contained a few superficial similarities to the opening chapters of Genesis. Only in Genesis do we see God existing from all eternity, long before the creation of the universe. God is the source of the universe and the power behind it. He is not a product of His creation!

LESSON OUTLINE

I. **LIGHTS IN THE SKY—** Gen. 1:14-19

II. **LIFE THROUGHOUT THE WORLD—**Gen. 1:20-25

Exposition: Verse by Verse

LIGHTS IN THE SKY

GEN. 1:14 And God said, Let there be lights in the firmament of the heaven to divide the day from the night; and let them be for signs, and for seasons, and for days, and years:

15 And let them be for lights in the firmament of the heaven to give light upon the earth: and it was so.

16 And God made two great lights; the greater light to rule the day, and the lesser light to rule the

night: he made the stars also.

17 And God set them in the firmament of the heaven to give light upon the earth,

18 And to rule over the day and over the night, and to divide the light from the darkness: and God saw that it was good.

19 And the evening and the morning were the fourth day.

Their purposes (Gen. 1:14-15). The fourth day of Creation parallels day one, in which light was created. On this day, God created the luminous bodies that would provide that light day and night. We are not told what the source of light was prior to this day, but on this fourth day the sun was created to rule the day and the moon and stars were created to rule the night. Were they there prior to this day without being previously revealed? Or did God Himself serve as the source of original light? Revelation 22:5 suggests that the latter idea is plausible.

Genesis 1:14-15 indicates four purposes for the heavenly luminaries. First, they were to distinguish day and night. This is parallel to the statement in verse 4 that when the original light was created, "God divided the light from the darkness," after which He "called the light Day, and the darkness he called Night." The specific location "in the firmament of the heaven" (vs. 14) describes the spatial relationship of these bodies of light with the earth.

The second purpose for these bodies was to provide signs that communicate to mankind. While those who promote astrology assign meaning through the signs of the zodiac, this is surely not what is meant. The luminaries are signs of the power and majesty of God, as seen in such Scripture verses as: "When I consider thy heavens, the work of thy fingers, the moon and the stars, which thou hast ordained; what is man, that thou art mindful of him? and the son of man, that thou visitest him?" (Ps. 8:3-4).

Psalm 19 tells us that "the heavens declare the glory of God; and the firmament sheweth his handiwork" (vs. 1). This message of God's greatness is communicated to the entire world (vss. 3-4).

The third purpose for these bodies was to distinguish seasons, which would also provide for the calendar of events God's people would later observe. Israel's feasts and other religious observations would occur according to the seasons and months of the year. Today we have seasons dependent on the position of these same luminaries. The fourth purpose was the illumination of the earth. By being placed high above, they would give light to the entire earth.

Their placement (Gen. 1:16-17). God made two of the lights to be the primary ones. The one, referred to as the "greater" light, was to be prominent during the day and the other, referred to as the "lesser" light, was to be prominent during the night. They are said to "rule" in those realms, that is, to have dominion over them, or to govern them. Daylight would be nonexistent without the sun, and on moonless nights the sky would be completely black apart from the stars. They do display their dominion.

The creation of the stars almost sounds like an afterthought: God also made the stars. They are in a different category from the prominent lights. When the sun comes out during the day, they disappear from sight completely, and when the moon comes out during the night, those nearby fade out or appear much dimmer. In fact, we tend to think of them as twinkling, suggesting a minor role in the night sky. In God's eyes, however, they are important and add beauty for us to enjoy.

God never intended that these luminaries be objects of worship, though we know this was the case in many ancient pagan nations. There even came a time when Israel fell into this false worship. In Mesopotamia, where Abraham came from, such worship was common, and in Egypt, the land from which Israel eventually would be delivered, the sun god was their primary god among hundreds of others. Such worldly influence is dangerous to God's children, and we must always be on guard against slipping into false theology.

The extremity of Israel's departure from God later in their history is recorded in the following terms: "And they left all the commandments of the Lord their God, and made them molten images, even two calves, and made a grove, and worshipped all the host of heaven, and served Baal" (II Kings 17:16). Even after seeing all that God had done for them throughout their history, they departed far from Him. That serves as a warning for every believer.

Their prominence (Gen. 1:18-19). The sun, moon, and stars were specifically placed "in the firmament of the heaven" (vs. 17) in order to shine light on the earth. In order for them to be effective immediately upon being created, God had to make them with the appearance of age, just as He did other things. Science tells us, for example, that the light we receive on earth from the stars comes from millions of light-years away. So God apparently created them with their light waves already spanning the distance to earth.

God's control in not only creating but also placing these bodies of light is obvious. He made them and set them right where He wanted them to be so that they would give the light on earth that He intended. In their specific placement, they accomplished exactly what He intended in ruling both day and night. Even this aspect of the creation speaks strongly of the work of a Creator and dispels the notion that everything evolved in a series of minute changes over long periods of time.

While the creation of the stars comes off almost as incidental, we know that was not really the case. The statement that God also made the stars is remarkable. "In the ancient Middle East, other religions worshiped, deified, and [mysticized] the stars. Israel's neighbors revered the stars and looked to them for guidance. In contrast, the biblical creation story gives the stars only the barest mention [and] . . . showed great contempt for ancient Babylonian astrology" (Radmacher, Allen, and House, eds., *Nelson's New Illustrated Bible Commentary,* Nelson).

Once again we read that after God commanded creative activity, "it was so" (Gen. 1:15) and "it was good" (vs. 18). Moses then completed his account of this part of the Creation by stating, "And the evening and the morning were the fourth day" (vs. 19). From then on the lights ruling day and night would be operative in this new world.

LIFE THROUGHOUT THE WORLD

20 And God said, Let the waters bring forth abundantly the moving creature that hath life, and fowl that may fly above the earth in the open firmament of heaven.

21 And God created great whales, and every living creature that moveth, which the waters brought forth abundantly, after their kind, and every winged fowl after his kind: and God saw that it was good.

22 And God blessed them, saying, Be fruitful, and multiply, and fill the waters in the seas, and let fowl multiply in the earth.

23 And the evening and the morning were the fifth day.

24 And God said, Let the earth bring forth the living creature after his kind, cattle, and creeping thing, and beast of the earth after his kind: and it was so.

25 And God made the beast of the earth after his kind, and cattle after

their kind, and every thing that creepeth upon the earth after his kind: and God saw that it was good.

Creatures in the water and air (Gen. 1:20-21).

On day two, God created the firmament with waters both above it and below it, leaving an expanse in between. On day three, He gathered the waters beneath the firmament into seas, making the dry land appear. Now on the fifth day, God ordered that the seas and the firmament be filled with aquatic and flying creatures. The creatures for the dry land would come on the next day. By then God completely filled His creation with living beings of every sort.

God ordered an abundance of living creatures to occupy His waters. "O Lord, how manifold are thy works! in wisdom hast thou made them all: the earth is full of thy riches. So is this great and wide sea, wherein are things creeping innumerable, both small and great beasts" (Ps. 104:24-25). Scientists tell us that the oceans cover 71 percent of the earth's surface, amounting to approximately 140 million square miles, and that the average depth is around twelve thousand feet.

Within that space there are nearly thirty thousand species of fish, with more being discovered continually. Among them are the "great whales" (Gen. 1:21). The Hebrew term refers to large sea creatures and includes whales (mammals), sharks (fish), and sea serpents. One of the largest creatures on record was a blue whale measuring 110 feet long. Another weighed 191 tons at capture. Huge whale sharks also exist, reaching up to 41 feet in length. These are a couple of examples of God's "great" water creatures.

On the other extreme are zooplankton, some measuring less than two micromillimeters. The same kind of diversity exists among the birds. A comparison of eagles with humming-birds, for example, helps us see God's variety. There are well over ten thousand known species, and more are being discovered regularly. To appreciate God's creative genius in the realm of feathered creatures, all one has to do is live in or visit a forested area, sit outside at nighttime or early morning, and listen!

Mandate to reproduce (Gen. 1:22-23).

For the first time we read that God blessed His creatures and commanded them to reproduce. This was never said about the plant life, so there is a distinction between that and these creatures. Both the creatures in the water and those in the air are addressed. One important aspect of this is their reproduction "after their kind" (vs. 21), again stated for both water and flying creatures. This would indicate reproduction along the lines of the species.

This simple statement refutes the teaching of evolution, which has fish and birds developing in a convoluted, eons-long process from a single original form. In reality, God set their species from the very beginning. We recognize that within species, there are sometimes mutations or development, but the basic groups have been in existence since Creation.

In a book titled *Creation: The Facts of Life,* Gary E. Parker examines the approaches of biochemistry to man's ancestors and makes the following observations: "1. Blood precipitation tests indicate the chimpanzee is man's closest relative. 2. Milk chemistry indicates that the donkey is man's closest relative. 3. Cholesterol level tests indicate that the garter snake is man's closest relative. 4. Tear enzyme chemistry indicates that the chicken is man's closest relative. 5. On the basis of another type of blood chemistry test, the butter bean is man's closest relative" (New Leaf Press).

How such tests were conducted is not discussed, but these results do reveal the extreme inaccuracy of evolutionary teaching. On the other hand, the facts stated in Scripture give us the truth about God's marvelous creative activities and give us reassurance of His absolute control over His creation.

Creatures on the earth (Gen. 1:24-25). Five times the phrase "after his kind" or "after their kind" is used in these two verses. There is no hint of anything evolving, least of all mankind (vss. 26-27). This was the climactic day of Creation, when the newly formed earth was populated. "The earth, which on the third day had been decked with flora in preparation for faunal life, is ready for its inhabitants on the corresponding sixth day" (Douglas, Norton, and Hildebrandt, eds., *New Commentary on the Whole Bible,* Tyndale). God began with the animal world.

Three categories of land animals are mentioned as having been created simultaneously: cattle, creeping things, and beasts of the earth. This categorization evidently is intended to cover comprehensively the entire animal kingdom. The term "cattle" probably refers to those animals that could be domesticated, while the term "beasts of the earth" probably refers to large wild animals not normally tamed in any way. The term "creeping things" refers to insects, worms, reptiles, and others low on the earth.

The cattle were herbivorous and capable of being used for labor while the wild beasts became carnivores with ravenous natures that would best be left in the wild. This probably included the dinosaurs like the behemoth mentioned in Job 40. What happened to the dinosaurs? They did exist, which is a well-known fact from archaeological discoveries, but since they have disappeared, we have to wonder about them. Their disappearance is probably connected to Noah's Flood.

The animals were apparently composed of the same elements as the earth since they are said to have been brought forth from the earth. Their bodies, like human bodies, go back to dust after death. Along with the fish and bird worlds, they also have conscious life like humans, unlike the vegetative world. Since they were not made in the image of God like mankind, though, they do not have eternal spirits. Next week, we are going to be reminded that we are God's greatest creation of all!
—*Keith E. Eggert.*

QUESTIONS

1. How does the fourth day of Creation parallel the first?
2. What are the four purposes in creating the luminaries?
3. What are the two primary luminaries, and what specifically were they created to do?
4. Why might we wrongly think the stars are less important in God's view?
5. How does the text emphasize God's complete control over the luminaries?
6. What did God create on the fifth day, and how does this parallel with days two and three?
7. What distinction do we see in the creation of these creatures?
8. What important aspect is noted regarding the reproduction of creatures?
9. What was created on day six?
10. What three categories of animals were created that day? How do they compare to man?
—*Keith E. Eggert.*

Preparing to Teach the Lesson

This week we continue our study of God's work in Creation, and we look specifically at the creatures He made to fill the sky, sea, and land. We also look at the role of light in the world. God was fully in control of every little detail as He prepared the world for us to live in. This week we look again at the heaven and the earth. This is the area and focus of God's activity for our learning this week.

TODAY'S AIM

Facts: to show the reader that God displays His glory through the creation, especially through the creation of light and life in this world.

Principle: to acknowledge that God is the Creator of all light and life.

Application: to show that we as Christians can see how the nature of God is reflected in all His creation.

INTRODUCING THE LESSON

Imagine a world without light. Aside from the fact that most life would not be possible, scientists tell us that long-term exposure to darkness without any sunlight can cause all kinds of physical and emotional problems. Depression is one of the major repercussions. In the physical realm, vitamin D, which our bodies produce from sunlight, is crucial to our health. In this week's lesson, we see how our Creator God has thought of everything that is necessary for our survival on this earth that He created.

This week, we explore more of what our God did in terms of creating life both in the sea and on land. The sun, moon, and stars constituted His major work on the fourth day of Creation. Light is preeminent in this section of creation and is crucial for our sustenance.

We often take our created world, especially light, for granted and forget that there is a Divine Planner behind it all looking out for us. While many people may tell us that all this came to be simply by chance, the Bible reminds us that God had a specific plan with us in mind as He spoke the earth and everything around us into existence. God brings light and life wherever He is.

DEVELOPING THE LESSON

1. Two lights in the sky (Gen. 1:14-19). God continued His creation on the fourth day. The God who lives in eternity now marked off time for His world. He gave us day and night, marking off these times and also the seasons with the sun and the moon. It is interesting that our calendars follow these two great lights just as the Bible indicates.

God set the sun, the greater light, to rule the day and the moon, the lesser light, along with the stars, to rule the night. Light was now separated from the darkness with the placement of the sun and the moon. God saw that all His work on day four, evening to morning, was good. Have the class discuss different ways in which light rules our earth. It is God Himself who gave us this light.

2. Creatures in the sea and in the air (Gen. 1:20-23). The work of God in Creation continued to progress, day by day. Until God spoke, the waters were a lifeless element. But when He spoke, they began bubbling with life. Remind the class that it is God's Spirit who gives us life. Birds and fish of every kind now filled the air and the seas with life and with the power to bear offspring after their kind. God is the source of all life.

On this fourth day of Creation, evening to morning, another full day displaying God's mighty work, the emphasis was on investing the earth with life. And although God has long since finished His creative work, we must realize that He is still active in our world. He is always working on our behalf to make our lives worthwhile and meaningful. Note that He is also showing us His attributes while He is working on our behalf. Our God is a living and active God. He brings life to all His creation throughout the universe. He is. And He does all this for us.

3. Creatures on the land (Gen. 1:24-25). The phrases "after his kind" and "after their kind," repeated again here, signify order in the universe and distinct planning on God's part. At this time He began the task of creating animals on earth. The once-empty earth was now teeming with all kinds of life. Cattle, reptiles, and other animals filled the earth through the spoken word of God. He then looked at all His creation and saw that it was all good.

What an amazing God we have who thought of everything we would need for life on earth! He is a God who pays attention to every little detail. It should be with a sense of mounting excitement that we follow every step of God's creative activity and arrive at His pronouncement of creation's goodness. In six exciting days He had fashioned the world and all that we need for life and sustenance. But the sixth day was not over, and God was not yet finished.

ILLUSTRATING THE LESSON

God had us in mind when He created the earth for us. He gave us lights to illuminate our world. God is the Author of light. The clearest light He has given us is the light of His Word.

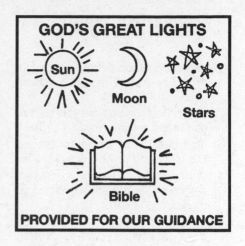

GOD'S GREAT LIGHTS
Sun
Moon
Stars
Bible
PROVIDED FOR OUR GUIDANCE

CONCLUDING THE LESSON

This week we saw how God had us in mind when He created this beautiful world for us to live in. He gave us both light and life to make our lives meaningful. Notice that these are two of the attributes of God that He now shares with us through the work of His hands. He wants us to know Him as we look at the creation He made just for us. This world did not come by chance as some would have us believe. God had a definite plan with us in mind.

It must be remembered that while the Bible is not a science textbook, it is fascinating that God would record all this for us so that we can learn about the beginnings of our world and that it all started with Him. The world around us should be a reminder that our Creator cares for us deeply and that we should praise His mighty name.

ANTICIPATING THE NEXT LESSON

In our lesson next week, we will see how God created mankind, His crowning creation. He made mankind in His image. We will learn that we are to be a reflection of our Creator. He also gave us power to rule over all creation.

—A.Koshy Muthalaly.

PRACTICAL POINTS

1. In creation, God demonstrates His mastery over time and space (Gen. 1:14).
2. When God has spoken, it is so. We can stand on His Word (vs. 15).
3. God designs all things to declare His glory and power (vss. 15-16).
4. We have no cause for fear when we know God watches day and night (vss. 17-19).
5. What God creates, He fills. God does not leave a void (vss. 20-21).
6. God sustains all life in all its variety, according to His perfect plan (vss. 22-23).
7. In God's control and perfect plan, His creation is still good (vss. 24-25).

—*Cheryl Y. Powell.*

RESEARCH AND DISCUSSION

1. In what ways has man corrupted God's design for the heavenly bodies?
2. What does the order of God's creation teach us about His character?
3. What common scientific knowledge can Christians cite to support the Creation account of Genesis? How should a Christian view scientific evidence that seems to contradict the Bible?
4. What does it mean when God calls His creation "good"? What does the goodness of creation teach us about the character of God?
5. What has been your most memorable experience with God's creation? What made that experience memorable?

—*Cheryl Y. Powell.*

ILLUSTRATED HIGH POINTS

He made the stars also

The stars are pretty awesome in size, quantity, and distance. Yet as God directed Moses to make a record of His creation, He simply said, "He made the stars also." Those are five words in English and actually only two in Hebrew.

Later, it took many chapters to give Israel directions for a tabernacle and the sacrifices by which they could approach God in worship.

The emphasis of the Bible is on the redemption of man. It was not all that difficult for God to create a universe. To redeem, however, took the sacrifice of His Son.

And creeping thing

God filled the earth with all types of animals and creeping things. Out of the estimated four hundred thousand various creeping things, the bombardier beetle is a fascinating creature.

His body combines two chemicals and then expels them in the face of a predator, which either kills it or drives it away.

The evolutionist says this is a great illustration of how the beetle evolved over millions of years. The creationist says this is an illustration of intelligent design. Who is right? Let Hebrews 11:3 be your guide.

God saw that it was good

Many go by the adage "the only good snake is a dead snake." Yes, there are many dangerous snakes in the world, but snakes are important to our natural ecosystems.

Snakes provide food for their natural predators. The feeding habits of snakes act as a natural form of pest control since snakes feed on a variety of harmful creatures.

Indeed, God wisely created the entire food chain for the survival of life on earth.

—*David A. Hamburg.*

Golden Text Illuminated

"God made two great lights; the greater light to rule the day, and the lesser light to rule the night: he made the stars also" (Genesis 1:16).

I used to love leading night hikes at camp. It was one of my camp duties that I truly enjoyed. There was nothing like having thirty campers walking behind me as I took them on a tour of the natural world in the nocturnal hours. I would point out constellations, teach them how bats found their way using sonar, and do activities that were not possible in the daylight hours.

The best part for me, however, had nothing to do with the night activities. It had to do with the campers' reactions. When I conducted a night hike, the girls I led usually started out with some measure of fear. They would timidly shuffle along, uncertain of the world at night and my ability to lead them safely in the darkness. By the end, they were walking behind me with complete confidence, even pleasure.

There have been times in my life when I have felt as though I were walking in darkness. Like the girls on the night hike, I found myself stumbling along in fear, hesitating to take a step in any direction. I yearned to turn back to safety, to the familiar.

When we are walking in the darkness, we may forget that daybreak is merely hours away. When the sun appears, we see our world clearly and walk unafraid (cf. John 11:9). Most of us do not even have to think about how we are placing our feet—we simply go forward.

It is when we find ourselves in crisis that we falter. We are lingering in spiritual darkness, afraid to move. We call out in fear, asking God to lift us out of the darkness. What we need to acknowledge is that God is with us in that spiritual night (Ps. 139:11-12).

What is our recurring problem? We have failed to trust God. When our way is clear and bright, trust is easy. In darkness, however, He sometimes asks us to do things that make little or no sense. We begin to question His ability to lead us safely through the night of our fears. We become paralyzed and stop moving.

The good news is that we can completely trust Him. Scripture tells us that Jesus is the Light of the World (John 8:12). He illuminates our path. As we keep our eyes on Him, we are surrounded by His light. He sees our paths, so He knows which step we should take next and where He is leading. Because of this, we can follow His lead confidently every day.

Are you facing darkness in some area of your life? Have you struggled and stumbled around, trying to stay on the path?

We do not see things clearly (I Cor. 13:12), and we cannot trust our own wisdom. We get tired and are tempted to give up, to just stay right there in the darkness. When we do that, we miss out on what He wants to show us.

If this sounds familiar, I would encourage you today to give up your stubbornness. Fall back into place behind the Lord and follow. After all, His vision is so much better than ours. His plans for us are always good (cf. Jer. 29:11), and He will not allow us to stumble as we walk with Him. Meanwhile, He has things there for you, even in the darkness. So what are you waiting for? Trust Him, and let Him guide you safely through.

—Jennifer Francis.

Heart of the Lesson

I love walking my dog on fall evenings when the harvest moon, swollen and orange, hangs above the horizon. The moon's beauty captivates me.

I read recently that the word "moon" is derived from an Old English word related to "month." One of the reasons God created the heavenly bodies was to mark times and seasons.

1. Sun, moon, and stars (Gen. 1:14-19). God spent the first four days of Creation preparing our world to support living creatures, both animals and humans. On the fourth day, God created the sun, the greater light, to rule the day and the moon, the lesser light, to rule the night. And He created the stars.

God's purpose in creating the sun, moon, and stars was to separate day and night; to provide signs to humanity (for example, in the end times, when God will pronounce judgment, the sun will become dark and the moon will turn to blood); to mark seasons (the sun and moon influence navigation and agriculture, and they help regulate the breeding and migration of animals and birds) (Keil and Delitzsch, *Commentary on the Old Testament,* Eerdmans); to delineate individual days and other time periods (the sun and moon help us mark time—for example, one rotation of the moon around the earth equals a month); and to light the earth.

God again saw that His creation was good. And His timing was perfect—now plant life had the means for photosynthesis as well as the sun's warmth to promote growth.

2. Marine life and fowl (Gen. 1:20-23). In contrast to God's creation of the earth, which He created from nothing, God's creation of living organisms was from existing matter on the earth. Matter is not eternal; God created it (Tenney, ed., *The Zondervan Pictorial Encyclopedia of the Bible,* Zondervan).

God spoke all manner of marine life into existence. He created more than a few creatures—He created in abundance. And from the ground God created all manner of birds to fly above the earth.

God saw that His creation on this fifth day was good and blessed both the aquatic animals and the birds. He gave them the charge to reproduce after their own kind, multiplying and filling the seas and earth. God wanted the oceans teeming with creatures and the skies filled with birds.

3. Animal life (Gen. 1:24-25). From the earth, God created animals in three categories: cattle, or domesticated animals; creeping things—small animals and reptiles; and beasts of the earth—wildlife.

These animals were to reproduce after their kind, creating more animals like them. God looked at the animals He had created and saw that they were good.

The Bible's Creation account teaches that God is the Creator of all things, both nonliving and living. God created living organisms to reproduce after their kind. Our world and the life in it is the result of God's power, not the result of a big bang or any other evolutionary construct. God Himself is the intelligence behind "Intelligent Design."

The beauty and intricacies of God's creation are witnesses to God's glory, power, and creativity. He created the earth to be a habitation where He and humanity would have fellowship. This week praise the Creator for the marvelous world He has provided, and remember to fellowship with Him through His Word.

—Ann Staatz.

World Missions

We believe Creation to be an uncontested fact because it is in the Bible. We assume our children believe it as well.

Unfortunately, Christian children across our nation are being so bombarded with the "science" of evolution and its "truth" that if they believe anything else, they are considered foolish and unscientific. Consequently, our schools and even some churches are becoming mission fields.

High school math teacher Brian Thigpen sees the damage being done by evolutionary teaching. "The evolutionary view of man leaves us without any moral compass or bearing. There is no intrinsic value to life. There is no right or wrong. We are just complex animals, and your imagination can run wild with how many foolish philosophies can develop with that worldview. We see many of them around us today."

What can we do to stop this godless worldview from permeating the mindset of our Christian children?

1. Be as intentional in teaching creation as the educational system is in teaching evolution. "Many churches aren't addressing evolution because they're saying 'Just have faith,'" says Thigpen. "But students are being fed the lie that the choice is between truth or God, instead of God is truth."

2. Do not assume they believe in creation just because it is in the Bible. "Students are presented with the idea that the science is completely clear, so if you don't believe it, you're a fool. Young people feel their choice is reality or the Bible."

3. Give them resources. There are excellent Christian sites out there to help answer their questions and equip them with truth. Brian's two favorites are Answers in Genesis (www.answersingenesis.org) and Institute for Creation Research (www.icr.org).

4. Show them inconsistencies and flaws in evolutionary theory that they are not hearing about in school. Richard Halvorson said in *The Harvard Crimson,* "Expressing hesitation about Darwin is . . . the unpardonable sin of academia. . . . Professors expressing doubts about evolution are often ostracized, demoted or fired" ("Confessions of a Skeptic," April 7, 2003).

The late Philip Skell was a professor at Penn State University. He admitted, "Many scientists make public statements about the theory that they would not defend privately to other scientists like me" ("Dr. Philip Skell's Open Letter to the South Carolina Education Oversight Committee").

"Something as simple as radiometric dating, one of their biggest 'proofs' of the old ages of things, gives evidence against itself," shares Thigpen. "Rock from the Mount St. Helens eruption in 1986 gave a radiometric age of 350,000 years. A 1954 eruption in Japan yielded an age of 3.5 million years."

5. Teach them that evolution takes more faith than creation. "Both evolution and creation require faith in the unseen; one rejects any consideration of God, the other acknowledges the fingerprint of God all around us."

6. Pray for them to be strong in their faith and courageous enough to defend it. "Satan is using the issue of evolution in a greater way than most parents realize. Though we'd like to ignore the issue, it's not going to ignore our children. If we can help them be prepared for the attacks of the enemy, they can not only stand strong in their own faith, but be a light for others also."

—Kimberly Rae.

The Jewish Aspect

There are many schools of thought in modern Judaism regarding the Genesis account of Creation versus evolutionary theory. Traditional Judaism, however, maintains that God created the universe. "This is the most fundamental concept of Judaism. Its implications are that only God has absolute ownership over Creation" (Troster, "Ten Jewish Teachings on Judaism and the Environment," www.greenfaith.org).

Rabbi Troster also states, "God's Creation is good. Creation is sufficient, structured and ordered. . . . It is also harmonious. It exists to serve God (Psalm 148). This order reflects God's wisdom . . . which is beyond human understanding."

Reform Judaism has daily blessings for the wonders of nature. "On seeing the large-scale wonders of nature, such as mountains, hills, deserts, seas, long rivers, lightning, and the sky in its purity," this prayer can be offered, "We praise You, Eternal God, Sovereign of the universe, who makes the works of creation" ("Daily Blessings: For Wonders of Nature," www.reformjudaism.org/practice/prayers-blessings/daily).

The Old Testament, and particularly the book of Psalms, is filled with exclamations of praise for the excellence of God and His creation. "The heavens declare the glory of God; and the firmament sheweth his handiwork" (19:1). "O Lord our Lord, how excellent is thy name in all the earth! who has set thy glory above the heavens" (8:1). These are just two examples of the psalmist's declaration of God's majesty.

Genesis 1:14 tells us that the lights were formed and placed in the firmament of heaven by God. They were created to serve such purposes as God willed they should. The lights were also created to serve as signs and for seasons. In Judaism, it is the earth's movement in relation to the sun and moon that determines the seasons and the calendar. In the Jewish calendar, a month occurs at every new moon.

It is God who created the great lights. This truth contrasted with the worship (in Egypt and Mesopotamia) of the celestial bodies. God revealed that the very stars, moons, and planets, which Israel's neighbors worshipped, were the products of His creation. The lights of heaven were made to serve Him. "To him that made great lights: for his mercy endureth for ever. The sun to rule by day: for his mercy endureth for ever. The moon and stars to rule by night: for his mercy endureth for ever. . . . O give thanks unto the God of heaven: for his mercy endureth for ever" (Ps. 136:7-9, 26).

Similarly, the moving creatures in the waters and the living creatures of every kind on the earth were made by God, and God saw that it was good (Gen. 1:21, 25). These creatures were created in great abundance. This can also be seen in Psalm 104:25: "So is this great and wide sea, wherein are things creeping innumerable, both small and great beasts."

God created all living things "after his [or their] kind" (Gen. 1:12, 21, 24, 25). The Hebrew word for "kind," *min,* designates a group or multiplicity of animals and implies boundaries between the groups. The word "emphasizes how the plants bearing fruit and the trees bearing fruit are created in all their kinds; that is, all kinds of plants and trees are created" (Hess, "The Meaning of mîn in the Hebrew Old Testament, Part 2," www.biologos.org). The creation of the animals completed the earth's preparation for God's greatest creation—mankind.

—*Deborah Markowitz Solan.*

Guiding the Superintendent

The Bible is God's story. The first chapter of Genesis is all about God and how He created the world as a perfect place for mankind to live and enjoy life.

The earth was originally described as "without form, and void" (Gen. 1:2). The first three days of Creation dealt with the "without form" situation (vss. 1-13). Light was created on the first day. God followed this the second day by separating the great water expanse into the oceans/lakes and a water canopy above the earth. To complete the basic structure of the earth, God filled the dry land with all its vegetation on the third day.

On days four through six, God completed His perfect creation by continuing to fill the void, or emptiness, of earth.

DEVOTIONAL OUTLINE

1. Fourth day of creation (Gen. 1:14-19). On the fourth day of Creation, God created in the heavens above the earth.

God had created light on the first day of Creation (Gen. 1:3). Now on the fourth day, the production of life came to be in the "firmament" (vs. 6). This word now expands from the idea of the atmosphere (vs. 7) to mean the entire universe (vss. 14-19).

Light generators—the sun, moon, and stars—were created for several reasons, such as to divide time into days, nights, seasons, and years (Gen. 1:14); to light the earth (vs. 15); and to have the sun to light the day while the moon and stars would light the night (vs. 16).

When God was finished with this vast creation, He evaluated it the way He did all His creation. It was good (Gen. 1:18). In keeping with Old Testament practice of evening marking the beginning of the day, the text identifies the fourth day as the evening and the morning. The text is clear that the Creation occurred over a period of six twenty-four-hour time periods.

2. Fifth day of creation (Gen. 1:20-23). With all the necessary heavenly bodies in place, God's attention turned to animal life.

Contrary to modern thinking, the great animals of the sea did not evolve over millions of years. All sea life was created on the same day.

"Let the waters bring forth abundantly the moving creature" (Gen. 1:20). Some of the greatest abundance of animal life can be found in the oceans. The original waters teemed with animals.

What God did for the oceans of the world He also did for the air above the earth by filling it with wildlife. God blessed His creation and ordered it to "be fruitful, and multiply, and fill the waters" (Gen. 1:22) and air above the earth with life. God's evaluation: it was all good.

3. Sixth day of creation (Gen. 1:24-25). The seas had been filled with animals and fish. The skies had been filled with all kinds of fowl. Now on the sixth day, God rounded out His creative activities by first creating the land animals. All kinds of wild animals and cattle now came forth to roam the earth. The earth was now ready for God's greatest creation—humans.

CHILDREN'S CORNER

text: **I Kings 17:8-16**
title: **A Widow Risks Everything**

In fulfillment of Elijah's prediction of no rain, the country dried up. Obeying the Lord, Elijah went to Zarephath and asked a destitute widow for a meal. She offered her last meal. In response to her faith, her food supply did not cease until the rains came and food could be obtained again.

—*Martin R. Dahlquist*

Scripture Lesson Text

GEN. 1:26 And God said, Let us make man in our image, after our likeness: and let them have dominion over the fish of the sea, and over the fowl of the air, and over the cattle, and over all the earth, and over every creeping thing that creepeth upon the earth.

27 So God created man in his own image, in the image of God created he him; male and female created he them.

28 And God blessed them, and God said unto them, Be fruitful, and multiply, and replenish the earth, and subdue it: and have dominion over the fish of the sea, and over the fowl of the air, and over every living thing that moveth upon the earth.

29 And God said, Behold, I have given you every herb bearing seed, which is upon the face of all the earth, and every tree, in the which is the fruit of a tree yielding seed; to you it shall be for meat.

30 And to every beast of the earth, and to every fowl of the air, and to every thing that creepeth upon the earth, wherein there is life, I have given every green herb for meat: and it was so.

31 And God saw every thing that he had made, and, behold, it was very good. And the evening and the morning were the sixth day.

2:1 Thus the heavens and the earth were finished, and all the host of them.

2 And on the seventh day God ended his work which he had made; and he rested on the seventh day from all his work which he had made.

3 And God blessed the seventh day, and sanctified it: because that in it he had rested from all his work which God created and made.

NOTES

The First Man

Lesson Text: Genesis 1:26—2:3

Related Scriptures: Psalm 8:3-9; Acts 17:24-28;
I Corinthians 15:45-50; Exodus 20:8-11

TIME: unknown   PLACE: Eden

GOLDEN TEXT—"God said, Let us make man in our image, after our likeness: and let them have dominion over the fish of the sea, and over the fowl of the air, and over the cattle, and over all the earth, and over every creeping thing that creepeth upon the earth" (Genesis 1:26).

Introduction

Francis Schaeffer, in his book titled *Escape from Reason* (InterVarsity), traced people's estimation of grace and nature. Discussion of these topics began with Thomas Aquinas (1225–1274) and continued through the days of the Renaissance.

Over a period of time, natural things became culturally more important than heavenly things and took precedence in man's thinking. Humanistic thinking became dominant, and spiritual thinking receded. Man became more and more the object of primary attention and importance, while God was pushed into the background.

Schaeffer pointed out that "man, being made in the image of God, was made to have a personal relationship with Him. Man's relationship is upward and not merely downward.... Modern man sees his relationship downward to the animal and to the machine. The Bible rejects this view of who man is. On the side of personality you are related to God."

LESSON OUTLINE

I. **THE CLIMAX OF CREATION—** Gen. 1:26-30

II. **GOD'S REST AFTER CRE-ATION**—Gen. 1:31–2:3

Exposition: Verse by Verse

THE CLIMAX OF CREATION

GEN. 1:26 And God said, Let us make man in our image, after our likeness: and let them have dominion over the fish of the sea, and over the fowl of the air, and over the cattle, and over all the earth, and over every creeping thing that creepeth upon the earth.

27 So God created man in his own

image, in the image of God created he him; male and female created he them.

28 And God blessed them, and God said unto them, Be fruitful, and multiply, and replenish the earth, and subdue it: and have dominion over the fish of the sea, and over the fowl of the air, and over every living thing that moveth upon the earth.

29 And God said, Behold, I have given you every herb bearing seed, which is upon the face of all the earth, and every tree, in the which is the fruit of a tree yielding seed; to you it shall be for meat.

30 And to every beast of the earth, and to every fowl of the air, and to every thing that creepeth upon the earth, wherein there is life, I have given every green herb for meat: and it was so.

A decision (Gen. 1:26). At the pinnacle of creation was a creature made in the image of God, having intellect, emotion, and will. This creature was vastly different from and superior to all the others. This one came about through a members-only consultation of the Triune God. After reading "Let the waters bring forth" (vs. 20) and "Let the earth bring forth" (vs. 24), we now read "Let us make" (vs. 26). The plurality of this source points us straight to the Triune God.

If we are to remain firm in our belief that man is a direct creation of God, we must maintain a firm belief in the validity of God's Word. A study of the area of theology called bibliology helps us understand that God's Word came directly from Him and can be fully trusted in what it says. Therefore, based on this one verse alone, we have no reason to give any credence to evolution as the source of mankind. We are direct creations of God, and there is no other creature anywhere near what we are.

The creation of man is treated as the highlight of the sixth day of Creation. Man was made to be the most authoritative creature on earth above all other creatures. The very fact that God deliberated shows that He had decided to make something different from all the others. Man was going to be made in God's own image and likeness, something that is not true of any of the other creatures. An astounding realization comes from this—here was one with whom God could have true relationship.

It is important to realize that the creation of man includes all of mankind. Every one of us is a reflection of God and, as such, is eternally valuable to Him. We will never be exactly like God, for He is the Supreme Creator. We can, however, reflect His character in our ability to act, to make decisions, to reveal attitudes, and to interact with His other creatures, both human and otherwise. We alone have the ability to think, to love, and to obey, and God should be the primary object of all these responses.

An action (Gen. 1:27). Once the divine council made the decision to make this special creature it was done: "So God created man in his own image, in the image of God created he him." The very fact that we have intellect, emotion, and will is both a great blessing and a possible hindrance. We noted that we all have the ability to think, love, and obey, which means we have a wide parameter of freedom as God's special creatures. That means that we can make choices, but these can be either good or bad.

We have the freedom to think as God thinks, but since He did not make us robots, we also have the freedom to think contrary to the way He thinks. We have the freedom to love Him and one another, but we also have the freedom to reject Him and His creatures. We have the freedom to obey Him and the teachings of His Word, but that means we also have the freedom to ignore and disobey them. All of this shows us that being made in the image of God is a great blessing, but it carries great responsibility as well.

In his book on Philippians called *Laugh Again,* Chuck Swindoll discussed these freedoms at length: "Because we are free to do these things, we are also free *not* to do them. We are free to make wrong choices—how well we know! In fact, we can continue to make them for so long we can wind up in our own self-made prison of consequences" (Nelson). He then explained that such living leads to bondage and addictions, which he referred to as freedom out of control.

We are the climax of God's creation, but with that comes the responsibility to be what He wants us to be. So while we rejoice in that privilege, we must also reflect seriously on the ramifications.

Genesis 1:27 indicates that God created both the man and his wife on the same day. The details for this are recorded in the next chapter, verses 18–25, where we are told specifically how God went about bringing Eve into the creation and to Adam. Men and women are equally valued and loved by God, and we do not have to fight for laws that declare such truth.

A blessing (Gen. 1:28). This is the second time we read "And God blessed them," the first referring to the sea creatures and birds (cf. vs. 22). Both blessings involve reproduction, and the one directed to mankind adds dominion. There are three phrases in the blessing, the first being generic and the second explaining the first in more detail. Both phrases deal with reproduction, with the third referring specifically to dominion. It all begins with the command "Be fruitful, and multiply," the same as given after the creation of the fish and birds.

We need to understand that this command was given to the heads of the human race (and to Noah later on); it was not intended to apply to every individual. Not every human being has been charged with having children; in fact, some are unable to. Nor is it intended to imply that people should have as many children as they possibly can. It does show, however, that human sexuality is from God and is to be rightfully used for procreation. It will be clear later that this is for married couples.

The second phrase in Genesis 1:28 expands on this thought with the command "replenish the earth, and subdue it." The Hebrew word translated "replenish" means "to fill." Along with reproducing, Adam and Eve were given the mandate to "subdue" the earth. The Hebrew word here indicates conquering and subjugating, that is, being in control of things. God's creation was good, and they were to see to it that it remained that way. He gave them the responsibility of keeping the environment and creatures under control.

This was further explained as their having dominion over the fish, the fowl, and every living creature on land. All these blessings were given to Adam and Eve while they were in their unfallen state. God knew that sin would ruin His creation and make it much more difficult to keep the world under control. Left to itself, it would not remain good, as it was when God first completed His creating.

A command (Gen. 1:29-30). Apparently man was originally created vegetarian. This changed only after Noah's Flood (9:3). God provided an inexhaustible supply of food by making all the herbs and fruit trees in such a way that they would replicate themselves by seeds. In this way, no matter how many people resulted from the reproductive process, they would never be without plenty. This was how God provided for the necessary energy needed for life and, at that time, the work of caring for the garden.

The Believer's Study Bible summarizes Genesis 1:29-30 as follows: "God provides for the needs of His creatures; the pagans believed men were created to feed the gods. God's statement about vegetation may indicate that originally God did not intend for life to be taken in order to provide food for man or beast, although this is not specifically prohibited in the text. Permission to do this specifically appears later, in 9:3" (Criswell, ed., Nelson).

Similar provision was made for the animal world. Every category other than those in the waters is mentioned as having been given herbs for food: beasts, birds, and everything that creeps. In this case, the mention of beasts would include both domesticated and wild animals. Just to be sure we understand, the author said this includes everything that has life. What is portrayed is a world where there was perfect harmony in the animal kingdom, which is very different from what we see today.

Isaiah 11 describes the return of this kind of world. A ruler described as "a rod out of the stem of Jesse, and a Branch" growing "out of his roots" (vs. 1) will reign on earth. At that time the animal world will again become peaceful. In a world without destruction, wolves and lambs will live together, leopards and goat kids will lie down and rest together, calves and young lions will be together, cows and bears will eat side by side, lions will eat straw like oxen, and babies will play with snakes (vss. 6-8).

GOD'S REST AFTER CREATION

31 And God saw every thing that he had made, and, behold, it was very good. And the evening and the morning were the sixth day.

2:1 Thus the heavens and the earth were finished, and all the host of them.

2 And on the seventh day God ended his work which he had made; and he rested on the seventh day from all his work which he had made.

3 And God blessed the seventh day, and sanctified it: because that in it he had rested from all his work which God created and made.

Completion (Gen. 1:31—2:1). In a summary statement, we read that at the end of the sixth day of Creation, "God saw every thing that he had made, and, behold, it was very good. . . .Thus the heavens and the earth were finished, and all the host of them." This was God's final evaluation of His work, although what follows in the second chapter contains further description. The universe had now reached its state of completion with all the components God wanted included in place. No further creation was necessary.

Six times God had looked at what He created and recognized it as good. Now as He took everything in view collectively, He pronounced it very good. In chapter 2, there is detailed explanation of His creation of mankind, included in this summary statement. God's complete pleasure should be an encouragement to us because it includes mankind and each of us in particular. There is often temptation to be dissatisfied with how we have been made or how we look, but we should remember that we are exactly what He wants!

The emphasis in Genesis 1 has been on the earth and everything created in relationship to it. The first verse of chapter 2 mentions the heavens and host of things in it that are associated with the earth. This gives a renewed emphasis on the entire universe, showing the greatness of God in a broader perspective. Our attention will be refocused on activity on the earth in the next verses, but a moment of contemplation on the vastness of God's creation is a good reminder.

"Everything in the universe . . . was still at this time exceedingly good, in God's own omniscient judgment. There could have been nothing that was *not* good in all creation: no struggle for existence, no disease, no pollution, no physical calamities (earthquakes, floods, etc.), no imbalance or lack of harmony, no disorder, no sin and, above all, *no death!*" (Morris, *The Genesis Record,* Baker).

Conclusion (Gen. 2:2-3). This is the only place in all of Scripture where we read of God resting. The statement does not indicate, of course, that He was exhausted or that there would be no further activity on His part in the future. The Bible indicates constant activity on our behalf from God to this day. The remainder of the Old Testament records His nonstop work on behalf of Israel, and all the New Testament records consistent activity on behalf of His church and children. So why did God rest on the seventh day?

The real meaning of God resting is that He ceased all His creative activity. It was not that He was tired, as we are after mowing a lawn and trimming weeds; rather, He had simply accomplished all that He had set out to do. When the necessary work for our salvation was completed on the cross, Jesus cried out, "It is finished!" (John 19:30); here likewise, the work of creation was done. There was nothing else to add to all that work. Several times it is mentioned that God finished all His work.

God then blessed the seventh day and set it apart as special, perhaps as a memorial of all He had done. In the Mosaic Law, the seventh day became the Sabbath, emphasizing the importance of resting from daily activity. Unlike God, we need regular rest, so this emphasis is found repeatedly in Scripture. It is also a time for leaving our regular activities alone and focusing on God and our worship of Him.

This special emphasis on a certain day of the week switched to Sunday for us because of the resurrection, but the pattern should still be observed. God did not command Adam not to work on the seventh day, but He included that in the Mosaic Law. The emphasis in the New Testament is on a day set aside in our lives for God. Anything we can do to honor Him on His day is surely pleasing in His sight.

—*Keith E. Eggert.*

QUESTIONS

1. How does the Bible portray the Triune God as making a decision on His climactic creative act?

2. How does our belief in the Bible help us accept creation instead of evolution?

3. In what way are we created in the image of God, and what position does this put us in?

4. In blessing mankind, what command did God give?

5. What did God specify as a food source for all His creatures?

6. What was the perfect animal world like, and when will we see this again?

7. How did God evaluate His completed work?

8. Why did God rest?

9. What did God do on the seventh day besides rest?

10. How is God's initial rest carried on in the Bible?

—*Keith E. Eggert.*

Preparing to Teach the Lesson

This week in our lesson, we explore together how man came to be on this earth. God had already created the animals, birds, and nature. He then embarked on His crowning creation—man. We also learn that God made man in His image and what this really means for us today.

TODAY'S AIM

Facts: to show how God created man and why He did.

Principle: to remember that God created man to rule over all the earth.

Application: to realize that if God has put us in charge of all the earth, then we have a responsibility to take care of all creation.

INTRODUCING THE LESSON

All around us we see the ingenuity of man. Big, heavy airplanes fly easily above us, and we communicate almost instantaneously with someone on the other side of the world. But nothing compares to the creation of man by a wonderful God. Our physical body is a wonder in itself. Every part has a unique function. Men and women are physically different, and yet we fit perfectly together. The psalmist said that we are "fearfully and wonderfully made" (Ps. 139:14).

Our lesson this week explores this great wonder of creation and helps us open a window into the heart of God as loving Creator.

DEVELOPING THE LESSON

1. Created in God's image (Gen. 1:26-27). The creation of man was no afterthought on God's part; it was deliberate and intentional. This is made clear by the picture the text gives of

God appearing to consult with Himself on the matter. The text uses the plural here: "Let us make man." This has usually been interpreted either as a sign of respect for God in the original language or as a veiled reference to the Trinity.

The Genesis account points out two special characteristics of man. First, man was to be made "in our image, after our likeness" (1:26). Second, God gave man many characteristics that reflect His, including rational thought, the ability to make conscious choices rather than merely act from instinct, and a full range of emotions. Yes, in these respects we share the nature of God. Third, we see that God put man in charge of all His creation, making him responsible for them.

We also see that besides giving us some of His own characteristics, God made mankind male and female. This was in His master plan for mankind. It is important to understand that we were created to be like God.

2. Fruitfulness and dominion (Gen. 1:28-31). Here we see three things that God did. First He blessed, then He provided, and finally He approved of all His creation. God blessed the first man and woman (note that the details of the creation of man and woman come later in chapter 2). The blessing came in the mandate for all life on the earth to multiply. Without God's blessing, there is no growth. This principle applies to all life and to every one of us.

We also see that God provided seed-bearing plants. This tells us that God is the Author of all life and has given us the ability to share in His work of life giving. When man tends the earth, it brings forth more life. This was also the provision for man's food. At this point, it appears that man's diet was vegetarian (there is no reference to the eating of animal flesh until Noah's time in Genesis 9:3).

Finally, we see how God again looked on in approval of all that He had done on the earth and said that it was very good. Notice that there is a greater degree of approval here than on previous occasions. Certainly this is because of the creation of man. Here was someone God could relate to on a personal level, for our God is personal in nature. Make sure your students understand that at every stage of creation, God was deliberate and had us in mind every step of the way.

3. A day for rest (Gen. 2:1-3). This section of the text sums up God's overall work in Creation. Your class should not miss the air of finality to the work of God that is brought out here. God created the earth in six days. Then on the seventh day, He rested from all the work that He had done.

There is a lesson for us here. When God begins something, He does not leave it unfinished. When He is finished, He stops, which is what it means to say that He rests. Emphasizing this truth, Genesis 2:3 says, "And God blessed the seventh day, and sanctified it." The day of rest follows work and is a day for renewal and for our sanctification. It is designed so that we can become a holy people who devote our time to God and honor Him.

This is also a picture of our heavenly rest when our work here on earth is done. We are told that God rested from His great work of creation. There is another principle in this that we cannot ignore. Rest always follows work. Only the one who works needs time for rest. God does not get tired and need rest for Himself, but He set an example for us in this matter. Our God is always working on our behalf in our world.

ILLUSTRATING THE LESSON

God created man to rule and protect His creation.

RULE AND PROTECT

GOD'S CREATION

CONCLUDING THE LESSON

The story of the creation of the first man shows us how much God loves us and how much He planned for us. We are constantly in His thoughts, and He cares so much for us. He shows this to us by allowing us to share in His creation. He has put us in charge of all His creation as His representatives on earth. We need to take this responsibility very seriously.

God also gave us the seventh day as a time of rest so that we can turn to Him from our labors of the week and honor Him. We dare not forget His goodness to us nor take for granted everything that He has provided to make life meaningful every single day.

ANTICIPATING THE NEXT LESSON

Next week we will explore the beginning of human history and man's first home in the Garden of Eden.

—*A. Koshy Muthalaly.*

PRACTICAL POINTS

1. We display God's image as we fulfill God's will and do His work in the world (Gen. 1:26).
2. God uniquely created mankind to have a relationship with Him, to glorify Him, and to fellowship with Him (vs. 27).
3. We care for the earth and all that God has created by recognizing God as the Owner and ourselves as stewards (vss. 28-30).
4. Everything God does is good (vs. 31).
5. God finishes what He starts—in His time and in His way (2:1).
6. We honor God when we work for Him, when we worship Him, and when we rest in Him (vss. 2-3).

—*Cheryl Y. Powell.*

RESEARCH AND DISCUSSION

1. What does it mean that God created man "in his own image" (Gen. 1:27)? In what ways is this true?
2. In what ways does our culture challenge God's design for sex? For gender roles? How are believers to respond to these challenges?
3. In what ways is man unique? How does man use that to honor God?
4. In what settings have you been given authority? How does God's command for the first man and woman challenge you in your own leadership?
5. What does it mean that God rested from His work? What did God intend by sanctifying the seventh day?

—*Cheryl Y. Powell.*

ILLUSTRATED HIGH POINTS

Make man in our image

A website catering to freethinkers referred to an illustration that appeared to be Michelangelo's *The Creation of Adam.* A closer look, however, shows Adam breathing life into God.

The article went on to praise this idea, claiming that since man cannot make sense out of the universe, he had to create a god as an explanation.

This is typical of man who seeks to change "the glory of the uncorruptible God into an image made like to corruptible man" (Rom. 1:23).

God created man

The fact that God is the Creator of the universe with Creation's climax being man is mentioned repeatedly throughout the Bible. There are numerous occasions in both the Old Testament and New Testament where various facets of Creation are affirmed.

Stuart Briscoe observed in connection with Psalm 8:5 and Hebrews 2:7, "'Slightly lower than the angels' is a whole lot better than slightly higher than the apes. Let's get the order straight. God, angelic beings, man, animals, and vegetables" (Sweeting, *Who Said That?* Moody).

It was very good

You have made many things throughout your lifetime. When you were finished, you probably observed your work and said, "That's pretty good."

Deep down, however, you knew that your "creation" had flaws—a nick, a scratch, a lump, or a mistake that perhaps only you could see. Everything man makes has some imperfection.

God, however, had no flaws in His creation. He pronounced it "very good."

—*David A. Hamburg.*

Golden Text Illuminated

"God said, Let us make man in our image, after our likeness: and let them have dominion over the fish of the sea, and over the fowl of the air, and over the cattle, and over all the earth, and over every creeping thing that creepeth upon the earth" (Genesis 1:26).

I love watching my husband and stepchildren. For me, there are few moments in life sweeter than the ones I spend doing that. Whether they are playing a game, completing a chore around the house, or just joking around, those times are precious for me to witness.

There are times, though, when the mannerisms of my stepchildren bring me an extra special smile. That happens when one of them does something like his father. Whether it is one of them standing exactly like his father or the other one repeating a phrase his father says, the mimicking of their dad always warms my heart. It reminds me of how much of him is in each of the kids. There is no mistaking that they are his children.

In the same way, we were created as God's own children. We are told that Adam was created in God's image. It was God's plan that people should live as His children.

Do not gloss over that. Let it sink in for a minute. Think of the children in your life, whether they are your own or someone else's. Have you ever seen them say or do something that completely mimics their parents? Did it make you smile when that happened?

What would it have been like to be created in God's own image in the time before sin entered the world? Adam was created to rule over this breathtaking world God had wrought. What was Adam really like? What was God's vision for a blameless man?

Our answer comes in Jesus, God's own Son. Jesus told us that whoever has seen Him has seen the Father (John 14:9). As we grow closer to Our Saviour, we see Him more clearly. When we grow closer to Jesus, we can better know both Him and His Father each day. Because of this, we can see what God intended for mankind from the very beginning.

As we as believers draw nearer to Christ, the benefit of walking in faith is that we begin to mimic Him. God is always sanctifying us, bringing us more in line with His original vision for our lives each day. When we take Christ as our example, we reflect Him more and more (II Cor. 3:18).

When I see my stepchildren's mimicry, it reminds me to think about whether I am reflecting Christ well. When people look at me, do they see Jesus? If not, what do I need to change? God's design for me is not identical to His design for other individuals. I know, though, that all believers are called to a family likeness to their Saviour. As I come alongside Him in this purpose, He will mold me into that perfect reflection of Him that He intended.

Do you reflect Jesus each day, or is there someone else that you have chosen to mimic? The person you choose to model yourself after is the person you will become. If you are modeling yourself after Jesus, then you will become like Him. If you are not, then you will find yourself drifting away from His design for you. That is a sobering thought. The question then, is, Who do you choose to mimic?

—Jennifer Francis.

Heart of the Lesson

I taught journalism at a Bible college for many years. In one assignment, I asked the students how their writing was a reflection of being created in God's image. Creativity is just one of the areas in which men and women bear God's image.

1. God creates man (Gen. 1:26-27). On the sixth day of Creation, before God created man, He again spoke. Before He did anything, God revealed His intention, saying, "Let us make man in our image."

The plural "us" can be seen as the Bible's first reference to the Trinity: God the Father, God the Son, and God the Holy Spirit. God's pattern and design for mankind was Himself. And all three Persons of the Godhead were involved in the Creation.

Being made in God's image means human beings reflect characteristics of God, such as self-awareness, ability to make moral choices, and personality. But the image also consists of a spiritual nature resulting from the breath of God (Keil and Delitzsch, *Commentary on the Old Testament,* Eerdmans).

The likeness of God in us is what distinguishes humanity from the animal world. God made a hierarchy in His creation, and human beings are at the top; they are the pinnacle of creation.

God created both male and female. Both sexes bear God's image. Both reflect their Creator.

2. God blesses man (Gen. 1:28-30). After blessing the man and woman, God charged them with the responsibility to be fruitful and multiply—have many children, who in turn would produce many more children down through the ages. They were to fill the earth, inhabiting all of it, not just the area where the first couple lived.

People are called upon to subdue the earth. They are to exercise power over it, make the earth productive, explore the earth, care for it, discover its treasures, and harness its resources.

Mankind is to have dominion over the earth and everything in it, including fish, fowl, and animals. They are to rule over earth's living creatures. God charged humanity with being stewards of His earth.

The first people were vegetarians. God explained that the man and woman were to eat a plant-based diet: grains and fruit. People would eat no meat until after the Flood.

3. God rests from His completed work (Gen. 1:31—2:3). After creating man, God said His work of creation was not just good but "very good."

God now had finished His work of creating the heavens and the earth and everything in them. He had equipped the earth with everything fish, fowl, animals, and humanity would need to live and thrive. After God ended His work of Creation, He rested on the seventh day. He was not tired, but He had completed His work.

God blessed the seventh day, His day of rest, and set it apart as holy. In doing so, He set a precedent for His people. Later, the nation of Israel would observe the seventh day as its Sabbath and cease from all work. People today also need a day of rest.

Another important lesson from the biblical account of God creating humanity is the implications of being made in God's image. Even though sin has tainted humanity, human beings are still image-bearers of God and retain the preeminent position in creation. All human lives, from babies in the womb to senior adults, are sacred and must be protected, regardless of infirmities or mental capacity.

—Ann Staatz.

World Missions

So many around our world do not know they are made in God's image and loved with His unconditional, everlasting love (Jer. 31:3). One of the ways this great news of value and worth is being carried to millions is through shoeboxes. Operation Christmas Child has given the love of Jesus to more than 124 million children around the world!

These boxes—filled with school supplies, hygiene items, toys and gifts—are so much more than humanitarian help at Christmas. They are tiny ambassadors for the gospel, and some have changed the lives of not just the children who received them, but their families and even entire villages.

How can a small shoebox do all that?

Angella in Malawi received a shoebox, got saved, and was instrumental in leading all ten members of her family to the Lord.

The shoebox Azima received in Cameroon had a note inside that said, "I might not know you, but always know that Jesus loves you and so do I." She had never been given a gift in her life. That night Azima received Jesus. "In times of sorrow and grief when I needed to be reminded of God's love, I would clutch my shoebox close to my heart and pray."

Against their father's wishes, she and her sisters sneaked out of the house to attend church. She began teaching the other children about Jesus. In time, her father came to the Lord. Now grown up, Azima packs shoeboxes for other children and includes a note about Jesus' love in each one.

Natasha, harmed by the nuclear disaster at Chernobyl, also had never received a gift before her shoebox. "I felt as though the world was crashing in around me." The shoebox gave her hope. "We were not forgotten. We were still loved."

In time, Natasha accepted Christ. "I am so thankful I was drawn to Him through that booklet in my shoebox," she said. Natasha has graduated from Liberty University and hopes to get a job in business that allows her to be involved in missions.

Elena's home in the former Soviet Union was cold and dirty. Her parents drank. She had nothing and would dream of Cinderella to get away from reality. "When I was at my lowest point—feeling unloved, worthless—God brought me a shoebox." Inside was "The Greatest Gift" booklet that told of the love of Jesus. "I had never heard of that kind of love before. I thought it was a fairy tale. The Creator of everything came down and died for someone like me? It gave me hope." After coming to the Lord, she organized shoebox-packing parties in college. Her plan for the future is to share God's love with orphans around the world.

In Cambodia, a struggling church had less than twenty people, and the villagers were not interested in coming. After the children received shoebox gifts and began The Greatest Journey discipleship program, parents became interested in what their children told them they were learning. The church now has about forty adults and fifty children attending, with hopes to reach their community for Christ.

Such a small gift with such huge, eternal possibilities!

Go to www.samaritanspurse.org to find out how you can send Jesus' love, in a shoebox, to the world!

—*Kimberly Rae.*

The Jewish Aspect

"And God said, Let us make man in our image, after our likeness" (Gen. 1:26). With these words, God made Adam, the first human being to walk the earth. "Man" is used in the generic sense, amplified by the phrase "male and female" (vs. 27). The Hebrew word for man, *adam,* indicates man's earthly nature—with the Hebrew word for ground being *adama.*

God also gave Adam dominion over the earth, the fish of the sea, the fowl of the air, and every living thing upon the earth. "In the name Adam, the word *dam* ['blood'] is preceded by the letter *aleph.* The letter *aleph* is also a word which means to teach or inculcate. It similarly indicates leadership, as implied by the related word *aluf* which means a general or tribal head. . . . By being in control instead of subject to the dominion of our impulses, man, who is created in the image of God, resembles God. In this connection, the name Adam also alludes to the name *adameh* which means I will liken myself, indicating one's ability to emulate God" (Baron, "The Meaning of 'Adam': Insights into the Hebrew Language," www.aish.com).

Having dominion defined man's unique relation to creation. Man was God's representative in ruling over the creation. The command to rule defined his relationship as above the rest of creation (Ps. 8:4-8). Man was created by God on the sixth day of Creation as the grand climax of all that God had accomplished in the week of Creation. The final act of Creation was that God joined the material and immaterial parts of man. Man's body was shaped from the dust, and he was also created in the image of God. The word "image" in Hebrew is *tzelem* and refers to the image, likeness, or resemblance of something. "The making of mankind constitutes the crescendo of the creation narrative of Chapter One. God creates man last, at the conclusion of six days of labor, an entire world of warm-up. This seems to signal that Man represents God's crowning achievement in creating the 'good world.'" (Waxman, "And God Saw That It Was Good," etzion.org.il/en).

There is much debate in Jewish commentary regarding the plural use of "us" and "our" in Genesis 1:26. With whom is God partnering when making mankind? Many Jewish scholars claim that God is referring to His ministering angels. Eli Hadar writes, "If you search the Bible, you will find that when the Almighty speaks of 'us' or 'our,' He is addressing His ministering angels. In fact, only two chapters later, God continues to use the pronoun 'us' as He speaks with His angels" (Orthodox Judaism, www.allexperts.com).

Approaching the text from a different angle, Gerald Sigal maintains, "In this verse the Hebrew verb 'created' appears in the singular form. If 'let us make man' indicates a numerical plurality, it would be followed in the NEXT verse by, 'And they created man in their image'" ("What is the meaning of God said: 'Let us make man in our image . . . ?" www.jewsforjudaism.org).

On the sixth day God finished the work that He had created and sanctified the seventh day for rest. "Shabbat . . . is the seventh day of the Jewish week and is the day of rest and abstention from work commanded by God. Shabbat involves two interrelated commandments: to remember (*zachor*) and to observe (*shamor*)" ("Shabbat: What is Shabbat?" www.jewishvirtuallibrary.org). God sanctified (set apart and made holy) this day for us to follow His example of rest.

—*Deborah Markowitz Solan.*

Guiding the Superintendent

The crown of creation is man. The universe and everything in it was created by God for man to enjoy. Genesis 1 presents man as the climax to the six days of Creation. Chapter 2 is also about the divine Creation but with a narrowed focus on man and his relationship to God.

DEVOTIONAL OUTLINE

1. God completed His works (Gen. 1:26-31). Everything God had already created was in preparation for the pinnacle of God's creation. The plan was specific. God the Father, God the Son, and God the Holy Spirit said, "Let us make" (Gen. 1:26). The image of God became God's pattern. They said, "in our image." There was a specific purpose for all this. Man was to "have dominion" over creation.

God created mankind as male and female. Together man and woman were called to reflect God to the world.

God blessed His creation of man and woman. He commissioned mankind with a task (Gen. 1:28). They were tasked with the responsibility of filling the earth. They were also given the task of ruling all the animals of the sea, sky, and land.

God provided all the food that His creation (both man and animal) would need. Green vegetation and every seed was provided for man and animals to eat.

The responsibilities before man were big ones. They were to rule over the creation; they were to multiply; they were to subdue creation; and, finally, it is implied that they were to cultivate the ground for their food.

Genesis 1 ends with God's final evaluation of His creation. Now it is not just "good" but "very good" (vs. 31).

2. God rested after completing His work (Gen. 2:1-3). The Creation account ends on a note of rest and celebration.

God was finished with His creative work. Three times the text uses the word "all" to emphasize that in creation God made everything. To further emphasize that creation was now complete, the text states that God "finished" (Gen. 2:1) and "ended his work" (vs. 2).

Having completed His creative activity, God rested. This was not the rest of exhaustion but the rest of completion. The task was complete.

God's resting did not indicate that God was now inactive. It is rather obvious that He was still very much involved with His creation. But while God was still involved with His creation, He was through with the original work of the Creation.

The seventh day became very special for God. He "sanctified" it (Gen. 2:3); that is, He set it apart for a very special purpose. The fourth commandment (Exod. 20:8-11) emphasizes that the seventh day is to be a day of rest for all. In honor of the resurrection of Christ, the church celebrates a day of rest on Sunday.

CHILDREN'S CORNER

text: **I Kings 17:17-24**
title: **Raised to Life!**

Because of an area-wide drought, Elijah sought refuge in the house of a widow. She was heartbroken when her son took sick and died. Elijah prayed over the boy's dead body, and the boy's life was restored to him. The widow was convinced that Elijah was God's prophet.

—*Martin R. Dahlquist.*

Scripture Lesson Text

GEN. 2:4 These are the generations of the heavens and of the earth when they were created, in the day that the LORD God made the earth and the heavens,

5 And every plant of the field before it was in the earth, and every herb of the field before it grew: for the LORD God had not caused it to rain upon the earth, and there was not a man to till the ground.

6 But there went up a mist from the earth, and watered the whole face of the ground.

7 And the LORD God formed man of the dust of the ground, and breathed into his nostrils the breath of life; and man became a living soul.

8 And the LORD God planted a garden eastward in Eden; and there he put the man whom he had formed.

9 And out of the ground made the LORD God to grow every tree that is pleasant to the sight, and good for food; the tree of life also in the midst of the garden, and the tree of knowledge of good and evil.

10 And a river went out of Eden to water the garden; and from thence it was parted, and became into four heads.

11 The name of the first is Pison: that is it which compasseth the whole land of Havilah, where there is gold;

12 And the gold of that land is good: there is bdellium and the onyx stone.

13 And the name of the second river is Gihon: the same is it that compasseth the whole land of Ethiopia.

14 And the name of the third river is Hiddekel: that is it which goeth toward the east of Assyria. And the fourth river is Euphrates.

NOTES

46

Man's First Home

Lesson Text: Genesis 2:4-14

Related Scriptures: Isaiah 51:1-3; Ezekiel 28:11-14

TIME: unknown   PLACE: Eden

GOLDEN TEXT—"God blessed the seventh day, and sanctified it: because that in it he had rested from all his work which God created and made" (Genesis 2:3).

Introduction

There is an adage that says, "Home is where the heart is." Various ideas might be communicated in this phrase. Perhaps it means that people long to be home more than anywhere else. Some think that it means that your true home is the place where the person you love the most is, so it is the place where you enjoy being more than anyplace else you could be.

At home we can be ourselves. We have a place where we can eat and sleep safely and where we are sheltered from the elements of the weather. Those who have no home or those who serve in military forces cannot enjoy such comforts. How thankful we should be for home!

Some Bible students think that what is recorded in Genesis 2 is a second account of Creation written by a different author. They often think this based on the different facts recorded in each chapter. A careful examination of those facts, however, reveals that added information is given in chapter 2—information that helps explain some of the events that occur later on in man's history.

LESSON OUTLINE

I. HOW THINGS BEGAN—
Gen. 2:4-7

II. HOW THINGS WERE
MAINTAINED—Gen. 2:8-14

Exposition: Verse by Verse

HOW THINGS BEGAN

GEN. 2:4 These are the generations of the heavens and of the earth when they were created, in the day that the LORD God made the earth and the heavens,

5 And every plant of the field before it was in the earth, and every herb of the field before it grew: for the LORD God had not caused it to rain upon the earth, and there was not a man to till the ground.

6 But there went up a mist from the earth, and watered the whole face of the ground.

7 And the LORD God formed man of the dust of the ground, and breathed into his nostrils the breath of life; and man became a living soul.

Initial creation (Gen. 2:4-5a). The phrase "these are the generations" translates the Hebrew expression *'elleh toledot,* used repeatedly in the book of Genesis to introduce new sections of information. Among other things revealed in this section (2:4—4:26) are the placement of Adam in Eden, the creation of Eve, and the entrance of sin into God's creation. What we also have in this section of Scripture are details of the sixth day not included in Genesis 1:1 through 2:3.

When we compare what we find in this text with what has already been recorded, several things show us different emphases. The Hebrew name used for God in the previous portion of Scripture is *Elohim,* meaning "the Strong One," but here the name used is *Yahweh,* meaning "the Covenant-keeping One." The first name shows God's transcendence over His creation, but the second emphasizes His immanence with His created beings. The God who created is the same God who controls the history of man.

The purpose of the previous section is to point to the facts of creation, but now we see an emphasis on God having a relationship with humans. While the world generally was the focus of attention earlier, now mankind becomes that focus. A subtle change of wording within Genesis 2:4 hints at this: from "of the heavens and of the earth" to "made the earth and the heavens," mentioning man's abiding place first. Mankind does appear to take center stage here.

Chronologically, we are taken back to the stage before plant life, and, therefore, prior to the creation of Adam. This was back to the time when God began preparing His creation for the entrance of mankind. At that time there were neither uncultivated or cultivated plants; so far nothing living was growing.

Initial moisture (Gen. 2:5b-6). There were two good reasons why there was no plant life: there had never been rain, and there was no person to cultivate anything. The absence of rain is one of the factors behind the theory of an original watery canopy over the earth. If correct, then that canopy burst open at the time of Noah's Flood, causing water to pour down upon the earth from above. This would explain the phrase "the windows of heaven were opened" in Genesis 7:11.

Longevity of life decreased greatly after the Flood, adding to the plausibility of a canopy over the earth. With a canopy, the harmful rays from the sun could have been hindered from reaching earth, allowing for longer lifetimes. This cannot be proved conclusively, of course, but the possibility remains.

Prior to rain, we are told that God used a mist coming up from the earth to water it. The idea seems to be that of an enveloping fog that came from below instead of above the surface of the earth. It might well be that the changes in temperature between days and nights caused a condensation from the waters that produced this fog. Unless it was a constant fog, the result was probably similar to a heavy dew that we sometimes find on our lawns and gardens in the early mornings.

Throughout Genesis 2, reference to God is repeatedly "Lord God," or *Yahweh Elohim.* It is used this way eleven times in twenty-two verses. Since the late eighteenth century, unbelieving biblical critics have used this fact to advance the argument that Genesis (indeed, the entire Pentateuch) was the work of multiple authors or editors. The claim is that the exclusive use of *Elohim* versus *Yahweh Elohim* reveals separate documents by individuals who knew of, or favored, only one designation or the other for Deity.

While space prevents us from touching on the great number of evidences that refute this view, suffice it to note that the use of one name or title rather than another points much more naturally to a simple change of emphasis. And while it would not be surprising to learn that Moses may have made use of earlier sources (whether written down or oral), in writing the entire Torah under the inspiration of the Holy Spirit, he would have understandably chosen different formulations to highlight different emphases.

What we find in the first two chapters of Genesis with the consistent use of different divine titles is the highlighting of a special truth. *Elohim* was used while describing all the details of creation, and now *Yahweh* is being used when the emphasis is on relationship with people. From this pattern, we gain the certainty that the great Creator of the universe is indeed the same God with whom we can have personal relationship and into whose family we can be adopted.

Initial man (Gen. 2:7). This verse contains information not given in chapter 1, namely that God took dust from the ground, forming Adam from it. The key word is "formed," because it explains what God did in this work. The Hebrew word is *yatsar,* and it refers to molding something in the way a potter works with clay. The potter does his work of molding and shaping with careful, loving movements. People are the work of a divine Artist, not accidental results from a process of evolution!

Look at God's words in Isaiah 45:9 when He spoke of the coming of Cyrus to chasten His people: "Woe unto him that striveth with his Maker! Let the potsherd strive with the potsherds of the earth. Shall the clay say to him that fashioneth it, What makest thou? or thy work, He hath no hands?" God then added, "I have made the earth, and created man upon it: I, even my hands, have stretched out the heavens, and all their host have I commanded" (vs. 12). We have been created deliberately and lovingly.

Man, a creature formed from inert dust, received a spark of immortality when God breathed into his nostrils the breath of life. Even though all the other living creatures had breath, Adam's life came directly from God's breath. Adam's body came from the earth, but his life came directly from God. Made of dust, he was transformed in a miraculous way into a living being through God's breath.

Our bodies are nothing more than worthless shells until brought alive by God. When He removes His life-giving breath, our bodies return to dust. The whole of our life and worth comes from God, not from personal achievements or abilities. The God of the universe has given us life, making each of us immeasurably valuable to Him. For anyone suffering from feelings of worthlessness leading to depression, it is important to remember that every person is unique and special to God.

HOW THINGS WERE MAINTAINED

8 And the Lord God planted a garden eastward in Eden; and there he put the man whom he had formed.

9 And out of the ground made the Lord God to grow every tree that is pleasant to the sight, and good for food; the tree of life also in the midst of the garden, and the tree of knowledge of good and evil.

10 And a river went out of Eden to

water the garden; and from thence it was parted, and became into four heads.

11 The name of the first is Pison: that is it which compasseth the whole land of Havilah, where there is gold;

12 And the gold of that land is good: there is bdellium and the onyx stone.

13 And the name of the second river is Gihon: the same is it that compasseth the whole land of Ethiopia.

14 And the name of the third river is Hiddekel: that is it which goeth toward the east of Assyria. And the fourth river is Euphrates.

The garden (Gen. 2:8-9). Just as God directly formed Adam, so He directly planted a special garden for him to live in. It was not by means of an impersonal command but rather by personal involvement. Did Adam observe this work? We have no way of knowing, but the text does say that God planted the garden and then placed Adam in it, as opposed to saying that He made the garden first and then formed Adam from dust within it. What we know is that it was an extraordinarily beautiful place just for him.

What we do not know is the exact location of this garden. We are told that it was toward the east, in Eden (a name meaning "pleasure" or "delight"). It is usually thought to have been in the area of Mesopotamia, a view based partly on the assumption of where Moses was when he wrote about it. Two of the rivers mentioned are there today, but is this where they were prior to the Flood? The fact that Adam was placed in such an ideal setting indicates God's deep love and special care for him.

While Genesis 2:8 seems to be a summary statement of fact, verse 9 reveals details about the formation of what grew there. Out of the dirt grew every tree that was beautiful to look at and every tree containing food for consuming. It was an orchard the likes of which has never been seen since. Included among these trees were two unique ones: the tree of life and the tree of the knowledge of good and evil. They were located right in the center of the garden and were the source of the first test of man's obedience.

In our finite understanding, we cannot fully comprehend all that was incorporated into these two trees. The tree of the knowledge of good and evil later proved to be an eye-opener for Adam and Eve, but they were exposed to more than they needed to know. They lived in a blissful place apart from evil and were meant to be protected there. How the tree of life would have stopped the aging process in human bodies, however, is unknown to science.

The main river (Gen. 2:10). God also caused a river to flow out of Eden for the purpose of keeping everything in the garden well watered. John MacArthur wrote this about the description of the river that proceeded out of the garden: "That is to say 'the source,' and likely refers to some great spring gushing up inside the garden from some subterranean reservoir. There was no rain at that time" (*The MacArthur Study Bible,* Nelson). The lush garden would have required the substantial amount of water provided this way.

Henry Morris speculated further that "the river would have to be supplied through a pressurized conduit from an underground reservoir of some kind, emerging under pressure as a sort of artesian spring. The fluid pressure, however, could not have been simple hydrostatic pressure (pressure resulting from gravitational flow of groundwater from a source area at a higher elevation), because this also would depend on rainfall" (*The Genesis Record,* Baker).

From this source, the river divided into four streams. In this way God made provision for the watering of the entire garden. We are not told the dimensions of the garden, but obviously God saw to it that it was well watered in its entirety.

The River Pison (Gen. 2:11-12). The Hebrew word for the name of this river is *pishon,* so it is almost always referred to as the River Pishon. It is said to have encircled Havilah. As with the other rivers mentioned here, however, we cannot be certain of the location of either the river or the country of Havilah, although it is thought to have been east of the land of Palestine in north-central Arabia.

This region was known for a particularly high-quality gold very pure in nature, along with bdellium and onyx stone. As far as we can tell, bdellium was either a pale gum resin valuable in the ancient world or perhaps pearl. Onyx stone is uncertain, but it might be a reference to some kind of precious stone like lapis lazuli. Whatever the special materials were, they are presented as valuable and highly regarded in the ancient world.

The other rivers (Gen. 2:13-14). The name of the second river was Gihon, and as with the Pison, we cannot place its location with any certainty. It is said to have encompassed the whole land of Ethiopia, sometimes called Cush, but this cannot be the Ethiopia of today. There was a land in the mountains east of Mesopotamia known by a similar Akkadian name: the land of the Kassites, so this is much more likely the location, but we cannot be certain.

It is fairly certain that the Assyrian name Hiddekel refers to the Tigris River, and, of course, the name Euphrates is familiar. The two run parallel to each other in the Mesopotamian valley and do at least give some indication that the Garden of Eden might have been located there. The problem with this, however, is that the topography of the earth's surface was vastly changed by the Flood in Noah's day; so there is no way to be absolutely certain of its location.

Man's initial existence was in a place with a nourishing river. He will also enjoy such a river in eternity, as described in Revelation 22:1-2. The river of life will be flowing from the throne of God and His Lamb, watering the tree of life forever.

—*Keith E. Eggert.*

QUESTIONS

1. What are some things revealed by the phrase "These are the generations"?
2. What differences do we find in this passage as compared to earlier?
3. What two reasons are given for there being no plant life?
4. Where did the necessary moisture come from for the plants?
5. What does the repeated use of the words "Lord God" indicate about our relationship with Him?
6. What does this chapter add about how God created Adam?
7. How do we know that God purposely prepared a special place for Adam to live?
8. Where did the first source of water for Eden come from?
9. What were the names of the four outflowing rivers?
10. What do we know about the location of Eden?

—*Keith E. Eggert.*

Preparing to Teach the Lesson

Throughout the ages, man has had questions about the beginning of the world, especially the very beginning of human history. How did we get here? Who made the earth and everything that is all around us? It is obvious that these things did not happen by chance, even though some have always thought so. The Bible makes it very clear that God is the Creator of the heaven and the earth. In our lesson this week, we explore some things about nature and the beginning of man.

TODAY'S AIM

Facts: to show how God provided for the needs of man and how man was created.

Principle: to acknowledge that God is the Creator of man and all of nature.

Application: to take time to honor the God who made us and gave us all things to enjoy.

INTRODUCING THE LESSON

When God began creating the earth, it was initially empty and barren. At the touch of God's Spirit, it was transformed into a place filled with life and usefulness. After God created the earth and everything in it, we read that He made man. The creation of man was very different from everything that He had created before this. The animals were not made to relate to God as man was. Man was special in God's eyes, and He created us to have a relationship with Him.

DEVELOPING THE LESSON

1. A world made ready for man (Gen. 2:4-7). There is no question that we are a special creation in God's eyes. Everything that He does is for us. The great God of the universe has His eyes on each of us and looks out for all our needs. God created the vast expanse of the heavens and earth in preparation for His creation of mankind.

After the grand summary of the six days of Creation in Genesis 1, chapter 2 takes us back to the beginning with a reminder that initially no life existed on the earth. Two reasons are given for this: "The Lord God had not caused it to rain upon the earth, and there was not a man to till the ground." Plants were created on the third day (1:12-13), but they needed someone to cultivate them. Rain also was not part of the earth's environment at this time. We are told that a mist rose up from the ground to water the whole earth.

We see that God had a plan, and He was putting things in place one by one. Nothing happened until God made it happen. He is the Author of all life on our planet. We dare not ignore the fact that He is still in charge of our creation and our world. Without His blessing, we cannot be sustained daily.

In Genesis 2:7 we are given specific details about man's creation. God took the dust of the earth, formed man's body from it, and breathed life into him. The Lord God created the very breath of life. The latter part of this verse says that "man became a living soul." God took the soil of the earth, which is the very lowest level of His creation, and infused it with the life of His Spirit, the very life-giving breath of God. This reminds us that until God gives us new life through His Spirit, we are dead in our sins.

Man was created with the very life-giving breath of God in order that he might become a living soul. Unlike the animals, man could relate to God spiritually, for he partook of His Spirit.

2. A garden home for man (Gen. 2:8-9). Here we see God providing for man again, and this time, He gave him a dwelling place. We are told that God planted a garden specifically for man "eastward in Eden." Although it cannot be known precisely where Eden was situated, many scholars locate it somewhere in the Tigris-Euphrates area (modern Iraq). The Garden of Eden is not a myth but was a real place in our world.

Once God had located and established a dwelling place for the first man, He then provided what was needed for his sustenance. God caused the ground to grow every tree that is appealing to the eyes and good for food. God does not just see to our needs; He delights in creating things for our enjoyment. Next we read of two mysterious trees that God put in the middle of the garden: the tree of life and the tree of the knowledge of good and evil. It is important to realize that sometimes God does some things that we do not always immediately understand. (These trees have a place later in the Genesis narrative.) But God always has a purpose for His actions. Some divine intentions take time to be discovered.

Ask your students why they think God put these trees right in the middle of the garden. What purpose was He trying to fulfill?

It seems most likely that God was putting the man to a test: Would he look to God to discern good from evil, or would he seek that knowledge on his own? The tree of life may have stood as a visible reminder that God was the Giver of all life and that all life depended on Him.

3. The rivers of Eden (Gen. 2:10-14). The Bible often provides detailed geographical information concerning the events it reports, but in the case of the earliest days of the earth before the Great Flood, such details can be tantalizing and mysterious.

Eden is described as the land of four rivers that were tributaries of one main river. The location of the first two rivers is difficult to pin down. Some associate the land of Havilah, where the Pison flowed, with northern Arabia. The Gihon is described as flowing around Ethiopia, but where that was in pre-Flood days is hard to say. The Hiddekel (Tigris) and Euphrates are rivers of Assyria and Babylon, pointing to present-day Iraq. But the Flood would have caused massive changes in topography, making today's location uncertain. What is certain is that these were real places, or the Bible would not have named them.

ILLUSTRATING THE LESSON

God gave the Garden of Eden to man as their dwelling place, and He continues to give what is good for humanity.

CONCLUDING THE LESSON

The garden was a beautiful place that God designed for man's complete security and enjoyment. Eden is long gone, but we have been promised an even better place in our Father's house (John 14:2-3).

ANTICIPATING THE NEXT LESSON

Next week we will learn how God made a suitable helper for Adam, the first man.

—A. Koshy Muthalaly.

PRACTICAL POINTS

1. God constantly reveals Himself so that all may know Him through His works (Gen. 2:4).
2. There is no void that God cannot fill and no barren place where God cannot bring life (vss. 5-6).
3. God's Spirit gives us life, and He gives that life its significance (vs. 7).
4. God teaches us by example in His creation, even as He provides for man's needs (vs. 8).
5. In a world filled with enticements and options, we honor God by choosing Him daily (vs. 9).
6. When we appreciate the beauty of the earth, we glorify our God, who created it (vss. 10-14).

—Cheryl Y. Powell.

RESEARCH AND DISCUSSION

1. What does this passage teach us about man's responsibility to the environment?
2. How does this passage help you help someone who suffers with low self-esteem?
3. In what ways are you creative? How has your use of your own creative talents given glory to God?
4. In what ways was the Garden of Eden a perfect home for the first man and first woman? What does this state of perfection teach us about God's character and His love for man?
5. Can you name another garden that is significant in Scripture? What happened there that makes it significant?

—Cheryl Y. Powell.

ILLUSTRATED HIGH POINTS

Dust of the ground

The Bible states that God created man out of the dust of the ground. Scientists in the laboratory claim that 96.2 percent of the human body is made up of oxygen, hydrogen, carbon, and nitrogen.

No one in the laboratory is suggesting that we collect these elements in their proper percentages, toss them in a giant mixer, and expect a human being to be produced. No, that takes the miracle from the divine Creator.

Breathed . . . the breath of life

God's activity has been described as "breathing." After He fashioned man out of a lump of clay, He gave him physical and spiritual life so that he could have fellowship with the Almighty.

Psalm 33:6 declares that God created the heavens by the "breath of his mouth." This is the psalmist's way of describing that God created millions of galaxies and trillions of stars out of nothing.

Our knowledge of these wonders comes from the fact that God inspired, or God breathed, the Bible. That guarantees its accuracy and sufficiency (II Tim. 3:16).

The Lord God planted a garden

Man's history started out with a beautiful garden. Sadly, man chose to sin despite the beauty and perfection of his home in the Garden of Eden.

In His love and grace, God ends the story of man with a glorious "garden city" described in Revelation 21 through 22. How can God provide such a blessed conclusion for sinful man? When Jesus submitted to the will of His Heavenly Father to suffer and die on the cross of Calvary, He died for the sins of the world.

—David A. Hamburg.

Golden Text Illuminated

"God blessed the seventh day, and sanctified it: because that in it he had rested from all his work which God created and made" (Genesis 2:3).

I always love coming home. Whether it is at the end of a grueling day at work or after a trip, there is nothing like stepping through my own front door. The sights and smells of my house welcome me into its peacefulness, and I am reminded of what a sanctuary it is for my family and me. It is a place where we can come together and let the world melt away for a while—a private haven. With my family there to welcome me, I am completely content.

When you think of home, what comes to mind? For each of us, home may look a little different. For one person, it may be a cottage set back from the road. For another, it is a stately house in the middle of town. For another, it is that little house in a quiet cul-de-sac.

For Adam, the first home was something completely different. It was not a house somewhere. In fact, home was a garden. Eden was a lush paradise, teeming with life. There were streams of sweet-tasting water in it. Lush plants teemed with flowers, while trees stretched to the sky. Animals walked placidly through the foliage. It was an outdoor utopia where man could live in harmony, delighting in its splendor.

It was more than just a place, however. For Adam, home was also about who was there. You see, Eden was home to Adam because God was there. Adam was able to walk right next to his Creator because God actually came down and walked in Eden (Gen. 3:8). Adam had direct, tangible access to Someone he loved dearly, just as you and I have with our families. Can you imagine that?

Sadly, we live in a world much different, a world rapidly deteriorating. It is difficult to imagine a perfect world because none of us have seen it. Many philosophers and writers have speculated about what it would be like, and each of them has his own version.

Our imaginations cannot come close to understanding it. Anything we think up fails to compare with God's original design. Why? Because God is infinitely wiser than we are (Isa. 55:8-9). It stands to reason that the world He created would go far beyond anything people could create. People can only create a flawed version of that world because they and all nature are flawed (cf. Rom. 8:20-22).

The good news is that we will not eternally live in a world of decay. Someday, when Christ returns, He will set everything right again. When that happens, the curse of sin will be ended. Then everything and all of God's people will be set free from the decay of this current age. All nature waits eagerly for that day of redemption.

As believers, we also know that we will one day be escorted into a new home (Revelation 21). In this home there is a place for each of us, prepared by Jesus Himself (John 14:2-3). Only in that day will we experience the world as God intended.

Are you looking forward to that day? If you are like me, you can hardly wait! Until then, though, we need to be good stewards of this world and its creatures. We may not be able to repeal the curse, but we can do our best to care for what is here now.

—Jennifer Francis.

Heart of the Lesson

When my aunt from the Midwest visited my family in the Northwest, she and I boated to Victoria, British Columbia. For the first time, I saw the Butchart Gardens. I had never before seen anything so beautiful. From the hints in Genesis 2, I suspect that Eden, the garden God planted for the first man, was even more magnificent.

1. The beginning of human history (Gen. 2:4-6). The second chapter in Genesis retells the Creation account with an emphasis on God's creation of man and his environment.

At the time when God created the Garden of Eden and provided a man to till the garden, a mist was watering the earth. Water rose up from within the earth and nourished the earth's entire surface.

2. The formation of man (Gen. 2:7). God spoke the animals into being. But when God created man, He personally took the dust of the ground and shaped it into a man. God had created the dust, and now He repurposed it to make a human being. God Himself brought about the body's design: arms, legs, toes, torso, head, ears, nose, eyes, muscles, internal organs, nerves, blood vessels, and so on. God was the Architect of it all.

God's spoken word had created the animals and brought them to life. But the Bible emphasizes the special care and love of God in creating man—He breathed into the man's nostrils the breath of life. Man was now a living being with personality, and he was made in God's image.

In this description of God's special act of Creation, God's personal name first appears in the Bible, the name that is sometimes written as Jehovah, or Yahweh. The sovereign God does not stay aloof from His creative work. We see that God is even more than our Creator. He is a personal God who desires a relationship with His creation.

3. The garden home of Eden (Gen. 2:8-14). God had the best in mind for the man He had just created. God Himself planted a garden in a region called Eden. The word "Eden" means "delight," or "pleasure," and suggests that this place was a pristine, beautiful home the man would enjoy. He placed the man in this garden.

God planted trees in the garden. He made it purposefully beautiful. I like to imagine my favorites—flowering cherries and weeping willows. Some trees produced fruit.

God planted two trees in the middle of the garden—the tree of life and the tree of knowledge of good and evil. These trees have special importance because they were the only trees in the garden that were named and because man's interaction with them would shape his destiny.

A river running through the garden watered it. Adam would have no worries about a source of water for the garden. As it left the garden, the river divided into four rivers: the Pishon, the Gihon, the Hiddekel (Tigris), and the Euphrates. These names give some clues as to where the garden might have been located—in Armenia, in Babylonia, or near the head of the Persian Gulf (Tenney, ed., *The Zondervan Pictorial Encyclopedia of the Bible,* Zondervan).

This passage reminds us that mankind is above the animals, as evidenced in the manner of our creation. We also see God's awareness of the first man's needs and the careful manner in which God provided for him. That same God loves us today and will supply all of our needs "according to his riches in glory by Christ Jesus" (Phil. 4:19).

—Ann Staatz.

World Missions

"You go to church on Friday?"

"Yes," the other missionaries told her. Sunday was a regular workday in that country. People would not be able to attend church if services were held on Sunday.

The new missionary believed that church on Friday could not be right. She struggled with her feelings but then decided to search the Scriptures for instruction about this. She was surprised to find that nowhere in the Bible is it commanded to have church on Sunday, or prayer meeting on Wednesday for that matter.

She was able to set aside her feelings about the day and worship God with joy alongside other believers—on Friday.

In missions, it is very important to adapt as much as possible, within biblical boundaries, to the culture of one's host country. God's church is made up of the body of Christ worshipping and serving Him. It is not our job to reproduce Western church culture, but rather to plant and nurture churches in Jesus' name.

Romans 14 talks of different cultural or personal standards that can be stumbling blocks to the cause of Christ—one of them being which day, if any, to esteem. The Scriptures give the principle of setting apart a day of rest as God did after Creation, but Jesus also said that this day was made for man rather than man for that day.

When building a ministry within another culture, one of the best things we can do is to allow the people themselves to play a decisive role in creating their own unique church experience according to their culture, so long as what they do follows biblical principles. The problem comes when we see our church as "real" and forget that much of what we consider church is cultural rather than biblical.

For example, there is no mention in the Bible of the need to have a steeple (or a roof for that matter!), a pulpit, offering plates, or pews. There are no instructions on whether genders should sit together or be segregated, whether babies should be in a nursery or kept in the service, or what the order of service should be or how long it should run (many churches overseas continue for hours longer than we would find comfortable and have musical instruments we would find quite strange).

Certain things we deem as normative are seen as the opposite in other cultures. In Bangladesh, an individual altar call is unwanted, as drawing attention to oneself is considered prideful. In Iraq, any picture of Jesus would be blasphemous to Muslims, who are not allowed pictures of any prophets. Flowers might turn away a Hindu.

Let us leave our own cultural norms behind and use only the Scriptures. If we were new believers in a remote country, who had never been to any church service, but we wanted to worship God together, what might church look like? What are the essentials?

Worshipping God "in spirit and in truth" is what is commanded (John 4:24). Beyond that, there is much liberty for cultures to do so in their own unique ways (II Cor. 3:17; Gal. 5:13). Let us not deny them that freedom, turning them into Western culture followers rather than Jesus followers. Let us support, guide, and help them create a church that honors God and reproduces itself. It may look strange to us, but to our Saviour such churches are beautiful.

—Kimberly Rae.

The Jewish Aspect

Eden (*Gan Eden*), also known as The Garden of Delight, The Garden of God, the Garden of Yahweh, and the Garden of Righteousness, was planted by God specifically for Adam and Eve, whom He had created. Eden "is derived from the Hebrew root *'dn,* meaning 'enjoyment.' The Hebrew word for garden (*gan*) suggests an enclosed (walled) or protected area where trees and plants flourish. . . . The land was without weeds . . . Man did not have to till the soil to produce food . . . man and woman are equal partners . . . in perfect covenant union with God" (www.agapebiblestudy.com/Genesis/Lesson_3. htm).

While some scholars consider the Garden of Eden mythological, the Bible describes a specific, geographic location with a single river that flowed out of it and then diverged into four rivers (Pison, Gihon, Hiddekel [Tigris], and Euphrates) whose courses were described and named. Some suggestions for its location are "the head of the Persian Gulf, in southern Mesopotamia (now Iraq) where the Tigris and Euphrates rivers run into the sea; in Iranian Azerbaijan, and in the vicinity of Tabriz, and in the Armenian Highlands or Armenian Plateau" ("Garden of Eden," en.wikipedia.org).

"The opinions of the most eminent Jewish authorities point to the location of Eden in Arabia. The 'four heads' or mouths of the rivers (=seas) are probably the Persian Gulf (east), the Gulf of Aden (south), the Caspian Sea (north), and the Red Sea (west)" ("Eden, Garden of," www.jewishencyclopedia.com).

"Among almost all nations, there are traditions of the original innocence of humans in the Garden of Eden. This was the 'golden age' to which the Greeks looked back. Men then lived a 'life free from care, and without labor and sorrow.

Old age was unknown; the body never lost its vigour; existence was a perpetual feast without a taint of evil. The earth brought forth spontaneously all things that were good in profuse abundance" (Easton, "Eden," www.christian answers.net/dictionary/eden). "Like the garden of the Lord; joy and gladness shall be found therein, thanksgiving, and the voice of melody" (Isa. 51:3).

The Garden of God is also described as being filled with every precious stone, including "sardius, topaz, and the diamond, the beryl, the onyx, and the jasper, the sapphire, the emerald, and the carbuncle, and gold" (Ezek. 28:13). Compare this to the stones described in the "holy Jerusalem, descending out of heaven from God," (Rev. 21:10; cf. vss. 19-20), leading some to believe in a "higher" *Gan Eden.* "The Talmudists and Cabalists agree that there are two gardens of Eden: one, the terrestrial, of abundant fertility and luxuriant vegetation; the other, celestial, the habitation of righteous, immortal souls" ("Eden, Garden of").

According to Jewish theology, history will complete itself; all mankind returns to the Garden of Eden. "According to Jewish eschatology, the higher Gan Eden is called the 'Garden of Righteousness.' It has been created since the beginning of the world, and will appear gloriously at the end of time. The righteous dwelling there will enjoy the sight of the heavenly *chayot* [heavenly beings described by Ezekiel] carrying the throne of God. Each of the righteous will walk with God, who will lead them in a dance. Its Jewish and non-Jewish inhabitants are 'clothed with garments of light and eternal life, and eat of the tree of life' (Enoch 58,3) near to God and His anointed ones" ("Garden of Eden").

—Deborah Markowitz Solan.

Guiding the Superintendent

In its account of Creation, Genesis 2 fills in some specific details related to the creation of mankind and his existence on earth.

DEVOTIONAL OUTLINE

1. Day one of Creation revisited (Gen. 2:4). A summary of Creation is given, with reference to how it was prepared for mankind. While in Genesis 1:1 the reader is told that Elohim (the powerful God) created the heavens and earth, in 2:4 the name of the Lord is added to the name of God, which adds a personal note to the connection between God and His creation.

2. Day three of Creation revisited (Gen. 2:5-6). The text gives more information about the water cycles of God's creation, which were established just before there was plant life. At this time there was no rain from the heavens. Rain would come regularly after the time of the Flood (chaps. 7—9). For now the land would be watered by "a mist from the earth" (1:6).

3. Day six of Creation revisited (Gen. 2:7-14). Several more details are now given that pertain to the creation of mankind.

Man was formed by God from "the dust of the ground" and the "breath of life" (Gen. 2:7). God made man of the very elements that make up the ground. The materials of which he consisted were no different. Of course, his external appearance was different.

At this point man was complete but still lifeless. Only life can create life. God breathed into man the breath of life. He was now a "living soul" (Gen. 2:7).

One cannot help noticing God's parental care for His new creation. In typical Hebrew style, Genesis 2:8 summarizes this care, and then verses 9-14 give the details.

God created a special place called Eden. Adam had already been created. One of the first things that he saw was the evidence of God's loving preparation of a place for him to live.

This garden was filled with all kinds of trees and plants that man would need to survive. The vegetation was both beautiful to look at and beneficial for food. In the middle of the garden, God placed two special trees—the tree of life and the tree of knowledge of good and evil.

Water is very necessary for life on earth. Without it, man could never survive. God created a river that flowed from Eden and then divided into four rivers. The locations and names of these rivers are all given in pre-Flood terms. The Flood erased most knowledge of their locations.

Suffice it to say God had provided all that mankind needed to survive and thrive in His new creation. It is evident that He had thought of everything that man would need. In this special garden, God placed the natural resources of gold, a precious metal, aromatic resins, and onyx stones.

Land, vegetation, water, and precious resources—God provided all that man would need.

CHILDREN'S CORNER

text: **I Kings 18:17-29**
title: **False Prophet Showdown**

Elijah the prophet of God challenged 450 prophets of Baal to a contest to determine whether Elijah's God or the prophet's god, Baal, was the true God. To make this determination, Elijah proposed a fire contest that seemed to be heavily weighted in favor of Baal. But God would prevail.

—*Martin R. Dahlquist.*

Scripture Lesson Text

GEN. 2:15 And the Lord God took the man, and put him into the garden of Eden to dress it and to keep it.

16 And the Lord God commanded the man, saying, Of every tree of the garden thou mayest freely eat:

17 But of the tree of the knowledge of good and evil, thou shalt not eat of it: for in the day that thou eatest thereof thou shalt surely die.

18 And the Lord God said, It is not good that the man should be alone; I will make him an help meet for him.

19 And out of the ground the Lord God formed every beast of the field, and every fowl of the air; and brought them unto Adam to see what he would call them: and whatsoever Adam called every living creature, that was the name thereof.

20 And Adam gave names to all cattle, and to the fowl of the air, and to every beast of the field; but for Adam there was not found an help meet for him.

21 And the Lord God caused a deep sleep to fall upon Adam, and he slept: and he took one of his ribs, and closed up the flesh instead thereof;

22 And the rib, which the Lord God had taken from man, made he a woman, and brought her unto the man.

23 And Adam said, This is now bone of my bones, and flesh of my flesh: she shall be called Woman, because she was taken out of Man.

24 Therefore shall a man leave his father and his mother, and shall cleave unto his wife: and they shall be one flesh.

25 And they were both naked, the man and his wife, and were not ashamed.

NOTES

A Suitable Helper for Adam

Lesson Text: Genesis 2:15-25

Related Scriptures: Proverbs 31:10-31; Malachi 2:13-16;
Matthew 19:3-9; I Corinthians 11:3-12

TIME: unknown   PLACE: Eden

GOLDEN TEXT—"The Lord God said, It is not good that the man should be alone; I will make him an help meet for him" (Genesis 2:18).

Introduction

Adam's world was beautiful and wonderful, but lonely. For the bulk of six days, God had been busy creating the universe. Light and darkness appeared, followed by a firmament. God then gathered the waters into their own areas, and the dry land of earth appeared. Luminaries were put in place to produce the light that had appeared on the first day. The waters were populated with swimming creatures next, along with the appearance of birds to fill the air above them. On the sixth day, God created creatures to live on the earth. This all culminated with the epitome of God's work: a man in His image.

One of the greatest blessings of God's creation is the privilege and joy of companionship and relationship. We learn this first in our families when we are children. This prepares us for future relationships. It is important for us to see where families started.

LESSON OUTLINE

I. **A NECESSARY BALANCE—**
    Gen. 2:15-17

II. **AN INCOMPLETE EXISTENCE—**
    Gen. 2:18-20

III. **A PERFECT COMPLETION—**
    Gen. 2:21-25

Exposition: Verse by Verse

A NECESSARY BALANCE

GEN. 2:15 And the Lord God took the man, and put him into the garden of Eden to dress it and to keep it.

16 And the Lord God command-ed the man, saying, Of every tree of the garden thou mayest freely eat:

17 But of the tree of the knowl-edge of good and evil, thou shalt not eat of it: for in the day that thou eat-est thereof thou shalt surely die.

A job to do (Gen. 2:15). God had planted a special garden in Eden in which He put Adam, the man He had created. We should not think of our regular vegetable gardens, however; rather, Eden was a place of delight and bliss and very much a place of paradise. Perhaps it would be more accurate to think of a botanical-type garden filled with fruit trees, shade trees, exotic trees, many types of flowers, and pools of water. The newly created animals probably roamed throughout this beautiful park-like setting.

God included every kind of tree that was pleasant to look at and produced delicious fruit along with two very special trees (Gen. 2:9). He provided a source of water through a river that parted into four streams (vs. 10). There was no rain at this time, so this provision was necessary for the continuance of the garden. Everything points to an idyllic situation for Adam.

About this setting and its perfection, Warren Wiersbe observed, "In this beautiful Garden, God provided both bounty and beauty; Adam and Eve had food to eat and God's lovely handiwork to enjoy. As yet, sin hadn't entered the Garden; so their happiness wasn't marred" (*The Bible Exposition Commentary,* Cook).

God had created Adam with a need for both enjoyment and active involvement, so He gave him a job to do. It was a significant responsibility—and a great honor—to care for God's beautiful creation. Adam's job of dressing and keeping was a spiritual service to God rather than the kind of job we normally think of. In fact, his work was a gift from God rather than punishment for sin, because sin had not yet entered the world. Adam was to serve and to guard the garden.

A command to obey (Gen. 2:16-17). God then instructed Adam that he was free to eat from every tree in the garden with one exception. The fruit of the tree of the knowledge of good and evil was off-limits and was not to be included in his diet. God did not offer an explanation but was, in essence, putting him under a test of obedience. Adam had been created with the freedom of choice. He was given liberty to enjoy every tree but this one, but relative to this tree, he was to obey God in leaving it alone. His response would reveal his loyalty and faith—or lack thereof.

Included in God's command was a stern warning: on the day that he ate from it, he would most assuredly die. Adam had the freedom to choose obedience, but God added an incentive— a steep price for disobedience. Disobedience would result in death. This was not limited to physical death. If it had been, Adam and Eve would perhaps have died upon taking their first bite. Should Adam disobey, there would be a separation from God that God did not intend.

Throughout Scripture it is evident that the term "death" refers to separation. When we die, the immaterial is separated from the material, leaving the body to be buried. Since we are born in a sinful state, we are spiritually separated from our Creator until we receive Jesus as our Saviour. All who are living today without having trusted in Jesus are living apart from God and have no hope of spending eternity with Him.

The ultimate death comes when a person dies without Jesus as personal Saviour, for then eternal separation occurs. The Bible teaches that those who are saved go immediately to heaven; those who are not saved will spend eternity in hell, apart from God. Physical death, then, is a symbol of spiritual death and reminds us of the importance of having a relationship with God through Jesus.

AN INCOMPLETE EXISTENCE

18 And the Lord God said, It is not good that the man should be alone; I will make him an help meet for him.

19 And out of the ground the LORD God formed every beast of the field, and every fowl of the air; and brought them unto Adam to see what he would call them: and whatsoever Adam called every living creature, that was the name thereof.

20 And Adam gave names to all cattle, and to the fowl of the air, and to every beast of the field; but for Adam there was not found an help meet for him.

God's observation (Gen. 2:18). Up to this point we have read a declaration made repeatedly about creation: God saw that it was good (1:4, 10, 12, 18, 21, 25, 31). Suddenly, and perhaps unexpectedly, God declared that something was *not* good! It is an indication that His creation was not yet complete, for something was still missing. We should note that in this chapter we are reading details about some areas that have already been revealed in summary form. Genesis 1:27 states that God made man in His image, both the male and the female.

In chapter 2, we get the impression that the creation of mankind was so important and significant that God wanted to reiterate this and did so by adding how He had accomplished the creation of the mate for Adam. God realized that Adam would not be completely happy alone in His creation. All the animals and birds had been created with mates, so it was not good that Adam was alone. One more step of creation, therefore, needed to be accomplished, and God knew exactly what He was going to do about it.

God determined to make a mate for Adam who would be "an help meet for him" (Gen. 2:18). The word "help" indicates someone who would aid Adam. The word "meet" indicates a counterpart—someone who would stand out as his opposite but who would be there to act alongside of him. It is significant to note that Eve was never meant to be inferior or treated as less than Adam. Ephesians 5:28-29 says clearly that husbands should love their wives as much as they love themselves and should nourish and cherish them.

Adam's task (Gen. 2:19-20). We probably tend to underestimate the intelligence of Adam, but when we read of his giving names to all the animals we ought to recognize a superior mind. The "prehistoric ages" are often dismissed as an era of extreme stupidity; in stark refutation of that view, God created Adam with a brain capable of creatively naming all the species of animals. His doing this also conveys dominion and authority over the animals, which, like Adam himself, had been created from the dust of the ground (cf. 1:24).

The text does not mean that Adam gave every individual animal a specific name but rather that he named the different kinds of species God brought before him. Their creation happened prior to God's statement that it was not good for Adam to be alone. It would be accurate to paraphrase Genesis 2:19 as saying that the Lord God had formed these creatures, after which He brought them to Adam for naming. God left the choices entirely up to him: "Whatsoever Adam called every living creature, that was the name thereof."

The mention of cattle probably included all animals that could be domesticated. All the birds are mentioned next, after which all the beasts of the field are specified. These were probably the wild beasts that were not capable of being tamed and used by mankind as pets or as working animals. Those of us who are creative imagine that this was an exhilarating time for Adam; those of us not so creative probably take it too much for granted!

At what point did Adam realize what was missing in his own life? The excitement of naming all the animals in Genesis 2:20 is followed abruptly by the contrasting conjunction "but": "but for Adam there was not found an help meet for him."

A PERFECT COMPLETION

21 And the LORD God caused a deep sleep to fall upon Adam, and he slept: and he took one of his ribs, and closed up the flesh instead thereof;

22 And the rib, which the LORD God had taken from man, made he a woman, and brought her unto the man.

23 And Adam said, This is now bone of my bones, and flesh of my flesh: she shall be called Woman, because she was taken out of Man.

24 Therefore shall a man leave his father and his mother, and shall cleave unto his wife: and they shall be one flesh.

25 And they were both naked, the man and his wife, and were not ashamed.

The woman (Gen. 2:21-22). There was nothing Adam could do about the situation, of course, because he did not have the creative power of God within him. God knew that, and He knew what He was going to do. He started by putting Adam to sleep. It was a deep sleep, not just a naptime slumber. There are medical procedures for which doctors numb a local area of the body without putting people to sleep. Most patients prefer a deep sleep, however, because our natural propensity is to not want to know what is happening.

After God put Adam to sleep, He performed a surgical procedure that involved opening up his flesh and removing a rib. After that, He closed up the place it was taken from with flesh. Obviously, this all took place without Adam's help; he was not even conscious. Eve was created by God and given to Adam as a gift. We should also

note that Eve was a creation made from preexisting material, since she was from the rib taken from Adam's body. God could create that way as easily as He could from nothing.

From that single rib, which is again emphasized as having been taken from the man, God made a woman, whom He then presented to him. If we read our Bibles with imagination (which we should always do), this is one of those moments we should like to reflect on. Adam had been busy naming creatures and had fallen asleep afterward, perhaps partly because of exhaustion, but also because God saw to it that he slept deeply. Try to imagine the look on his face when he awoke and saw Eve walking toward him!

Scripture is very clear in stating that wives are gifts from God Himself. "A virtuous woman is a crown to her husband" (Prov. 12:4). "Whoso findeth a wife findeth a good thing, and obtaineth favour of the Lord" (18:22). "House and riches are the inheritance of fathers: and a prudent wife is from the Lord" (19:14). The description of a good wife in Proverbs 31:10-31 confirms the value that Christian husbands should place on their wives. Everything about their creation says we should never see them as inferior.

The relationship (Gen. 2:23-24). We read Adam's statement rather matter-of-factly most of the time, but this was truly an outburst of excitement! "This is now" means "at last!" "Bone of my bones" sums up Adam's appraisal. "Adam's wording is poetic and exalted; seeing Eve was a shocking and exhilarating experience because the match was perfect. Here was a mirror of himself, someone just like him, and yet different!" (Radmacher, Allen, and House, eds., *Nelson's New Illustrated Bible Commentary,* Nelson). Adam now had the joy of naming someone just for him: Woman!

As Moses recorded these things that

he had not witnessed but had received directly from God, God had him include His view of marriage. As God established marriage through this first couple, it is clear that His intention was that it involve a man and a woman. The man's role includes leaving his parents and giving himself completely to the woman. The Hebrew word translated "leave" means to loosen or relinquish, and the word for "cleave" means to cling or adhere. A man is to put his wife above his parents.

When a marriage takes place the spouse is to become (after God) the number one person in one's life and is to remain in that position throughout life. Even when children come into the family, the husband and wife should still esteem each other as most important. Child psychologists tell us that children receive their greatest sense of security when they see their parents completely devoted to each other. It is important that believing parents love each other deeply and not fight in front of the children.

When the Apostle Paul picked up this subject in his letter to the Ephesians, he reminded them of the importance of a man loving his wife in a sacrificial way (5:25), for marriage is a reflection of Christ and the church. Paul concluded with, "Nevertheless let every one of you in particular so love his wife even as himself; and the wife see that she reverence her husband" (vs. 33). This is what started in the Garden of Eden!

The innocence (Gen. 2:25). Adam and Eve were totally innocent, open, and trusting with each other. This is clear in the statement that they were naked and without shame. The perfect relationship they enjoyed is what God intended for all of mankind who followed. Sadly, the entrance of sin into God's beautiful and perfect creation ruined this. Now we must put forth constant effort to make our marriages succeed, and we must rely on God to enable us to fulfill our individual roles.

The encouraging truth is that we who are born again and part of the family of God have the indwelling Holy Spirit to give us the ability to have marriages far above those seen in many unbelievers. For some of us, God has plans that do not include marriage. For those of us who are given this privilege, we should do everything we can to make it the best it can be. Whatever we do, we must resist the world's notion that we can end our relationship whenever we are not happy.

—Keith E. Eggert.

QUESTIONS

1. What responsibilities did God give Adam in the garden?
2. What did God say about the trees in the garden?
3. What was the prohibition God gave, and how did God reinforce the need for obedience?
4. How do we know that God was not speaking merely about physical death?
5. What did God mean by the statement "it is not good" (Gen. 2:18)?
6. What is conveyed by the words "an help meet for him" (vs. 20)?
7. What task did God give Adam, and what did this task accomplish?
8. How did God meet Adam's need, and how did Adam respond afterward?
9. What guidelines do we find for marriage in the relationship between Adam and Eve?
10. How is the perfection of this first relationship expressed?

—Keith E. Eggert.

Preparing to Teach the Lesson

The first man is now settled in his new home, the Garden of Eden. Our Creator God looked at Adam and saw that he was alone and needed someone like him for companionship. In our lesson this week, we explore how God created a suitable helper for him.

TODAY'S AIM

Facts: to show that God saw a need for Adam and made another human being suitable for him.

Principle: to remember that God created woman to be with man.

Application: to remember that husbands and wives we are called to honor God's plan for marriage.

INTRODUCING THE LESSON

Throughout this quarter we have become aware of a God who sees our needs and works hard on our behalf to prepare everything to meet those needs. We are the objects of His love and affection. He loves us dearly.

Have you ever been alone and lonely? Is it not strange that loneliness can happen even in a crowd? There may be hundreds of people all around us, but we may feel isolated because we cannot make that human connection. We were created to be social beings.

While the creation of Adam was amazing, to say the least, something was missing. God knew exactly what it was and moved to fill that missing space. God did something about it, and His answer was incredible! In our lesson, we explore the creation of the first woman and what it meant for Adam.

DEVELOPING THE LESSON

1. A task complete (Gen. 2:15-17). Last week we saw how the garden was prepared as a home for Adam to live in.

He was then given work to do. It is important to note that the concept of work was God's idea! And it came at the very beginning of human history. Remind the class that work was not a consequence of the Fall of Adam and Eve into sin. Adam was called to work in the garden "to dress it and to keep it." God had a plan to keep Adam productive.

We then find that God allowed Adam absolute freedom to eat from any of the trees that were in the garden. They were placed there to provide food. But there was one exception. He was not allowed to eat of the fruit of the tree of the knowledge of good and evil. The Bible does not give us much detail about this special tree that was prohibited to Adam. Its name implies that eating the fruit had something to do with the ability to discern good from evil.

It must be noted that at this time sin had not entered into the world. However, we can safely infer that God gave man freedom to choose to obey or disobey Him. He did not make man a robot but gave him a heart and free will to choose to follow Him. This tree was a test of obedience to God.

God's prohibition came with a consequence. "For in the day that thou eatest thereof thou shalt surely die" (Gen. 2:17). The immediate consequence spoken of here was separation from God. But physical death also would be an eventual, unavoidable result.

2. A companion for Adam (Gen. 2:18-22). We see how God pinpointed a fundamental need and filled that need for Adam. The animals and birds had also been created out of the soil; they were now brought to Adam. He gave them names, but they could not fill the unique human need for companionship. Yet as Adam saw them all in pairs of male and female, he must have become aware of what was missing in his own case.

Then God put Adam to sleep. While he slept, God took a rib from his side, closed the flesh back up, and created Eve, the first woman. Taking the rib from Adam's side suggests equal companionship. She was someone of his own kind whom he could relate to. Finally, after seeing all the male-female partnerships in the animal world, Adam had a partner to connect with. God had thought of everything. God is amazing in the way He has provided.

3. An outburst of joy (Gen. 2:23-25). When Adam saw Eve for the first time upon awakening from his deep sleep, he exclaimed with joy that she was his own flesh and bone, someone like him in many ways and so unlike the animals around him. She was specially designed for him alone, and Adam knew this. God could not have done better! She would be called "woman" because she was taken out of man.

The account here goes on to relate this to the basis for marriage today—that a man should leave his parents and be joined to his wife in a new and exclusive relationship. They were to be one unit functioning together as one. If you have time, lead a discussion on how husbands and wives can more effectively demonstrate their one-flesh unity.

Genesis 2:25 highlights the purity of the marriage bond. Adam and his wife were naked and not ashamed. Shame is a sign of sin. (We will study more of this in lesson 6.) Being unashamed and not aware of one's nakedness was a state of absolute purity before God and each other. Take a moment to look at the concept of shame and how it is related to sin. How can we as Christians deal with shame? What does the Bible tell us about this?

ILLUSTRATING THE LESSON

When God gave Adam a companion perfectly suited to him, He set the foundations for marriage.

THE GIFT OF MARRIAGE

God

ONE COUPLE FOR LIFE

CONCLUDING THE LESSON

It is important to realize that when God created man, He designed us to have fellowship with Him. But He also created us with the capacity to be moral and sexual beings. We have the ability to use our free will to choose to worship Him. We also have the ability to procreate. For this, God gave us marriage, one man with one woman for life. In giving Eve to Adam, God also showed us the divine principle of marriage for mankind.

ANTICIPATING THE NEXT LESSON

In our lesson next week, we will see how Adam and Eve made a reckless choice to disobey the God who had done so much for them. We learn how their perfect world was shattered around them because of one dreadful decision to disobey the God who loved them so.
—*A. Koshy Muthalaly.*

PRACTICAL POINTS

1. Work has always been part of God's design for man (Gen. 2:15).
2. Our choices either bring us closer to God or further away from Him (vss. 16-17).
3. God perfectly fills our need for companionship (vs. 18).
4. As we devote ourselves to God's work, we see Him at work meeting our needs (vss. 19-20).
5. Men and women are created with different roles, but they have equal responsibility to glorify God (vss. 21-22).
6. As one flesh, whatever affects one partner affects both (vs. 23).
7. Believers stand on the truth and goodness of God's plan in a world that rejects Him (vss. 24-25).
   —*Cheryl Y. Powell.*

RESEARCH AND DISCUSSION

1. Why do you think that God would place a tree in the Garden of Eden but forbid man to eat of its fruit?
2. How does Adam's work help us understand man's relationship with God?
3. How is it significant that God views man's aloneness as "not good"? What does God's assessment teach us about our relationships today?
4. Do you think it is possible to be in a right relationship with God if you are not in a right relationship with your spouse? Why or why not?
5. What lessons can a Christian draw from this passage to begin restoring broken relationships?
   —*Cheryl Y. Powell.*

ILLUSTRATED HIGH POINTS

Took one of his ribs

Matthew Henry's comment on the creation of woman is well-known. It is, however, worth repeating and would result in much blessing and harmony in marriage if followed.

He said, "The woman was made of a rib out of the side of Adam; not made out of his head to rule over him, nor out of his feet to be trampled upon by him, but out of his side to be equal with him, under his arm to be protected, and near his heart to be beloved" (*Matthew Henry's Commentary on the Whole Bible,* Hendrickson).

Leave . . . cleave

The basics of a good marriage were introduced by God in the very beginning. First, there needs to be a proper separation from parents so that the couple can resolve their own problems without outside interference. It is important for parents to help (allow) their children to learn the responsibility of their own independence.

Second, there needs to be a whole-hearted and permanent attachment to the other. They are to "cleave" to one another. Third, there is to be a God-sealed sexual bond ("one flesh").

These basics also declare that adultery and polygamy have no place in a God-ordained marriage.

Cleave unto his wife

Cleaving means that the husband is to "glue" himself to his wife. This should make them one forever.

Too many enter into marriage with the mistaken idea that if things do not work out, they can get a divorce and start over. God's intention from the beginning was and still is " 'till death do us part" (cf. Matt. 19:5-6).
   —*David A. Hamburg.*

Golden Text Illuminated

"The Lord God said, It is not good that the man should be alone; I will make him an help meet for him" (Genesis 2:18).

As I approached my wedding, I found myself reflecting on it a lot. What does it mean to be a wife? This lesson reveals God's heart for marriage and its intent.

It began with Adam. Everything was brand-new. It was just God, Adam, and the animals. Although Adam lived in paradise and enjoyed an amazing communion with God, there was something missing.

Adam was alone. Although he loved God, there was no other earthly being who could relate to him. God knew that Adam needed an earthly companion who could help him and be his companion along life's way.

In literary circles, a foil is a character that serves as a contrast to another. The foil is often quite distinct in nature from the character being contrasted. This can serve to emphasize traits in both characters that might get overlooked otherwise. In some ways Eve was Adam's foil.

In the first marriage, God provided in Eve someone similar to Adam, but also distinctly different. Eve was not like any being Adam had ever seen. She looked, thought, and even experienced emotions in a way that was unique to her. She was not merely a female copy of Adam.

How many of you have a mate who seems to be your exact opposite? My husband and I fit the bill. He loves math; I like English. He enjoys westerns; I like classic historical movies. What is both strange and amazing is how our strengths complement each other's weaknesses.

This blending of two people is what God intended. He knew that we would need this intertwining in order to face the challenges in life. He saw that people had a need for companionship.

That is why Christian couples should not work independently of each other (I Cor. 11:11). They are not separate but a unit ordained in a lifelong covenant before God (Matt. 19:5). With Christ as their Head, they become that "threefold cord . . . not quickly broken" (Eccles. 4:12).

God knows each person before he is even born (cf. Ps. 139:16), so He knows both members of a couple. He knows the right timing to bring a couple together. Since He also knows what is best for each of us, we can trust Him to bring us that person designed specifically to share our lives. When we remain faithful and committed to our spouse, we exercise trust in His wisdom in the area of marriage.

Is this always easy? Hardly! I know that my husband is God's answer for my earthly companion, however. That is why I see it through, even when it is tough. We are no longer two people but one unit (Eph. 5:31). Our marriage covenant is not just for us but for God as well.

Are you married? If you are, how well are you doing at truly giving yourself to this relationship? Ask God to show you how to grow in love and understanding.

Are you single? Do not despair. There are reasons for whatever state God has us in at this time. Remember, Paul was single and one of the Lord's greatest missionaries. It may simply be that the timing is not right and that you still have things that you can best do while you are single.

Whatever the case, we can praise God for the blessings of companionship that marriage brings.

—*Jennifer Francis.*

Heart of the Lesson

A marriage counselor once told me about an around-the-world trip he took alone when he was a young man. For many months, he explored various cultures. But by the end of the trip he was frustrated because he had no one with whom to share his experiences. He was ready to come home.

When God created Adam, Adam was alone in a big world. God was aware of Adam's need for companionship, and He made provision for it.

1. Life in the garden (Gen. 2:15-17). God placed Adam in the garden God had created to be Adam's home. Adam's job was to cultivate the garden and care for it. As part of his orientation to the garden, he was instructed that he could eat from any tree but the tree of the knowledge of good and evil. Eating its fruit, God warned, would bring certain death—physical and spiritual.

2. Loneliness in the garden (Gen. 2:18-20). God knew that Adam's solitary condition as the only human being on earth was a negative. Adam needed a helper—someone to work alongside him, someone with whom to share his life. Besides, as a lone person, Adam would have been unable to fulfill God's later instruction to be fruitful, multiply, and fill the earth.

To prepare Adam for the woman God was about to make, God charged him with naming the animals and birds. The Scripture text notes that God wanted to see what Adam would call them. God is interested in His creation, both past and present. God cares about your life.

Naming the animals acquainted Adam with them and helped him understand his relationship to them—He was their lord. As Adam completed this first God-given task in the garden, he realized that no living creatures were like him. Out of the host of created life, he was unique and special, but he was alone.

3. Marriage in the garden (Gen. 2:21-25). God placed Adam into a deep sleep—as if he were undergoing anesthesia. Then God completed the first surgery and removed one of Adam's ribs. Afterward, God closed up the flesh around the rib and the incision.

From Adam's rib God fashioned a woman. Then God brought her to him. This was an arranged marriage with God as both Matchmaker and Creator of the persons involved! Adam responded with joy when he saw the woman. He recognized immediately that she was of his kind. She was a person. And she must have been beautiful. Adam blurted out that she was bone of his bone and flesh of his flesh. He sensed a oneness with her. They were soul mates, meant for each other. She was his perfect complement.

Genesis declares that because of the way God created man and woman, when a man marries he should leave his parents and cleave to his wife, forming a stronger and different bond with her than he had in the parent-child relationship. The two become one flesh. They complete each other and become united in a special way.

Adam and his wife were naked but felt no shame. God had created and brought them together naked, completely open to each other.

Marriage is not a cultural invention; "it was instituted by God" (Barton, ed., *Life Application Study Bible,* Tyndale). God knew Adam's need and created the woman to be his *helper,* not his servant. She was to be a companion and co-laborer with him, but Adam was created first, and he was to be the leader.

—*Ann Staatz.*

World Missions

A wife can make or break her husband's ministry, and even more than that, his spirit. The Bible says a wife can either be a gift from God (Prov. 19:14) and "crown to her husband," or she can be "as rottenness in his bones" (Prov. 12:4). That is clearly evident in missionary stories throughout history. For some, the wife was a team partner who helped make the ministry great. For others, her resistance and complaining damaged the work on the field.

Marriage, whether on the mission field overseas or in our local communities, is intended to portray the relationship between Christ and His church. If a missionary wife refuses God's call or goes but maintains a resentful spirit, she conveys the opposite message to the lost than what God intends.

It is easy to see this in a foreign context, but what about in our own marriages? What message are we giving to the mission field all around us?

We women in the West are not known for having meek and quiet spirits, not with slogans such as "I am woman; hear me roar."

However, like missionary women on the foreign field, we are called to step away from any aspect of the culture that does not align with our eternal culture—the kingdom of God. Anything that goes against God's principles for living should be rejected, and we should choose God's way instead.

This means our marriages should look different than the world's. When I lived in a Muslim country, I wrote down a few lessons I learned about being a wife among lost women. I knew they watched our lives. They paid close attention to my marriage.

There are people watching our marriages here as well. Perhaps some of the lessons I learned will resonate. Here they are:

1. I must find my value in Christ, not in how much I accomplish.

2. A meek and quiet spirit is a learned spirit—it is not a valued spirit in America, but each of us can develop it.

3. Take photos with lost friends and evaluate how I look different. Are my clothing, hair, posture, and other characteristics appropriate for their understanding of holy living?

4. Reverence my husband—how I treat him in front of our lost friends is *very* important—no interrupting, belittling jokes about men, correcting, or criticizing.

5. God brought more opportunities for spiritual discussion from how I raised my children than any other subject   my daily choices about living mattered.

6. The days I set aside my agenda for God's were happy days.

7. Making my home a place of joy is one of the most valuable things I can do for the Lord.

8. Joyful submission, as unto the Lord, shows I am obeying out of love and gratitude for the love and goodness shown to me by God. This is vastly different from forced oppression.

We wives have a significant calling. When God declared it was not good for man to be alone, it was the first time in creation that something was not good. We were needed. We still are.

The world is watching. Will we choose to be the helpmeets God created us to be, for His glory? Our marriages can honor God and advance His kingdom greatly.

—*Kimberly Rae.*

The Jewish Aspect

Although God called all of His creation "very good" (Gen. 1:31), when He saw that man was alone, He said, "It is not good . . . I will make him an help meet for him" (2:18). Fashioned out of man, woman became man's counterpart and companion.

As Adam slept, God took one of his ribs, made a woman, and then brought her to him (Gen. 2:21-22). Adam declared, she was "bone of my bones and flesh of my flesh" (vs. 23). "Bone of my bones" is a Hebrew idiom meaning "exact counterpart," "perfect partner," "completer of me." Adam called her "woman," or *ishah,* because she was taken out of man (*ish*)—she had her source in him.

"The creation of Eve, according to Rabbi Joshua [ben Hananiah], is that: 'God deliberated from what member He would create woman, and He reasoned with Himself thus: I must not create her from Adam's head, for she would be a proud person, and hold her head high. If I create her from the eye, then she will wish to pry into all things; if from the ear, she will wish to hear all things; if from the mouth, she will talk much; if from the heart, she will envy people; if from the hand, she will desire to take all things; if from the feet, she will be a gadabout. Therefore I will create her from the member which is hid, that is the rib, which is not even seen when man is naked'" (Eve, www.wikipedia.org).

God called the woman a "help meet" (Gen. 2:20). "The relationship between this first pair of humans is also expressed by the term *ezer ke-negdo,* translated 'helper as his partner.'. . . This unusual phrase probably indicates mutuality. The noun *helper* can mean either 'an assistant' (subordinate) or 'an expert' (superior); but the modifying prepositional phrase, used only here in the Bible, apparently means 'equal to'" (Meyers, "Eve: Bible," www.jwa.org).

Adam was created without any flaws or shortcomings, but in order for him to fulfill God's mandate of filling the earth and exercising dominion over it, he needed help. As created, he was incomplete for the task. In the Psalms, the word "help" is frequently used in describing the Lord. The term "meet" translates a Hebrew word for "opposite." "Literally it is 'according to the opposite of him,' meaning that she will [complement] and correspond to him" ("Genesis Chapter 2 Continued," www.bible-studys.org).

Adam gave the woman the name Eve "because she was the mother of all living" (Gen. 3:20). "Eve" in Hebrew is *hawwah,* meaning "living one" or "source of life" and is derived from the Hebrew word *hawah,* which means "to breathe" or the related word *haya,* meaning "to live." The name described her function and destiny in spiritual history of which she was the beginning.

Proverbs 31:10 declares that the value of a virtuous woman "is far above rubies." She works with her hands to care for the needs of her family, she speaks wisdom and shows kindness, and she is called blessed by her children and husband (vss. 13-28).

God instructed that "a man [shall] leave his father and his mother, and shall cleave unto his wife: and they shall be one flesh" (Gen. 2:24). The marital relationship was established as the first human institution. A man and his wife are combined in physical and spiritual unity. "One flesh" speaks of a complete unity of parts making a whole. The term also carries a sense of a permanent or indissoluble union.

—Deborah Markowitz Solan.

Guiding the Superintendent

Man is God's highest creation. Because he is, more is said in the Bible about his creation than about any other part of what God did. This week's lesson focuses first on God's provision of a place for the first man to live and food for him to eat. But one thing was still missing. Adam needed a companion. God provided this in a most unique way.

DEVOTIONAL OUTLINE

1. Placed in Eden (Gen. 2:15-17).
As we saw in the previous lesson, God had created the perfect place for man to dwell and supplied it with all the natural and mineral resources that were needed to live (vss. 4-14). Adam was now placed in God's perfect garden. He was tasked by God "to dress [the garden] and to keep it" (vs. 15).

The produce of the trees was available for man's food. There was one exception. Adam was not to eat of the tree of knowledge of good and evil. Only one reason is given—eating from this tree would bring death. Death should be understood here in terms of separation. To refuse to obey God would lead to being separated from God. This tree would become a major problem for Adam and Eve in Genesis 3. It would become the focus of the major test of man's obedience to God.

2. A perfect helpmate (Gen. 2:18-25).
Up to this point, every time God evaluated creation He said it was good. Now for the first time in the book of Genesis, the reader is told that God saw that something was not good. It was not good "that the man [male] should be alone."

To help Adam understand this, God instructed him to inspect all the animals and name them. In the process, Adam noticed that there was not "an help meet for him" (Gen. 2:20).

Man was incomplete, and this was not good. The situation was not evil, but it was unfinished. The term "help meet" has the idea of equality and completeness. There is no suggestion of inferiority. The word "help" is used many times of God (cf. Gen. 49:25; Deut. 33:7; Ps. 121:1-2).

While man was in a deep sleep, God took a rib (the word can be translated "side") from him and made the first woman, Adam's perfect and complementary helpmate (Gen. 2:21-22). As humanity is the pinnacle of Creation in chapter 1, so now Eve is the climax of Creation in chapter 2.

Waking from his sleep, Adam burst into an exclamation of praise about his new companion. He called her woman, for she had come from man.

Our passage closes with a comment from the author (Moses) explaining that a man was to separate from his parents when he joined his wife.

CHILDREN'S CORNER

text: I Kings 18:30-40
title: **Only One True God**

After many hours of frantic activity, the prophets of Baal were unable to get their god to respond. Their god did not exist.

Elijah stepped forward, called the people to him, and built an altar of stone. He placed wood and a sacrifice on it. Then he ordered that water be poured on this setup three different times. He called on God to answer. Fire immediately came from heaven and devoured the entire sacrifice and altar. The people were convinced and cried out to Elijah's God, "The Lord, he is the God" (I Kings 18:39).

—Martin R. Dahlquist.

Scripture Lesson Text

GEN. 3:1 Now the serpent was more subtil than any beast of the field which the Lord God had made. And he said unto the woman, Yea, hath God said, Ye shall not eat of every tree of the garden?

2 And the woman said unto the serpent, We may eat of the fruit of the trees of the garden:

3 But of the fruit of the tree which is in the midst of the garden, God hath said, Ye shall not eat of it, neither shall ye touch it, lest ye die.

4 And the serpent said unto the woman, Ye shall not surely die:

5 For God doth know that in the day ye eat thereof, then your eyes shall be opened, and ye shall be as gods, knowing good and evil.

6 And when the woman saw that the tree was good for food, and that it was pleasant to the eyes, and a tree to be desired to make one wise, she took of the fruit thereof, and did eat, and gave also unto her husband with her; and he did eat.

7 And the eyes of them both were opened, and they knew that they were naked; and they sewed fig leaves together, and made themselves aprons.

8 And they heard the voice of the Lord God walking in the garden in the cool of the day: and Adam and his wife hid themselves from the presence of the Lord God amongst the trees of the garden.

9 And the Lord God called unto Adam, and said unto him, Where art thou?

10 And he said, I heard thy voice in the garden, and I was afraid, because I was naked; and I hid myself.

11 And he said, Who told thee that thou wast naked? Hast thou eaten of the tree, whereof I commanded thee that thou shouldest not eat?

12 And the man said, The woman whom thou gavest to be with me, she gave me of the tree, and I did eat.

13 And the Lord God said unto the woman, What is this that thou hast done? And the woman said, The serpent beguiled me, and I did eat.

NOTES

A Reckless Choice

Lesson Text: Genesis 3:1-13

Related Scriptures: Matthew 4:1-11; John 8:42-45; James 1:13-15

TIME: unknown   PLACE: Eden

GOLDEN TEXT—"And when the woman saw that the tree was good for food, and that it was pleasant to the eyes, and a tree to be desired to make one wise, she took of the fruit thereof, and did eat, and gave also unto her husband with her; and he did eat" (Genesis 3:6).

Introduction

In his book *The Grand Weaver* (Zondervan), Ravi Zacharias tells the story of "a man aboard a plane who propositioned a woman sitting next to him for one million dollars. She glared at him but . . . [t]he pair set the time, terms, and conditions. Just before he left the plane, he sputtered, "I-I have to admit, ma'am, I have sort of, ah, led you into a lie. I, um, I really don't have a million dollars. Would you consider the proposition for just—ah, say—ah, ten dollars?'

"On the verge of smacking him across the face for such an insult, she snapped back, 'What do you think I am?'"

"'That has already been established,' he replied. 'Now we're just haggling over the price.'"

Zacharias then pointed out the importance of a moral framework.

LESSON OUTLINE

I. COURTING DISASTER—
   Gen. 3:1-7

II. REFUSING ACCOUNTABILITY—
   Gen. 3:8-13

Exposition: Verse by Verse

COURTING DISASTER

GEN. 3:1 Now the serpent was more subtil than any beast of the field which the LORD God had made. And he said unto the woman, Yea, hath God said, Ye shall not eat of every tree of the garden?

2 And the woman said unto the serpent, We may eat of the fruit of the trees of the garden:

3 But of the fruit of the tree which is in the midst of the garden, God hath said, Ye shall not eat of it, neither shall ye touch it, lest ye die.

4 And the serpent said unto the woman, Ye shall not surely die:

5 For God doth know that in the day ye eat thereof, then your eyes shall be opened, and ye shall be as gods, knowing good and evil.

6 And when the woman saw that the tree was good for food, and that it was pleasant to the eyes, and a tree to be desired to make one wise, she took of the fruit thereof, and did eat, and gave also unto her husband with her; and he did eat.

7 And the eyes of them both were opened, and they knew that they were naked; and they sewed fig leaves together, and made themselves aprons.

A sly question (Gen. 3:1). This chapter opens by introducing us to a serpent (a snake) that talked with Eve. John later clearly identified Satan with this serpent: "And the great dragon was cast out, that old serpent, called the Devil, and Satan, which deceiveth the whole world" (Rev. 12:9; cf. 20:2). Apparently, Satan possessed and took control of a literal snake, which was probably a beautiful, upright creature before the Fall.

While Satan's question to Eve might sound innocent, we must read it in its context: "the serpent was more subtil than any beast of the field which the Lord God had made" (Gen. 3:1). The Hebrew word translated "subtil" means "cunning" or "crafty." It sounds like a simple request for information only, but the question was worded in such a way as to cast doubt on what God had said to her. The insinuation was that maybe she had misunderstood Him.

Satan's means of getting to Eve and inducing her to fall was through her mind. He wanted her to rethink what she thought she had understood from God. Maybe what she was thinking was not exactly what God had meant. Had God restricted her in some way, and if so, was this right and kind of Him? Were other possibilities available? The implication was that perhaps disobedience was an option. Maybe God's motives were improper and completely unnecessary. Was she absolutely certain about that prohibition?

Satan focused totally on the one tree God had told Adam and Eve not to eat from. He ignored (and hoped she would also ignore) the magnanimous generosity of God in allowing them to eat from every other tree in the garden (Gen. 2:16). The two warnings we should see in the encounter are the way Satan works negatively in our minds and the way he points us away from the many blessings we already enjoy. He wants us to focus on what seems to be a lack of God's blessing instead of all God has done for us.

An uncertain answer (Gen. 3:2-3). Eve was faced with her first temptation. Temptation often comes to us in subtle, misleading ways that cause us to think that if we give in to it we will enjoy something that would otherwise be missed. How we respond to temptation is crucial to our relationship with God. Eve responded by misquoting what God had said, a dangerous and subtle response any time we face temptation. How often people misquote God's Word or take something out of context to validate their actions.

First, Eve added to what God had said by claiming that she and Adam were not even to touch the tree. Granted, touching the fruit would increase the temptation, but the fact is that God had not put this restriction on them. They could have enjoyed the beauty and feel of the fruit as long as they did not eat it. It was a simple matter of obeying the parameters God had set for them. We wonder whether Adam, in passing along to Eve this prohibition, said that she should not even touch it, and she included it as from God.

Eve may also have weakened God's warning of death somewhat. The words "lest ye die" in Genesis 3:3 could be taken as an understanding of something that *might* happen. By contrast, God had said to Adam, "In the day that thou eatest thereof thou shalt surely die" (2:17). There was no uncertainty in what God had warned; His wording was expressed most emphatically.

"Eve would come to understand that God's Word is not just generally true; it is absolutely and precisely true. God says what He means—and He means what He says. This understanding of the absolute authority of God's Word is necessary for mankind to acknowledge so he might respond in a God-honoring manner" (Anders, ed., *Holman Old Testament Commentary,* B&H).

An underhanded accusation (Gen. 3:4-5). Everything we have read in the first two chapters of Genesis tells us that God is good. Now Satan implied to Eve that God was not so good after all! The thought was planted in her mind that in the single prohibition placed on them, God was being selfish and restrictive. Satan lied by accusing God of lying, and in doing this he implied that God's motives were less than honorable. In reality, God had nothing but the best for mankind in mind, but Satan implied the opposite.

Satan's direct refutation of God's warning was a bold-faced lie. They certainly would not die, he claimed. At this point the doubt already lurking in Eve's mind would tempt her to deny or dismiss what God had said. Now that Satan had her thinking negatively about God, it would not be so difficult to get her to act contrary to what He had said. What an important warning for us! When we come to the point of thinking negatively about God, we are open to the temptation to disobey Him. Such thinking puts us on the dangerous pathway of spiritual destruction.

Satan went further. He claimed that as soon as they ate from the forbidden tree, their eyes would be opened and they would be like God, knowing good and evil. The accusation was that God was withholding special privileges from them, reinforcing the insinuation that God was not good. Satan made it sound as if God were jealously trying to keep Adam and Eve from enjoying their full potential. That thought opened the way for doubting that God would really punish disobedience. It led to seeing sin as less than serious, paving the way for an act of direct disobedience.

A self-indulgent response (Gen. 3:6-7). As we read in verse 6, what was forbidden looked good, pleasant, and desirable. Is that not often the case for us too? "These verses provide both the record of the historical Fall of man and the archetypal temptation. This passage is a perfect case study of temptation, for sin cannot be blamed on environment or heredity" (Walvoord and Zuck, eds., *The Bible Knowledge Commentary,* Cook). The process of falling into sin included looking at the fruit, seeing it as pleasant, and taking what was desirable.

The connection to the warning in I John 2:16 is unmistakable: "For all that is in the world, the lust of the flesh, and the lust of the eyes, and the pride of life, is not of the Father, but is of the world." In temptation we want to fulfill our physical desires, crave the pleasures we see, and pridefully determine to have what we want. It has often been said that there is nothing so important as being careful of what we look at. Satan can use what we see to get us to fall.

Eve's contemplation of the seemingly obvious benefits of disobeying God led her to take of the fruit and eat it. Her response was entirely guided by human rationalization, which was captive to her personal physical, natural desires. In that moment of action, she shut out of her mind what God had said and acted instead on what seemed good to her. It is a reflection of the attitude seen in so many people, who simply throw caution to the wind and go ahead with what they want to do. Yet how dangerous to ignore God!

Eve then gave some of the fruit to Adam, and he ate too. Immediately, they saw things in a different way. Their nakedness had never been a problem before, but now they were ashamed and felt guilty (Gen. 3:7; cf. 2:25). They did not become divine as Satan had implied, but they had a new understanding of good and evil. They had a new awareness of themselves and felt a need to cover up. Their innocence was gone. Their reckless choice resulted in permanent change that would affect them and all their descendants from then on.

REFUSING ACCOUNTABILITY

8 And they heard the voice of the Lord God walking in the garden in the cool of the day: and Adam and his wife hid themselves from the presence of the Lord God amongst the trees of the garden.

9 And the Lord God called unto Adam, and said unto him, Where art thou?

10 And he said, I heard thy voice in the garden, and I was afraid, because I was naked; and I hid myself.

11 And he said, Who told thee that thou wast naked? Hast thou eaten of the tree, whereof I commanded thee that thou shouldest not eat?

12 And the man said, The woman whom thou gavest to be with me, she gave me of the tree, and I did eat.

13 And the Lord God said unto the woman, What is this that thou hast done? And the woman said, The serpent beguiled me, and I did eat.

Trying to hide (Gen. 3:8). Adam and Eve did not immediately die physically, but they experienced a separation from God they had never known before. It was a spiritual death; they were now alienated from God. In the Bible, death refers to separation. In physical death, the immaterial part of us leaves the material. In spiritual death, there is a separation or chasm between us and God. All unsaved people are spiritually dead. In eternal death, the person is separated from God permanently and forever.

Evidence of their new alienation from God is seen in the couple's attempt to hide from Him when they heard Him coming to them in the garden. It was the time of evening cooling. Perhaps God regularly came at that time to have a chat with them. Normally, they would have greeted Him eagerly, but this day was different. This time they cowered behind some bushes or trees in order not to be seen. It reminds us of Jonah's silly attempt to flee from the Lord's presence (Jonah 1:3).

What a sad commentary following the beauty of creation, the special privilege of having been made in the image of God, and the unbroken fellowship that had been enjoyed with their Creator! It is a stark reminder for every one of us that the only way we can completely enjoy God's presence is to be right with Him through wholehearted obedience to His Word. Even when we have to give up things we greatly desire, we ultimately discover that closeness with God is far better than acting outside of His will.

Trying to explain (Gen. 3:9-10). Into the serenity of the cool evening came the Lord God for His time with His creatures. Strangely, however, they were not waiting for Him. So God asked Adam a question He had never asked before: "Where art thou?" God already knew, of course, but He had always enjoyed such a personal relationship with these two that He spoke on their level. He was also about to force them to admit their guilt and confess their wrong actions.

It was a pathetic scene. Adam and Eve, who supposedly were now like God, knowing good and evil, were hiding from the God who had created them. The trees they had been told to enjoy now became a hiding place. We immediately see the first effects of the Fall, including the need for confession of sin and the acceptance of God's way of forgiving that sin. We should note that God took the initiative in reaching out to His sinning children, as He continues to do today. He is a loving God who wants to forgive.

Adam's response was, "I heard thy voice in the garden, and I was afraid, because I was naked; and I hid myself" (Gen. 3:10). Three things stand out in this response. First, he was afraid of God for the first time ever. This was not the respect we often speak of when we refer to the fear of God; it was a genuine sense of being afraid to face God and what might follow. Second, Adam was afraid because he was naked, something that had never bothered him before. Third, he attempted the impossible act of hiding from God.

Trying to blame (Gen. 3:11-13). Human nature comes to the fore as God continued His questioning. "Who told thee that thou wast naked? Hast thou eaten of the tree, whereof I commanded thee that thou shouldest not eat?" Our natural propensity when under such interrogation is to say, "It was not my fault!" We do our best to blame someone else for our weaknesses and failures, which is another evidence of the fallen nature we received from Adam. Sometimes it is very hard to accept responsibility!

Adam ignored God's first question and went straight to answering the second one. He blamed Eve. There is further implication here. In essence, Adam was saying, "It's really Your fault, God, because You gave me this woman, who led me into disobedience!"

Leaving Adam's insinuation unanswered for the moment, the Lord turned to the woman and asked her about her involvement, to which she essentially responded, "The serpent is to blame!" We would like to laugh at this ludicrous exchange, except for the fact that we see our own natural tendencies in this situation.

When Eve said the serpent had beguiled her, she was saying that he had led her astray by mentally deceiving her. This, of course, was true, but it was still necessary for her to accept responsibility for her own actions. She did this in part when she admitted that she had eaten the fruit after falling for the serpent's trickery.

Many people today do their best to avoid admitting wrong. It is easier to blame our situation on somebody else, our environment, our homelife, or our genetics. We show spiritual maturity, however, when we can face wrongdoing by admitting and confessing our failures.

—*Keith E. Eggert.*

QUESTIONS

1. On what did Satan concentrate his efforts in attempting to get Eve to fall into sin?

2. What were his questions seeking to get her to doubt?

3. What does this show about where Satan wants us to direct our thoughts?

4. How did Eve add to what God had said to Adam?

5. What did Satan say that was a direct lie about God's words?

6. What three-pronged challenge do we face in temptation?

7. What changed for Adam and Eve after they ate the fruit?

8. How do we know Adam and Eve felt alienated from God?

9. What was Adam's pathetic response to God's question?

10. What do we see about human nature in their explanations?

—*Keith E. Eggert.*

Preparing to Teach the Lesson

This week we learn how one reckless choice to disobey God led to a miserable state of affairs. We learn that God gave man free will. He wants us to be able to choose Him and His ways so that we may reap the blessings He has for us.

TODAY'S AIM

Facts: to show how one reckless choice to disobey God caused man to fall from God's favor.

Principle: to remember that disobedience to God leads to broken fellowship with Him.

Application: to realize that if we seek God's blessing, then we must be prepared to obey Him in all things.

INTRODUCING THE LESSON

When it comes to driving a motor vehicle, people can learn all too suddenly that failing to obey the rules of the road can have disastrous results. While many accidents have causes that are beyond the driver's control, far too many occur because the driver thought he could ignore a particular prohibition. Excessive speed, failure to yield, impulsive lane changing, disobedience to the laws against texting while driving—these are some of the reckless choices that can lead to tragedy.

Our lesson this week keeps us in the Garden of Eden with the first man and woman, and we can learn from their bad decision. Some choices have dire consequences.

DEVELOPING THE LESSON

1. The temptation (Gen.3:1-5). Temptations are all around us. In their new home, Adam and Eve faced only one temptation, but it appears to have taken them by surprise. This was partly because the enticement was subtle.

Temptations do not come with warning signs. Scripture reminds us that Satan can transform himself into an angel of light (II Cor. 11:14). This week's text, Genesis 3:1-13, opens with a warning about the nature of the serpent. He was "more subtil than any beast of the field which the Lord God had made." The word "subtil" is an older spelling for "subtle," or cunning.

We have to ask ourselves how an evil creature like the serpent, the devil, got into the beautiful garden. Isaiah 14 and Ezekiel 28 give us some explanation about his origins. For our purposes in this lesson, it suffices to recognize that the evil one is alive and well even today. If we are not careful, he will cause us to fall into disobedience. It is important to note that the first couple was minding their own business when the serpent struck up a conversation. He initiated the Fall.

Satan, the serpent, first planted seeds of doubt in Eve's mind. Did God really say that they could not eat of all the trees in the garden? Of course not! But that is where Satan started. Eve was quick to respond that it was only one particular tree that was forbidden. She said they were not to eat it or even touch it, or they would die. (The prohibition against touching, if valid, is not recorded in the instructions to Adam.)

The serpent was very quick to respond. He said that they really would not die. The reason God did not want them to eat was that their eyes would be opened and they would know good and evil as He did. Doubt had been sown. Who would not want to know good and evil? The temptation was beginning to take effect, and Eve was listening closely (as was, presumably, Adam).

2. The wrong choice (Gen. 3:6-7).

Notice that temptation is always slick and attractive. Adam and Eve fell for the temptation. The fruit was pleasant to the eyes and good for food, and it would make one wise. Here was everything that appealed to the human senses. Temptation always appeals to the flesh first. Notice the warning in I John 2:16, where we are cautioned against temptations that come through the eyes, the flesh, and the pride of life.

Notice also that the covering of fig leaves that Adam and Eve made for themselves was grossly inadequate. Remind the class that we cannot cover up our own sin. We need a Saviour, and that Saviour is our Lord Jesus. The price has already been paid for us.

3. The ruin (Gen. 3:8-13).

Sin always brings ruin in its wake. Adam and Eve's disobedience immediately brought about a broken relationship with God. Up to this time, God had made a practice of walking with them in the garden. Now they were afraid of Him. When He called, they hid themselves. This would be a good place to note that even today it is God who comes searching for sinful man.

Adam and Eve also realized that they were naked. Sin brought about an awareness of nakedness. They were no longer innocent. When God pinned them down about eating the forbidden fruit, Adam blamed Eve. She then blamed the serpent for their wrong choices.

Drive home the point that sin and disobedience come with a costly price tag, and they break our relationship with the One who created us to be with Him. Lead your students in a discussion of some strategies that will help them consistently make the right choices. Remind them that the Holy Spirit has promised to be with us to guide us into all truth.

ILLUSTRATING THE LESSON

We have the power to choose good or evil. Foolish choices turn us from God.

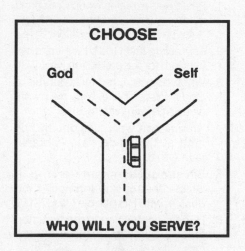

CONCLUDING THE LESSON

We all have to make several choices every day. We have the power to choose good or evil. The latter will leave us with regrets. Good choices will leave us with a right relationship with God. The choices we make every day also affect all other relationships for good or ill. We learned that the evil one seeks to trick us into taking the easy road. Often the easy road leads us to destruction. Right choices lead us on a path to peace.

Remind the class that sinful choices never lead down the right path. They always cause pain in the end. If we are to see God's blessing, then we have to make godly choices, which lead to life.

ANTICIPATING THE NEXT LESSON

Next week we will explore the dreadful consequences of sin experienced by Adam and Eve and what we can learn from some of their regrets. We learn that sin brings only punishment and death from a holy God. Sin also spoiled what God had so lovingly planned for His creation.

—A. Koshy Muthalaly.

PRACTICAL POINTS

1. Real trouble begins when Christians dwell on what God forbids and forget what God provides (Gen. 3:1).
2. Appreciate that God's love limits our freedom for our protection (vss. 2-3).
3. When tempted, remind yourself of God's Word, believe it, and walk away from sin (vss. 4-5).
4. No one can walk by sight and by faith at the same time. Choose faith (vs. 6).
5. Sin produces shame and guilt which destroy the intimacy God desires with His people (vss. 7-10).
6. Honest confession is the first step to reconciliation, not the last resort (vss. 11-13).

—Cheryl Y. Powell.

RESEARCH AND DISCUSSION

1. What does the Bible teach about Satan (cf. Gen. 3:1-5; Job 1:6-12; Isa. 14:12-23; Ezek. 28:13-19)? Why do you think it is important that the people of God know these things about Satan?
2. How is it significant that Satan appeared to Eve as a serpent (cf. Num. 21:8-9; John 3:14; Rev. 12:9, 20:2)?
3. In what ways have you seen yourself or others be deceived by Satan? What strategies can help a Christian avoid being deceived today?
4. Why do you think that Satan presented the temptation to Eve, the woman, and not to Adam, the man?
5. In what ways do men and women today desire to make themselves equal to God?

—Cheryl Y. Powell.

ILLUSTRATED HIGH POINTS

More subtil

Satan is described as "more subtil." Various translations of this verse use a variety of synonyms: crafty, cunning, clever, shrewdest, sneakier. Ezekiel 28:12 says that Lucifer was "full of wisdom." One might think that man is in a hopeless situation.

Satan is a powerful enemy, but Eve possessed the same weapon Jesus used when He was tempted—the words of God (Matt. 4:4, 7, 10). We too can use this same weapon, which is always lethal to our enemy.

The serpent

Whenever there is a tragic mass shooting incident, such as the twenty children (ages six and seven) and six adults killed at the Sandy Hook Elementary School in Newtown, Connecticut, there is a call for more stringent gun control and the old serpent, who is a liar, gains the upper hand (cf. John 8:44).

Stricter gun control may help some, but what we need is a greater presentation of the gospel of Christ.

The woman whom thou gavest to be with me

A Connecticut prison warden was asked in an interview whether she believed criminals could be rehabilitated. She said, "Most people who do bad things are under the influence of drugs and alcohol; get rid of the drug problem—you'll get rid of overcrowding."

Just as Adam and Eve tried to cover their guilt by blaming others, people today blame a variety of things rather than hold people responsible for their sinful choices. True rehabilitation comes through the gospel.

—David A. Hamburg.

Golden Text Illuminated

"And when the woman saw that the tree was good for food, and that it was pleasant to the eyes, and a tree to be desired to make one wise, she took of the fruit thereof, and did eat, and gave also unto her husband with her; and he did eat" (Genesis 3:6).

My friend Sandi and I were late. We were both section leaders of the band. Our previous director had left, and we had yet to meet the new one. It was the first day of band camp. We had seven minutes to make a trip that normally took fifteen.

What did we do? I am guessing that most of you know. Did we drive safely and arrive late? We did not. Instead, we turned up the radio, gunned the engine, and careened down the roads at breakneck speed. We arrived with a minute to spare, peeling into the parking lot and causing people to stare.

Have you ever made a decision like that one? I suspect that most of us would admit that we have. Whether it stems from youthful folly, thoughtlessness, or something else, each of us has made choices that were not the wisest.

Such was the case with Adam and Eve. They ran into the earth's first devious salesman. Picture the situation. Eve was young and naive. The devil came to her, speaking words that sounded logical. He gave her a reason why she could not do without the fruit of that one tree. He gave her a false line, leading her to believe that things would be better if she and Adam would just eat.

We all are thinking that we would not fall for this. But let us be honest with ourselves. Have we not all fallen for a similar lie at some point or other? Has Satan ever prompted you into what you knew was sin, yet you made the choice to do it anyway?

The reality is that we all have fallen into this trap. It is easy to condemn Adam and Eve, until we look back at ourselves. We all are prone to sin (cf. I Kings 8:46). In our fleshly nature we are vulnerable to it. Adam and Eve were prey to Satan's enticements, and we can be pulled into his web as well.

How do we combat this? First, we need to remember that believers do not live under the dominion of the sinful flesh. We have been given a new nature when we receive Christ and are regenerated. Because of this, we already have victory.

Second, we need to be aware when Satan is knocking on the door of our hearts and minds. Scripture tells us that he seeks to devour us (I Pet. 5:8). His suggestions will have persuasive power. Many of them may seem harmless at the time. We might even think that what he suggests is the right thing to do.

That is why we must put on God's armor to protect us (cf. Eph. 6:11-13). When we protect ourselves with God's armor, we are able to discern Satan's attacks and stand against them. We can be steadfast when we are tempted.

What if we have already made a bad choice? We can seek forgiveness for it. We may not be able to undo all the consequences, but we can repent of our sinful decisions and trust God to be gracious.

Are you feeling tempted? Have you already fallen into reckless behavior? God can redeem and rescue you. He is always there, so seek Him and ask for His help.

—Jennifer Francis.

Heart of the Lesson

One summer afternoon, my mother allowed me to ride my bicycle to my friend Suzy's house. But I was to call my mother sometime that afternoon and be home by five o'clock.

Suzy lived near the beach, and we had such a wonderful time there that I forgot to call my mother. In fact, I lost all track of time. When I got home well past six o'clock, I faced my mother's wrath. And I also had to live with the consequences of my long afternoon in the sun—a painful sunburn. Disobedience leads to trouble.

1. Treachery in the garden (Gen. 3:1-6). Satan came as a crafty serpent when he approached Adam and Eve in the garden. Through the serpent, Satan questioned God's command about eating fruit from the garden. He twisted God's words, implying the couple could eat no fruit. Eve corrected the serpent, saying that only the fruit of the tree in the middle of the garden was off-limits. Death would result if they ate from it.

The serpent called God a liar. He said they would not die. He wanted Eve to believe God was withholding something good from her and to question His love. Doubt often is a precursor to sin. The serpent said if she ate the fruit, her eyes would be opened, she would know good and evil, and she would be like God.

To be like God is to be a reflection of God's holy character. Satan's idea of how to be like God was distorted. He was trying to persuade Eve "to be her own god" (Barton, *Life Application Study Bible,* Tyndale).

God gave Adam and Eve the ability to make choices. Sadly, Eve ate the fruit and gave some to her husband. Now Adam had a choice. He knew what God had said. He had watched his wife partake and had made no move to stop her. He took the fruit and ate, deliberately disobeying God.

2. Loss of innocence (Gen. 3:7). The couple did not immediately die physically. But their innocence was gone. Now that their eyes were open to evil, nakedness felt wrong. They stitched fig-leaf aprons to wear. They had never considered clothing before.

3. Confrontation by God (Gen. 3:8-13). Ordinarily, Adam and Eve had walked with God. But now when they heard Him coming, they just wanted to hide. Their sin was separating them from God. God asked Adam where he was. God knew, but he wanted Adam and Eve to face their sin and confess it. Adam told God that he was afraid because he was naked. "Who told thee that thou wast naked?" God asked Adam. "Hast thou eaten of the tree?" Adam made excuses. He blamed Eve, saying she had given him the fruit.

When God asked Eve what she had done, she too made excuses, saying the serpent had deceived her. But her own weakness had caused her to sin. She could have conferred with her husband. She could have said she needed to talk it over with God.

Neither Adam nor Eve had tried to resist the temptation. Together they should have been strong. But they disobeyed God. As father and mother of the human race and as representatives of it, they caused sin to enter the human heart.

As believers, we face daily choices to obey God. When temptation comes, call on God's power. Look for the ways of escape God has promised. Seek the counsel of godly people who will help you discern truth. And then make a godly choice.

—Ann Staatz.

World Missions

The choices we make daily, small and great, add up to either a life of great eternal purpose or a small life merely chasing temporary desires.

If we set our minds "on things above, not on things on the earth" (Col. 3:2), we will have an eternal perspective and make choices that advance God's kingdom and honor God. If our treasure is here on earth, that will be reflected in how we think and act instead.

Richard Wurmbrand, suffering for Christ in a Soviet prison, once said, "I saw Christians dancing for joy in Communist prisons. Christians don't have to feel it when they are beaten. While in a Romanian jail, I was caught preaching. This was strictly forbidden. The Communist guards took me out and beat me with a heavy stick. While they hit me, I thought about the continuation of the sermon. I was too busy to feel pain. They threw me back in the cell and departed. I said, 'Now, gentlemen, let us continue.'"

That kind of perspective does not come naturally or by accident. It comes with practice—taking every thought into captivity (II Cor. 10:5) and choosing to put Christ above ourselves and His purpose above even our own lives.

The day Eve chose to eat the fruit, she turned away from the words of God and chose the words of Satan instead. She allowed herself to be convinced that God did not really want what was best for her and that Satan's way was easier, better, more appealing, and would make her happy.

To truly make an impact for God in this world, we have to choose the voice of God over any other voice, even our own. Again, this is not something that comes without intention and self-denial.

In 1948, all the missionaries were kicked out of China and told to never return. One missionary determined that she was going to go back anyway. On the dock before the ship left, Dawson Trotman, founder of the Navigators, met with her to pray. Before she left, he gave her a verse, one to help her get through whatever she might face.

The woman was captured, imprisoned, and tortured for her faith. The guards encouraged many to kill themselves. Some did. The missionary was not exempt from the temptation to consider it, but she resisted and for two years endured suffering that did great damage to her body and her mind.

When she was finally set free, the missionary woman returned home and sought out Dawson Trotman to thank him for the verse he gave her. It had sustained her in her most painful hours, when she was close to breaking.

That verse saved her life. When Mr. Trotman told this story, his listeners wanted to know what the special verse was.

He would not say.

They insisted. What was the one verse that would preserve a life through hardship and persecution?

Finally, Mr. Trotman responded with a small statement: "There are hundreds of them."

Every day we make choices about what to think, how to feel, how to act, and how to respond to the actions of others. Those choices are based on the words we listen to. If we want to make a difference, we have to choose God's words over any other. His words can give life to us, and through us to the lost in our world.

—Kimberly Rae.

The Jewish Aspect

In the perfect world where God had placed Adam and Eve, He gave only one commandment for them to follow—not to eat of the fruit of the tree of the knowledge of good and evil. God said they could eat of every other tree in the garden except this one, "for in the day that thou eatest thereof thou shalt surely die" (Gen. 2:17).

The knowledge of good and evil is a "merism," the combination of two contrasting words, which then refer to an entirety. The knowledge of good and evil (two opposites) in Hebrew meant all knowledge—knowledge of everything. Adam and Eve already had a knowledge of what was good.

"In Jewish tradition, the Tree of Knowledge and the eating of its fruit represents the beginning of the mixture of good and evil together. Before that time, the two were separate, and evil had only a nebulous existence in potential. While free choice did exist before eating the fruit, evil existed as an entity separate from the human psyche, and it was not in human nature to desire it. Eating and internalizing the forbidden fruit changed this and thus was born the *yeitzer hara,* the Evil Inclination.

"In Rashi's notes on Genesis 3:3, the first sin came about because Eve added an additional clause to the Divine command: *Neither shall you touch it.* By saying this, Eve added to YHWH's command and thereby came to detract from it, as it is written: *Do not add to His Words* (Proverbs 30:6)" ("Tree of the knowledge of good and evil," en.wikipedia.org). "Rashi" is a popular acronym for Rabbi Shlomo Yitzchaki, who lived in medieval France and wrote extensive commentaries on both the Old Testament and the Talmud.

The woman chose to eat because "the tree was good for food, . . . pleasant to the eyes, and a tree to . . . make one wise" (Gen. 3:6). The tree appealed to the lust of her eyes and the lust for wisdom to make one wise. Eve chose to listen to "the serpent [who] was more subtil than any beast of the field which the Lord God had made" (vs. 1). More "subtil," in this context, means "crafty" (cf. Job 5:12; 15:5). The rebellion of Satan (the serpent) had already occurred (Ezek. 28:1-18; Isa. 14:12-15), and in the Garden of Eden, he tempted Eve to be like God. This was also why he had been thrown out of heaven—for wanting to be like God.

Both Adam and Eve ate the fruit, and their eyes were opened, bringing to them the sudden realization that they were naked. They therefore made coverings for themselves by sewing fig leaves together. They had started out naked and unashamed, but after disobeying God, they were filled with shame and guilt.

"Before eating from the Tree, Adam and Eve saw each other first and foremost as souls. They knew the soul is the essence of a human being, with the body serving merely as a protective covering. Since Adam and Eve were focused on the spiritual side, they weren't self-conscious about their bodies.

"However, after eating from the Tree, human perception of the physical world changed. The physical senses enticed as if possessing a value of their own. Adam and Eve's 'eyes opened' to a focus on the body. The body had become a distraction from the soul and when this happened, Adam and Eve were ashamed of their naked bodies" (www.jewishpathways.com/chumash-themes/garden-eden). They had gone from being innocent souls to sinful ones, and this permanently discolored their outward relationships.

—Deborah Markowitz Solan.

Guiding the Superintendent

Creation did not remain perfect very long. Satan stepped into the picture and tempted the first man and woman by seeming to offer them something better than what God had given them. Satan implied that God really did not have their best interests at heart.

DEVOTIONAL OUTLINE

1. First temptation to sin (Gen. 3:1-6). Adam and Eve were in the new garden prepared by God. They had all that was needed for life and happiness. Then Satan came onto the scene. Life would never be the same for Adam and Eve or, for that matter, for everyone and everything after them.

Satan's temptation took a very specific route. First, he got Adam and Eve to question what God had clearly said (cf. Gen. 2:17). "Yea, hath God said, Ye shall not eat of every tree of the garden?" (3:1). Now God's clear words were open to debate. Eve attempted to fight off Satan by saying that they could eat from all the trees but one; she also added that God said it would bring death (vs. 3).

Satan followed with a strong denial. "Ye shall not surely die" (Gen. 3:4). Eve had two choices—God's plan or Satan's plan.

Satan was clearly denying what God had said and indicating that God was withholding the truth from Eve. Satan stated that by eating from the tree she would become like God. Satan had attacked the divine barriers. The first people were left to their natural desires and appetites. Eve "saw . . . took . . . and gave also unto her husband" (Gen. 3:6). After she gave it to Adam, he also ate the fruit. It was all over. Sin had now entered the human race.

2. First effects of sin (Gen. 3:7-13). Immediately, the first effects of sin were felt—shame. Adam and Eve were so ashamed that they tried to hide, from each other and from God as well. Adam and Eve made some clothes out of fig leaves in an attempt to hide their nakedness. In their folly, they also tried to hide from God. The Fall had taken place. Sin has such a disastrous effect that it strains and severs relationships.

Shame quickly turned to fear. The all-seeing God found Adam trying to evade Him. His simple question pointed toward a new distance in relationship: "Where art thou?" (Gen. 3:9). Adam had to admit that he was afraid and did not want God to see him naked.

God was not through confronting Adam. He continued with this obvious question: "Hast thou eaten of the tree?" (vs. 11). Adam had a chance to own his failure but instead chose to blame Eve. The third effect of sin was trying to evade responsibility. Adam blamed his wife for their troubles. God turned to Eve, who blamed Satan.

The rapid effects of sin were felt. Instead of taking responsibility, neither the man nor the woman would acknowledge guilt.

CHILDREN'S CORNER

text: **I Kings 18:41—19:8**
title: **The Running Prophet**

Having defeated the wicked prophets of Baal, Elijah prophesied that a flooding rain would soon come. He outran King Ahab back to the city.

Jezebel soon found out that Elijah had killed all the prophets of Baal. She threatened to end his life immediately. The prophet ran into the desert. There he was met by an angel who encouraged him with some food.

—Martin R. Dahlquist.

Scripture Lesson Text

GEN. 3:14 And the LORD God said unto the serpent, Because thou hast done this, thou art cursed above all cattle, and above every beast of the field; upon thy belly shalt thou go, and dust shalt thou eat all the days of thy life:

15 And I will put enmity between thee and the woman, and between thy seed and her seed; it shall bruise thy head, and thou shalt bruise his heel.

16 Unto the woman he said, I will greatly multiply thy sorrow and thy conception; in sorrow thou shalt bring forth children; and thy desire shall be to thy husband, and he shall rule over thee.

17 And unto Adam he said, Because thou hast hearkened unto the voice of thy wife, and hast eaten of the tree, of which I commanded thee, saying, Thou shalt not eat of it: cursed is the ground for thy sake; in sorrow shalt thou eat of it all the days of thy life;

18 Thorns also and thistles shall it bring forth to thee; and thou shalt eat the herb of the field;

19 In the sweat of thy face shalt thou eat bread, till thou return unto the ground; for out of it wast thou taken: for dust thou art, and unto dust shalt thou return.

20 And Adam called his wife's name Eve; because she was the mother of all living.

21 Unto Adam also and to his wife did the LORD God make coats of skins, and clothed them.

22 And the LORD God said, Behold, the man is become as one of us, to know good and evil: and now, lest he put forth his hand, and take also of the tree of life, and eat, and live for ever:

23 Therefore the LORD God sent him forth from the garden of Eden, to till the ground from whence he was taken.

24 So he drove out the man; and he placed at the east of the garden of Eden Cherubims, and a flaming sword which turned every way, to keep the way of the tree of life.

NOTES

Dreadful Consequences

Lesson Text: Genesis 3:14-24

Related Scriptures: Romans 5:12-19; 8:19-23; Revelation 12:3-11

TIME: unknown   PLACE: Eden

GOLDEN TEXT—"Because thou hast . . . eaten of the tree, of which I commanded thee, saying, Thou shalt not eat of it: cursed is the ground for thy sake; in sorrow shalt thou eat of it all the days of thy life" (Genesis 3:17).

Introduction

One of the principles of life is that of cause and effect. Various types of actions lead to certain results, which cannot be voided once those actions have been taken. Many of these are automatically built into the laws and course of nature. If we jump off a rooftop (cause), we will have a crash landing (effect), very possibly with a broken leg. If we drive too fast on an icy road, we will likely go into a dangerous slide. If we overeat, we will gain weight.

In the spiritual realm, there are also important cause-and-effect situations. If we neglect prayer on a regular basis, we will live life without spiritual guidance and make many errors in judgment. If we neglect Bible reading on a regular basis, we will be ignorant of God's will and ways and have a shallow understanding of the Christian life. If we attend church regularly, we will have fellowship and the support of brothers and sisters in Christ during times of trial and testing.

LESSON OUTLINE

I. JUDGMENT—Gen. 3:14-19

II. PROTECTION—Gen. 3:20-24

Exposition: Verse by Verse

JUDGMENT

GEN. 3:14 And the LORD God said unto the serpent, Because thou hast done this, thou art cursed above all cattle, and above every beast of the field; upon thy belly shalt thou go, and dust shalt thou eat all the days of thy life:

15 And I will put enmity between thee and the woman, and between thy seed and her seed; it shall bruise thy head, and thou shalt bruise his heel.

16 Unto the woman he said, I will greatly multiply thy sorrow and thy conception; in sorrow thou shalt bring forth children; and thy desire shall be to thy husband, and he shall rule over thee.

17 And unto Adam he said, Because thou hast hearkened unto the voice of thy wife, and hast eaten of the tree, of which I commanded thee, saying, Thou shalt not eat of it: cursed is the ground for thy sake; in sorrow shalt thou eat of it all the days of thy life;

18 Thorns also and thistles shall it bring forth to thee; and thou shalt eat the herb of the field;

19 In the sweat of thy face shalt thou eat bread, till thou return unto the ground; for out of it wast thou taken: for dust thou art, and unto dust shalt thou return.

On the serpent (Gen. 3:14-15). Looking at the situation from a human perspective, we might say that God's original plans and hopes had been dashed to pieces and that it was now time for plan B instead of plan A. This is only a human perspective, because, of course, God knew ahead of time what was going to happen. Yet knowing we are made in God's image and experience feelings of disappointment over certain failures, we have no doubt that God had a feeling of disappointment too.

He had put Adam and Eve in a perfect setting and wanted them to enjoy to the fullest all He had given them. Now, because of their disobedience to His command about the tree of knowledge of good and evil, He had no choice but to bring His judgment upon them. He began with the serpent since it had led them into this disobedience. In His statements, we hear God address the literal serpent, but the application moves to the spiritual being that used the creature to effect the Fall.

Because of Adam and Eve's disobedience, the entire creation fell under a curse from God, including the whole animal kingdom. The serpent, or snake, however, was uniquely cursed because of its role in the Fall. The implication is that it was originally a beautiful, upright creature. Under the curse, it would now slither on the ground and appear to eat dust. Eating dust is a figurative statement depicting a sign of deep humiliation. While some people like and enjoy snakes, most loathe them.

That antagonism between snakes and humans is pointed out in Genesis 3:15, where God is now really addressing Satan. The double meaning here refers both to hatred between snakes and women and to the hatred between Satan and the woman who would be the mother of Jesus. Jesus, the Seed of Mary, would bruise Satan's head while Satan would bruise His heel. The statement alludes to Satan's temporary victory over Jesus on the cross contrasted with Jesus' permanent victory over Satan at the end.

Genesis 3:15 has been called by many Bible students the Protevangelium, meaning "the first gospel," because it foretells our Redeemer. Paul told the Romans, "The God of peace shall bruise Satan under your feet shortly" (Rom. 16:20), and John later described Satan as being thrown into a bottomless pit for one thousand years (Rev. 20:2-3) and ultimately into the lake of fire and brimstone (vs. 10). The good news is that we are on the side of the Victor in this battle.

On the woman (Gen. 3:16). Giving birth to children now held the outlook of being intensely painful. There would be great joy in conceiving and bearing children, but it would be tempered by the pain of the actual birth process. God's wording makes it sound as if there would have been some pain in childbirth without the Fall, but now He said it would be greatly multiplied or significantly increased. God then foretold a second consequence for Eve: "Thy desire shall be to thy husband, and he shall rule over thee."

There are those who think this judgment might refer to sexual desire, but the most likely interpretation seems to be that the woman would desire to rule over the man, indicating an innate desire to dominate him. While this might seem unlikely to believing women who have no problem submitting to their husbands, there is plenty of evidence among worldly women pointing to a determination not to be dominated.

There is a parallel construction in Genesis 4:7 that also indicates this meaning. God said to Cain, "If thou doest well, shalt thou not be accepted? and if thou doest not well, sin lieth at the door. And unto thee shall be his desire, and thou shalt rule over him." In both verses we observe a desire to take over. God told Cain that when sin tried to take over, he should have power over it. God told Eve that women would experience a desire to be independent or even in charge, but each was to follow her husband's leadership.

John MacArthur noted, "Sin has turned the harmonious system of God ordained roles into distasteful struggles of self-will. Lifelong companions, husbands and wives, will need God's help in getting along as a result. The woman's desire will be to lord it over her husband, but the husband will rule by divine design (Eph. 5:22-25)" (*The MacArthur Study Bible,* Nelson).

On the man (Gen. 3:17). Because of his disobedience, Adam was going to have to work harder in order to grow the things necessary for their sustenance. They had sinned in what they ate; now what they ate was going to be a lot harder to come by. Adam was specifically reminded that he was the one who had been given the command about the tree, for God told him it was his hearkening to Eve that was bringing this judgment on him. Was he so passive that he was afraid to speak up when Eve was tempting him with the fruit?

Since the ground was now cursed, Adam's work to gain food from it would be a struggle. The same Hebrew word was used for telling Eve her childbearing would be in sorrow, and it signifies labor or pain. Having to work was not the punishment; Adam had been placed in the garden to tend it. That, however, would have been a pleasurable experience. Now he was going to encounter hindrances that would make the work much harder and would require a lot more exertion than before, and it would be a lifetime requirement.

Detailed results (Gen. 3:18-19). Paul told the Roman believers that the sufferings we experience here pale in comparison to the glory we will enjoy in heaven (Rom. 8:18). We are eager for this change to occur because we have been "made subject to vanity" (vs. 20) and given over to "the bondage of corruption" (vs. 21). What caused this undesirable condition? The sin that Adam and Eve committed brought the curse upon God's creation, and now we too wait for our ultimate redemption (vs. 23).

"For the creature was made subject to vanity, not willingly, but by reason of him who hath subjected the same in hope, because the creature itself also shall be delivered from the bondage of corruption into the glorious liberty of the children of God. For we know that the whole creation groaneth and travaileth in pain together until now. And not only they, but ourselves also, . . . even we ourselves groan within ourselves, waiting for the adoption, to wit, the redemption of our body" (Rom. 8:20-23).

What would Adam experience that was proof of this destructive situation? Thorns and thistles would grow and become nuisances as they mixed in with the grain. So he was going to have to deal with those first if he wanted to eat. The toil would be so strenuous that he would sweat profusely as his body labored to maintain a steady internal temperature. This kind of work was going to be required until the day of his death, when God said he would return to the dust from which he had been created.

None of this was the way God had originally intended it to be. What God had just described was a reversal of the condition of the land He started with. Useless weeds that had no benefit for human beings would now grow with the good crops. While all this sounds very harsh, the grace of God is still evident in that He would provide for the needs of the people as they labored.

PROTECTION

20 And Adam called his wife's name Eve; because she was the mother of all living.

21 Unto Adam also and to his wife did the LORD God make coats of skins, and clothed them.

22 And the LORD God said, Behold, the man is become as one of us, to know good and evil: and now, lest he put forth his hand, and take also of the tree of life, and eat, and live for ever:

23 Therefore the LORD God sent him forth from the garden of Eden, to till the ground from whence he was taken.

24 So he drove out the man; and he placed at the east of the garden of Eden Cherubims, and a flaming sword which turned every way, to keep the way of the tree of life.

A name and clothing (Gen. 3:20-21). Two specific events are recorded in these verses: Adam named his wife Eve, and God made clothes for them. Adam had previously called Eve "Woman," but now he replaced that with a new name, one that revealed his faith. By calling her "Eve" (*havvah*), a name meaning "life" or "living," he was accepting the fact that they were not going to die physically right then and that she would become "the mother of all living," that is, of all future humans.

Adam believed that life was going to continue in spite of the curse God had pronounced, so his name for Eve expressed both his faith and his hope for the future. He understood that Eve would bear children and that human life was going to continue. We are not told what he came to understand about physical death, but he knew at this point that life was going to go on for them and those who would follow in the next generations. The word "Woman" looked back at her origin; "Eve" looked ahead to what was still coming.

Adam and Eve had tried to cover themselves by using fig leaves, but this was inadequate, so God saw to it that they received something suitable and that would last much longer. The text does not say that He killed animals to provide skins for them, but the implication is certainly there. The only other option would be to create skins from nothing. The death of animals and the shedding of their blood might be intended to look ahead to the death of Jesus and the provision of salvation through His shed blood.

Removal from the garden (Gen. 3:22-23). Once again the Triune God conferred within Himself and determined that the people must never be allowed to eat from the tree of life. Their understanding of good and evil had been awakened, making them to that extent more like their Creator than before, but in a perverse and deficient way. God knew that for them to live forever in their fallen condition was unthinkable, and we should be thankful that He did not allow it! Imagine the horror of living forever in human bodies prone to sin and in a fallen state.

God, therefore, took immediate action to prevent such an unthinkable condition. He sent Adam and Eve out of the garden and into territory where Adam would have to work hard in order to sustain himself.

The Fall involved a significant shift in thinking. "God had not done evil, as man had, in order to know what was good and evil. But God, in his omniscience, knows what is good and evil and makes decisions accordingly. Man however, had obtained this knowledge by committing evil. Now man would seek to act like God in making decisions based on his inadequate knowledge of good and evil. He would no longer accept God's word as the final authority" (Anders, ed., *Holman Old Testament Commentary*, B&H).

In some way, the tree of life stopped the aging process and would have enabled Adam and Eve to live forever. With all of creation now under a curse from God, this was not a desirable thing. God's grace and mercy protected His people from eating from this tree. The tree of life, however, is going to appear again!

John was shown heaven while on the island of Patmos and recorded that an angel showed him "a pure river of water of life, clear as crystal, proceeding out of the throne of God and of the Lamb. In the midst of the street of it, and on either side of the river, was there the tree of life, which bare twelve manner of fruits, and yielded her fruit every month: and the leaves of the tree were for the healing of the nations. And there shall be no more curse" (Rev. 22:1-3).

Placement of a guard (Gen. 3:24). God made doubly sure that Adam and Eve would never eat from the tree of life by not only removing them from the garden but also stationing cherubim in front of it to keep them out. First, He drove out the man and his wife. God banished, or expelled, them forcefully. Then on the east side, which was evidently the entrance, He put the cherubim. The direction is probably significant in light of the fact that the tabernacle and temple built later both faced east.

Cherubim are portrayed consistently in the Old Testament as angelic beings that surround and protect God's presence. They are like holy bodyguards. At the garden, they protected mankind from doing something that would have eternal consequences of separation from God, and in doing so, protected God's holy plan for them. It was of utmost importance that Adam and Eve never eat of that tree. If they did, a terrible, irreversible condition would occur.

All this came about because Eve listened to the serpent and Adam listened to Eve. How important it is that we not listen to misleading voices, but only to the truth!

—Keith E. Eggert.

QUESTIONS

1. Why is a purely human perspective insufficient in speaking of God's plans for His creation?

2. Why was the serpent uniquely cursed among all creation? What happened to it?

3. What prophetic significance is found in Genesis 3:15?

4. What was now in store for the woman in the areas of childbearing and marriage?

5. What specific punishment was reserved for the man?

6. What were some things that would make work harder?

7. What did Adam do for his wife, and how did this show faith?

8. What did God do to cover them more effectively?

9. What was God's assessment of Adam and Eve's condition, and what did He do about it?

10. How did God ensure that no one would reach the tree of life?

—Keith E. Eggert.

Preparing to Teach the Lesson

We have a painful lesson to digest this week because we see the consequences of sin and the punishments that were given out to Adam and Eve. The serpent was also punished. This lesson should make us think twice about sin when we are tempted to engage in it.

TODAY'S AIM

Facts: to understand that sin separates us from God.

Principle: to realize that it is by God's mercy that salvation is offered.

Application: to personally trust Jesus as Saviour and Lord.

INTRODUCING THE LESSON

Perhaps we all remember times when we as children were taken back to the store by our parents to return some small item that we had taken without permission. We had to say that we were sorry, and we found it humiliating. But it was necessary for us to learn that sin has real consequences. There is always a consequence to sin. This week we learn the consequences that came to Adam and Eve for their disobedience—consequences that are still with us today.

DEVELOPING THE LESSON

1. A rendering of judgments (Gen. 3:14-19). It must be made very clear at the very beginning that God hates sin and will punish all sin. In this section of Scripture, we read that the serpent was the first to be judged. He was cursed above all cattle and above every living thing. He would slither on his belly from then on. We are not told how he moved before that. Finally, sin brought in perpetual enmity between the serpent and man. Mankind and the serpent (Satan) would be in perpetual conflict.

This enmity is detailed in Genesis 3:15. It would be between the serpent and the woman and her offspring. The phrase "and her seed" also looks ahead to the virgin birth that would bring forth our Redeemer many years in the future. The Bible contains many prophetic truths just under the surface of the text, and we are to dig for them (cf. Prov. 2:4).

We are also told that while the seed of the woman would be bruised in the heel (a veiled reference to the crucifixion), the serpent would be utterly bruised in the head. This was fulfilled when Jesus conquered death at His resurrection. It is worth noting that even before man sinned, God had planned his redemption.

Judgment next was pronounced on the woman (Gen. 3:16). She would bear children in sorrow and pain. It is clear from later texts (4:1-2; 5:3-4) that Cain and Abel and the other children were born after the Fall. We are also told that the man would rule his wife. She would be subject to his leadership.

Finally, judgment was rendered on the man (Gen. 3:17-19). Note that there are some very harsh words here. After God listed Adam's sins (listening to the woman and eating of the tree), He spelled out his punishment. The ground would be cursed, and he would toil for all that he would eat all his days. We must note that there was work before the Fall of man. Adam was tasked with tending the garden. But the labor now became toilsome and difficult because the ground was cursed. Thorns and thistles would hamper the work. Adam would have to provide food by the sweat of his brow.

All this came as a result of sin. The final part of this curse was death—man would return to the dust from which he came. It must be noted that man was created to have fellowship with his

Creator, and now that was broken because of sin.

Reflect with your class on how sin always brings destruction.

2. A touch of divine mercy (Gen. 3:20-21). In the midst of sin's devastating consequences, a glimpse of God's grace is given. Adam named his wife Eve (the name means "life" or "living") because all human life would come through her. She would be the first mother in the world. Adam gave her a place of honor under God, recognizing her important status.

Then we read that God gave them garments of animal skins to cover their nakedness. You will remember that immediately after their disobedience, they had sought to cover themselves with fig leaves. Their effort was wholly inadequate. The fact that God Himself gave them another covering is a sign of His grace. Through sin came shame. God moved to take away, or at least alleviate, that shame. This idea of covering shows up repeatedly in the Bible as something that God does for sinful mankind.

Remind the class that the covering God provides for our sins was not an afterthought but a deliberate plan from since the beginning of time. Jesus' blood is the covering for our sins.

3. A permanent and bitter exile (Gen. 3:22-24). We have already talked about the fact that the consequence of sin is separation from our holy God. Here we see that Adam and Eve had lost their innocence. They were aware of right and wrong, having chosen the wrong. They knew good and evil, and evil was now lodged within them. God did not want them to eat from the tree of life in this condition and "live forever." So they were cast out of the garden to work hard tilling soil that was far from ideal. Sin had made life difficult.

There is yet one more grave consequence of sin here. God prevented them from coming back into the gar-

den. Angels brandishing flaming swords guarded the entrance. Adam and Eve had no access to the tree of life. Sin prevents us from realizing eternal life and breaks our relationship with God. God had a greater plan for the salvation of mankind, but the main lesson here is that sin separates us from God and carries profound consequences (cf. Rom. 3:23; Jas. 1:15).

ILLUSTRATING THE LESSON

Sin separates us from God and brings severe consequences upon us.

CONCLUDING THE LESSON

In our society today, we seem to have lost our sense of what sin is. What our grandparents considered sin does not seem to be considered sin anymore.

Adam and Eve knew what was morally right and wrong. We need to make right choices and be aware of sin's consequences.

ANTICIPATING THE NEXT LESSON

Next week we will explore how sin in our world brought about the first murder. We learn about the death of Abel, killed by his own brother. Sin brought about bloodshed.

—A. Koshy Muthalaly.

PRACTICAL POINTS

1. When we choose sin, we also choose its consequences (Gen. 3:14-15).
2. Sin destroys our relationship with God and exposes us to pain that God never intended for us (vs. 16).
3. Disobedience allows toil and sorrow to infect relationships, activities, and places that once brought us joy (vss. 17-19).
4. When your life seems to lie in shambles, trust God and look to Him as your hope for restoration (vs. 20).
5. God always cares for His own (vs. 21).
6. God's grace limits the consequences of man's sin (vss. 22-24).
   —Cheryl Y. Powell.

RESEARCH AND DISCUSSION

1. What happens when man tries to separate an action from its consequences? Where have you seen attempts to do so in your own life or in the world around you?
2. How do we use consequences to train our children? How does awareness of consequences affect an adult's decision making?
3. How does Genesis 3:14-15 encourage you on days when it appears to your human understanding that Satan has the upper hand in our world?
4. How does it encourage you that God revealed His plan for salvation even as He punished Adam and Eve for their sin?
5. Why did God not simply leave us trapped in that separated life?
   —Cheryl Y. Powell.

ILLUSTRATED HIGH POINTS

The Lord God said

J. Hudson Taylor said, "No sin is small. It is against an infinite God and may have consequences immeasurable. No grain of sand is small in the mechanism of a watch."

Indeed, Adam and Eve only ate fruit from a forbidden tree, but their sin has had repercussions throughout time on billions of people. Every time Eve brought forth a new baby, the agony caused her to remember. When Adam hacked at the weeds and thistles in his garden, he remembered.

The serpent

God's curse upon the serpent seems to indicate a change in its appearance and mobility. Today there are around three thousand different species of snakes. They range from the four-inch threadsnake of Barbados to thirty-foot pythons. Most snakes are harmless, while others are very dangerous. Six hundred species are venomous.

Satan is called a serpent in Revelation 12:9 and 20:2. He continues to operate subtly and is not easily avoided, but he is a defeated enemy (Heb. 2:14; I John 3:8).

Enmity between thee and the woman

Growing up in New England, we saw snakes in our yard and along the river where we swam and fished. It was good to know that there were not many dangerous snakes in our area.

Dealing with Satan, however, is much more difficult than dealing with snakes. First, snakes generally do not attack humans, but Satan does. Second, Satan can be resisted (Jas. 4:7) and defeated through faith and obedience to God and His Word.
—David A. Hamburg.

Golden Text Illuminated

"Because thou hast . . . eaten of the tree, of which I commanded thee, saying, Thou shalt not eat of it: cursed is the ground for thy sake; in sorrow shalt thou eat of it all the days of thy life" (Genesis 3:17).

"This will only end in tears." I cannot tell you how many times I have either heard or said this. It usually comes out of my mouth when I or someone I know is about to do something that is not wise. Although we know it is not wise, many times we end up doing it anyway. We end up regretting that decision when we injure ourselves or someone else. Sometimes, thankfully, the results of our choices are only minor.

Sadly for Adam and Eve, and for us, the consequences of their decision were not so minor. They made a foolish decision to disobey God's directive. Because of it, they were driven out of paradise. Their beloved home was lost to them. They were forced into an unknown landscape to live out their lives.

That was only the start. They would now be forced to provide for themselves. Before this they did not have to strive for things. Now they would have to work, experience pain and suffering, and endure hardship. Ultimately, they would face death.

The worst part, though, was knowing how far-reaching the consequences were to be. Imagine knowing that because of you, everyone else after you would be forced into pain and toil. The entire planet would experience this (Rom. 8:20). Adam and Eve had to carry that guilt, knowing that their own children would one day see the results.

More important, that special communion they shared with God was broken. Since God cannot tolerate sin in His presence (Ps. 5:5), a rift formed in the intimacy that was once there. It had even created a rift between Adam and Eve themselves. Even their relationship was marred.

To them it must have been a nightmare. They were being driven from their home and were at odds with each other and God. The ease and simplicity of living was gone, never to return. What despair they must have felt!

When we look at our world, it is easy to share in that despair. As believers, however, we need not indulge in an attitude of hopelessness. Although our world is deteriorating around us, we have hope for the future.

Why? For believers, this world is only a way station, a stopping place. There is a better world waiting for us, one that has been prepared specifically for those who trust Jesus Christ as Saviour (John 14:2). Christ told us that He is creating a new world, one that is perfect and suited for us. It is a world without sin. Because of this, we will not be subject to sin's consequences in that world. All of that will be erased, like a vapor. Jesus has saved us from that curse.

Someday there will be redemption for this fallen planet. We know that the created order has been waiting for this redemption (Rom. 8:22). Until then, we need to be vigilant working for God's kingdom.

How can you take part in God's redemptive work? What is your role? While we cannot turn back the consequences of sin in this world, we know that they do not have to be eternal. That is news that a dying world needs to hear.

—*Jennifer Francis.*

Heart of the Lesson

Every time I pull out a morning glory snaking up my raspberry bushes, I am reminded of the Fall, the entry of sin into the world. My gardening hobby reminds me of Adam's sin and the resulting curse on nature.

After God confronted Adam and Eve with their sin, God revealed to them the consequences they now faced.

1. Consequences of sin for the serpent (Gen. 3:14-15). God addressed the serpent first. Because it had cooperated with Satan and had exalted itself above man, its curse would be beyond that of the other animals.

The serpent would have to slither on its belly through the dust. This implies that before the curse, the serpent did not crawl on its belly or appear as it does today. The serpent may well have been attractive; Eve was evidently not repulsed by it.

The woman and her offspring and the serpent and its offspring would be enemies. But the seed of the woman eventually would crush the serpent's head, while the serpent would only bruise the seed's heel. Here God offered hope in the midst of death and despair. Jesus would redeem mankind through His death and resurrection and thus strike a death blow to Satan.

2. Consequences of sin for the couple (Gen. 3:16-20). Because Eve had acted outside of her husband's influence, listened to the serpent, and led her husband into sin, God punished her with a craving for her husband "and with subjection to the man" (Keil and Delitzsch, *Commentary on the Old Testament,* Eerdmans).

After the Fall, men would tend to selfishly dominate women, something God did not originally intend. We see extremes of this domination, particularly in cultures that do not follow God's Word. Lawrence O. Richards wrote that such dominance "is a consequence of sin. Why perpetuate it in the Christian home?" (*The Bible Reader's Companion,* Cook). Intimidation is not headship or leadership.

Eve also would experience painful childbirth. The curse on Eve affected these two areas of life that women cherish: marriage and raising children.

Because Adam had listened to his wife, he "repudiated his superiority to the rest of creation. . . . nature would henceforth offer resistance to his will" (Keil and Delitzsch). Unlike in the garden, work would be hard, a constant fight to survive. Subduing the earth would become a difficult task. And eventually, Adam would return to the dust from which he came. The curse affected work, a vital aspect of life for men.

3. Provision for the couple (Gen. 3:21). Fig leaves were inadequate clothing. So God clothed Adam and Eve with animal skins, which was a loving, merciful act. Because of their sin, an animal had to die. This was their first experience of a death and a foreshadowing of the sacrificial system to come.

4. Expulsion from the garden (Gen. 3:22-24). God knew Adam and Eve might be tempted to eat from the tree of life. Then they and their descendants would live forever in a sinful state. So God banished them from the garden and placed cherubim—heavenly beings—and a flaming sword to block the way to the tree of life.

God offered hope to Adam and Eve, and He offers hope today. By faith in Jesus and His sacrifice for our sin, we can have forgiveness and a restored relationship with God the Father.

—*Ann Staatz.*

World Missions

Sin, grace, salvation, hope— all the truths needed for eternity with God are in God's Holy Word to be read and received. Yet, how can people believe those words if they do not have them?

The Voice of the Martyrs (VOM) has insinuated copies of God's Word into over fifty hostile or restricted areas. One pastor in Sudan rode for nine hours on a donkey to get Bibles and attend a conference. He said it was worth it. "Most of us did not have Bibles, and you could find a church having only one Bible for the pastor. Now we have more that we can share."

We take so much for granted. We have never known what it is like to risk our lives to read God's Word by candlelight or to have only one precious page of the Bible to commit to memory before passing it along.

During monsoon season in the Nuba Mountains, God's people can spend days digging trenches through mud-filled roads to get trucks of Bibles through, watching out for cargo planes with bombs.

One believer took a Bible deep into a jungle in India. Now that village is no longer predominantly Hindu; seventy percent of them have been saved.

In another part of India, workers deliver Bibles using everything from camels to canoes, through terrible heat and pressure from hostile enemies.

One way workers are making headway is through audio versions of the Bible. An audio Bible can be listened to in dangerous situations without raising suspicion in the way a physical book would.

Another way is through *The Action Bible* for children. "Children's Bibles are very much an unmet need in the world's most restricted and hostile areas," says a VOM worker. "Persecutors know that the way to win is to win the new generation."

God's Word is powerful. In one country in the Middle East, believers were smuggling Bibles when they were stopped by officers. While being questioned, they noticed the director reading one of their Bibles. He began wiping away tears. Later, he came into the room and said, "Allow them to take all the New Testaments." Then he told them, "I apologize for keeping you. How much the sayings of Christ have affected me! You should not just bring these books in suitcase by suitcase, but ship by ship."

What VOM workers do is dangerous. Anyone caught with a copy of God's Word in North Korea "will almost certainly be sentenced to imprisonment in a labor camp. In Iran, Christians caught distributing Bibles are sent to prison," says their magazine (2016 Special Photo Issue).

The Voice of the Martyrs' president, Jim Dau, says, "One of the most frequent questions I hear is, 'Will this type of persecution come to America?' While I can't know for certain, I believe it will. . . . Knowing this, we should be even more resolved to read God's Word daily and treasure it in our hearts. . . . Pick up a Bible and allow the Word to take root in your heart, making you a 'bold' Christian" (Jas. 1:21-25).

And while we still have the freedom, let us share the Word of God with others. We can give Bibles to the lost around us and also worldwide at www.persecution.com/Bibles. VOM already has the names of 178,875 people who have asked for one.

—Kimberly Rae.

The Jewish Aspect

Isaiah 14:12-14 gives us a strong hint that before man was created, Satan led a rebellion against God and was cast out of heaven. In the Garden of Eden, he continued his rebellion, enticing Eve to question and disobey God. "Eve saw no wrong in the masterpiece of satanic subtle suggestion. Satan did not tell her to sin, but insinuated in the cleverest way that there was nothing to worry about in eating the forbidden fruit . . . . Adam made no effort to restrain Eve from eating of the fruit although the divine prohibition was addressed to him as well as to Eve" (www.biblegateway.com/resources/all-women-Bible/Eve). He too ate the forbidden fruit, and when asked by God what he had done, he not only blamed Eve but also implied blame on God Himself (Gen. 3:12).

After Adam and Eve ate and realized the catastrophic consequences that they had caused in the world, they tried to hide from God. They were embarrassed by their nakedness and were ashamed to be in the presence of God. When Adam and Eve ate from the tree, it changed the entire human experience for all of mankind. What began as a perfect union of man and woman in complete and total harmony—with each another, with all living things, and with God—immediately changed to the reality of pain, sorrow, labor, shame, subjection, and judgment.

The woman sinned in acting independently of her husband. The man sinned in abandoning his leadership and following the wrongful action of his wife. For woman, pain in childbirth would be a constant reminder that a woman gave birth to sin in the human race and passed it on to all her children. Eve's relationship with Adam became marked by a burdensome power struggle. "Unto the woman [God] said, I will greatly multiply thy sorrow and thy conception; in sorrow thou shalt bring forth children; and thy desire shall be to thy husband, and he shall rule over thee" (Gen. 3:16).

Sin turned the harmonious system of God-ordained roles into distasteful struggles of self-will. Adam obeyed the voice of Eve and not God, which was the first marital role reversal. He was then told that the fields would produce not only grain but also weeds. God responded to Adam and Eve's disobedience by fusing good and bad into the very fabric of the natural world. In God's punishment for Adam, He cursed the ground so that it would produce only what man worked from it. Prior to the Fall, crops would freely yield food. After the Fall, man would have to work hard, sweat, and then return to the ground when he died.

God made coats of skins to clothe Adam and Eve. He rejected the covering they had made because it represented their own effort. The wonderful invention of fastening animal pelts together was ascribed by the ancient Hebrews to God. Animals had to be slain to cover the sins of man.

God also sent them from the Garden of Eden to till the ground and to prevent them from eating of the tree of life. This was to protect them from living forever in their fallen condition. He placed cherubim and a flaming sword that turned every way to guard the tree of life.

He also cursed the serpent and put enmity between the serpent and the woman. He promised, "I will put enmity between thee [the serpent] and the woman, and between thy seed and her seed; it shall bruise thy head, and thou shalt bruise his heel"(Gen. 3:15). In so doing, He established what some refer to as the Adamic covenant, in which He promised redemption through the seed of the woman.

—Deborah Markowitz Solan.

Guiding the Superintendent

It did not take long for sin to have its horrible effects on humanity. Sin would bring death and pain to all of man's relationships—marriage, family, and work.

As promised, God would initiate judgment and punishment, but it would be a punishment that would be both corrective and redemptive.

DEVOTIONAL OUTLINE

1. Judgment (Gen. 3:14-19). The first to receive God's judgment was the serpent. It would be cursed to crawl in the dust. The judgment then expanded to Satan, the force behind the serpent.

Genesis 3:15 is known as the protoevangelium. In the midst of great judgment, there is hope. The first prophecy in the Bible said that the serpent would strike the heel of the seed of man and that the seed of the woman (which later Scripture would identify as Jesus Christ) would crush the serpent, or Satan. The blow to Satan would be fatal.

Next, the woman was judged. She would now experience pain in childbirth. She would also suffer in her relationship to her husband. God said, "He shall rule over thee" (Gen. 3:16). Adam too would experience pain as he made a living out of the dust of the ground. Ultimately, the prospect of (physical) death would be felt by man. He would return to the dust from which he came.

Among the results of sin, mankind struggles in three key relationships: marriage, work, and children.

2. Redemption (Gen. 3:20-24). God stepped in to rescue His sinful creatures. Adam named his wife "Eve," which means the mother of all the living. Adam was responding to God's promise in verse 16. He did not look at their past sin but to the future and God's promise.

God took steps to restore His fallen creatures. He provided them with "coats of skins" (Gen. 3:21) to cover their nakedness. When sin first caused Adam to realize his nakedness, he attempted to cover himself with leaves (vs. 7). Man was now taught a key biblical lesson. Only God can provide a substitute to cover man's sinfulness.

The most striking punishment for mankind after the Fall was death. God was concerned that mankind not have access to the tree of life and live forever. They had to die. Man and woman were now expelled from the garden. But the door to salvation was open, and it would be the death of Jesus Christ that would accomplish salvation. Only through a death would death be extinguished (I Cor. 15:54-55).

Human life would never again be found in the original garden (Gen. 3:24). But life would go on. Adam would till the ground, but it would be of poorer quality (vs. 19).

"And he [Adam] died" (Gen. 5:5). God's punishment of death now fell on Adam and all his descendants.

CHILDREN'S CORNER

text: **I Kings 19:9-19**
title: **Elijah Set Straight**

After facing a death threat from Jezebel, Elijah fled into the desert. God appeared to him and asked why he was there. Elijah was burned out emotionally. He pled with God to take his life. He thought he was the only one left to defend God. God ministered to Elijah and then gave him a task to do. Elijah was reminded that he was not the only God-follower left. The Lord had seven thousand people who were still His followers.

—Martin R. Dahlquist.

Scripture Lesson Text

GEN. 4:1 And Adam knew Eve his wife; and she conceived, and bare Cain, and said, I have gotten a man from the LORD.

2 And she again bare his brother Abel. And Abel was a keeper of sheep, but Cain was a tiller of the ground.

3 And in process of time it came to pass, that Cain brought of the fruit of the ground an offering unto the LORD.

4 And Abel, he also brought of the firstlings of his flock and of the fat thereof. And the LORD had respect unto Abel and to his offering:

5 But unto Cain and to his offering he had not respect. And Cain was very wroth, and his countenance fell.

6 And the LORD said unto Cain, Why art thou wroth? and why is thy countenance fallen?

7 If thou doest well, shalt thou not be accepted? and if thou doest not well, sin lieth at the door. And unto thee shall be his desire, and thou shalt rule over him.

8 And Cain talked with Abel his brother: and it came to pass, when they were in the field, that Cain rose up against Abel his brother, and slew him.

9 And the LORD said unto Cain, Where is Abel thy brother? And he said, I know not: Am I my brother's keeper?

10 And he said, What hast thou done? the voice of thy brother's blood crieth unto me from the ground.

11 And now art thou cursed from the earth, which hath opened her mouth to receive thy brother's blood from thy hand;

12 When thou tillest the ground, it shall not henceforth yield unto thee her strength; a fugitive and a vagabond shalt thou be in the earth.

13 And Cain said unto the LORD, My punishment is greater than I can bear.

14 Behold, thou hast driven me out this day from the face of the earth; and from thy face shall I be hid; and I shall be a fugitive and a vagabond in the earth; and it shall come to pass, that every one that findeth me shall slay me.

15 And the LORD said unto him, Therefore whosoever slayeth Cain, vengeance shall be taken on him sevenfold. And the LORD set a mark upon Cain, lest any finding him should kill him.

16 And Cain went out from the presence of the LORD, and dwelt in the land of Nod, on the east of Eden.

NOTES

The First Murder

Lesson Text: Genesis 4:1-16

Related Scriptures: Matthew 23:29-36; John 15:19-25;
I John 3:10-15; Hebrews 12:22-24

TIME: unknown   PLACE: unknown

GOLDEN TEXT—"And [God] said, What hast thou done? the voice of thy brother's blood crieth unto me from the ground" (Genesis 4:10).

Introduction

A fun thing to do on the bank of a river is skipping rocks. When a small, flat rock is thrown at a shallow angle, it will skip several times across the surface of the water. Ripples roll across the surface of the water, gradually growing larger in size.

In last week's lesson we saw some of the results of Adam and Eve's sin, particularly the judgments God pronounced upon them. This week we will see that, like the ripples rolling across the surface of water, there were more and expanding results. We tend to think that our actions are confined to our own lives, but the reality is that what we do affects others.

The perfect world of Adam and Eve was marred when they disobeyed God by eating from the tree of knowledge of good and evil.

LESSON OUTLINE

I. **A DEVELOPING PROBLEM—**
   Gen. 4:1-5

II. **A FATEFUL RECKONING—**
   Gen. 4:6-12

III. **A PRESSING CONCERN—**
   Gen. 4:13-16

Exposition: Verse by Verse

A DEVELOPING PROBLEM

GEN. 4:1 And Adam knew Eve his wife; and she conceived, and bare Cain, and said, I have gotten a man from the LORD.

2 And she again bare his brother Abel. And Abel was a keeper of sheep, but Cain was a tiller of the ground.

3 And in process of time it came to pass, that Cain brought of the fruit of the ground an offering unto the LORD.

4 And Abel, he also brought of the firstlings of his flock and of the fat thereof. And the LORD had respect

unto Abel and to his offering:

5 But unto Cain and to his offering he had not respect. And Cain was very wroth, and his countenance fell.

Two sons (Gen. 4:1-2). In this context the word "knew" is a euphemism for sexual intercourse, after which Eve conceived and gave birth to Cain. The name Cain in Hebrew sounds much like the Hebrew verb that means "to acquire" or "to get." Though it was usually the father in Scripture who named the children, in this case Eve did so. She explained that she had received a man from the Lord, so perhaps she thought this might be the seed that God had promised her (3:15). It is commendable that she recognized her son was from God.

The name Abel is from a word that means "empty" or "vanity," referring to something transitory like a vapor or breath. In naming Cain, Eve recognized that new life comes from God. In naming Abel, she recognized that human life on earth is relatively brief compared to the existence of God and that which is eternal. Both facts are true, of course, and remind us that God is the Giver of this brief life and should be the only one to take life. (Of course, He can direct authorities to do so in fulfilling the demands of justice.)

The two boys grew and chose two different occupations, apparently based on their different interests. Abel became a shepherd, probably caring for both sheep and goats, and Cain became a farmer, working with the soil. Both of these were commendable occupations needed for the survival of the people. Abel is mentioned first in verse 2 without explanation, even though he was the second son born. Perhaps this points to his affinity toward religious dedication as revealed in the upcoming offerings.

Two offerings (Gen. 4:3-4a). We cannot know how much time elapsed between verses 2 and 3, but verse 3 begins by observing that some amount of time had passed before what is described next. Both men seem to have been thoroughly settled in their life's work and came to a point in time when they wanted to show gratitude to God. They chose their offerings from their lines of work, so Cain's offering was from what he had produced by his working of the soil and Abel's offering was from his flocks.

Abel is specifically said to have brought from the firstborn of his flocks, with special attention called to his use of their fat. This naturally leads us to wonder, Had God previously given some instructions? When offerings are later described in the book of Leviticus, these two things are mentioned as important. It was specified for many of the animal sacrifices that the first-born be offered, and in each of the sacrifices there were special instructions regarding the burning of the fat.

It is also possible that the details about Abel's offering merely indicate he was bringing the best that he had. There are no such corresponding words describing Cain's offering. If that is the intended contrast, we get a clear indication that Abel was more spiritually minded than Cain and understood that God deserved nothing but the best. Such a mind-set is a good reminder for us. God always deserves our best, not our leftovers.

Two responses (Gen. 4:4b-5). The next statement, "And the Lord had respect unto Abel and to his offering: but unto Cain and to his offering he had not respect," has long been the subject of discussion and debate. In Leviticus, both grain and animal offerings are described as being acceptable to God. The question remains, therefore, as to why God accepted Abel's offering but not Cain's.

The simplest explanation of God's acceptance of Abel's offering is found in Hebrews 11:4, where we read that "by faith Abel offered unto God a more excellent sacrifice than Cain, by which he obtained witness that he was righteous, God testifying of his gifts." But what did Abel have that Cain did not? Some believe the difference was in their attitudes rather than in the specific offerings. In Genesis 4:4-5 the name of the person is mentioned prior to the offering in each case, indicating that it was the person God responded to.

Others believe that God must have given instruction about the necessity of shedding blood for the offerings, although we have no record of it. John MacArthur wrote, "Abel's offering was acceptable, not just because it was an animal, nor just because it was the very best of what he had, nor even that it was the culmination of a zealous heart for God; but, because it was in every way obediently given according to what God must have revealed (though not recorded in Genesis)" (*The MacArthur Study Bible,* Nelson).

Cain's attitude was clearly a problem—whether it was a lack of faith in not bringing the firstfruits and his best or a case of direct disobedience. We do know that God cares about both the intentions of our hearts and the quality of what we give. In some way, Cain displeased God in his offering.

A FATEFUL RECKONING

6 And the LORD said unto Cain, Why art thou wroth? and why is thy countenance fallen?

7 If thou doest well, shalt thou not be accepted? and if thou doest not well, sin lieth at the door. And unto thee shall be his desire, and thou shalt rule over him.

8 And Cain talked with Abel his brother: and it came to pass, when they were in the field, that Cain rose up against Abel his brother, and slew him.

9 And the LORD said unto Cain, Where is Abel thy brother? And he said, I know not: Am I my brother's keeper?

10 And he said, What hast thou done? the voice of thy brother's blood crieth unto me from the ground.

11 And now art thou cursed from the earth, which hath opened her mouth to receive thy brother's blood from thy hand;

12 When thou tillest the ground, it shall not henceforth yield unto thee her strength; a fugitive and a vagabond shalt thou be in the earth.

God's challenge to Cain (Gen. 4:6-7). The rejection of his offering made Cain very angry, causing him to go into a deep sulk that showed in his countenance. When God saw this, He asked Cain two questions: "Why art thou wroth? and why is thy countenance fallen?" The Hebrew word translated "wroth" is *harah* and means "to glow" or "grow warm," which figuratively refers to blazing up! Cain had a temper tantrum, and he could not hide it. Such extreme emotions on our part cannot be hidden from those around us.

We do not know definitively why God rejected Cain and his sacrifice, nor do we know how God indicated this. But He obviously had done so clearly enough, and Cain reacted with anger and resentment. Moreover, his attitude did not improve after he was addressed by God but only intensified, for the attack on Abel came after God had made it clear to Cain that he could still find acceptance if he did well. On the other hand, sin was at his door, and he would fail if he did not conquer it.

The word behind "lieth" in Genesis 4:7 carries the picture of crouching like an animal ready for a sneak attack. Cain's anger blocked him from choosing the right response. He needed to master his anger and desire for revenge, but his anger—coupled with envy toward his brother—proved too strong, and he was not able (or willing) to change. What a strong warning to us about the danger of allowing sinful attitudes to control our thinking! Sinful actions follow, and we find ourselves in deep rebellion against God.

Cain's angry reaction (Gen. 4:8). Cain allowed his anger and resentment to build, leading to an extreme and unprecedented act: the murder of his brother. Since he had dismissed God's gracious correction, Cain's relationship with Him deteriorated to the extent that it destroyed his relationship with his brother. This pattern, established so early in mankind's existence, recurs repeatedly today. When we are not in right relationship with God, we cannot be in right relationship with one another. Anger, envy, selfishness, strife, and bitterness will damage all human relationships.

Anger is an especially powerful emotion that is warned about in many texts of Scripture. It becomes the means leading to violence and the potential of committing many sins against people and God. It is imperative that we allow the Spirit of God to give us victory over this destructive emotion.

God's question to Cain (Gen. 4:9). Cain's action was quickly met by a direct question from God: "Where is Abel thy brother?" God already knew, of course, but He wanted to give Cain an opportunity to confess. Instead, Cain, like his parents, tried to hide from the truth by claiming ignorance and lack of responsibility for his brother's well-being. Again we see a callous indifference toward both God and his brother. What a revelation of human irresponsibility it is to see Cain so angry with God that his only means of getting back at Him was to kill his brother!

God's judgment on Cain (Gen. 4:10-12). "There's a definite parallel between God's dealings with Cain in Genesis 4 and His dealings with Adam and Eve in chapter 3. In both instances, the Lord asked questions, not to get information (for He knows everything) but to give the culprits opportunity to tell the truth and confess their sins. In both instances, the sinners were evasive and tried to cover up what they had done" (Wiersbe, *The Bible Exposition Commentary,* Cook). In neither case did God allow this to happen.

Just as Adam and Eve had faced judgment from God, so now did Cain. God immediately let Cain know that He was aware of what had occurred and then proceeded to tell him what the consequences would be. This is the third curse recorded in Genesis (the first, in 3:14, was on the serpent; the second, in verse 17, the ground) and the first to fall directly on a human. It fell on Cain because of his brother's shed blood, which God said was received by the earth. Cain's curse, therefore, was that the ground would resist his attempts to cultivate it and receive its produce.

The twofold curse expanded beyond the resistance of the ground to yield crops. Cain would now become a vagabond wandering over that ground. He would no longer be able to enjoy the settledness of farming; God himself had become resistant to him, which caused him to lose previous blessings of family closeness and productive work. Even so, God was gracious in that He did not take Cain's life.

A PRESSING CONCERN

13 And Cain said unto the LORD, My punishment is greater than I can bear.

14 Behold, thou hast driven me out this day from the face of the earth; and from thy face shall I be hid; and I shall be a fugitive and a vagabond in the earth; and it shall come to pass, that every one that findeth me shall slay me.

15 And the LORD said unto him, Therefore whosoever slayeth Cain, vengeance shall be taken on him sevenfold. And the LORD set a mark upon Cain, lest any finding him should kill him.

16 And Cain went out from the presence of the LORD, and dwelt in the land of Nod, on the east of Eden.

Cain's fear (Gen. 4:13-14). Cain's response was one of self-pity rather than remorse over what he had done. He was distressed by his punishment, but he did not repent of his actions. His fear was expressed in his complaint that the punishment was more than he could bear and that he would now be a loner and hunted by others. Instead of expressing a submissive attitude, his statement appears to blame God: "Thou hast driven me out this day from the face of the earth; and from thy face shall I be hid."

Cain feared that in being driven away from everybody, he would be hidden from God Himself. Accordingly, being a fugitive and vagabond would result in constant wandering with no means of protection available to him. His greatest fear was that anyone finding him would kill him. He viewed all relationships as broken, from his relationship with God to his relationships with all other human beings. Such alienation led to great fear in his heart.

There is a severe warning in this passage about the cost of sin. The first result of sin is separation from God. Unbelievers are separated because they have no relationship with God to begin with. Believers can lose the closeness of fellowship with Him when they allow sin to come between them and God. Alienation from God is just the beginning of the potential for alienation and fear between us and other people in our lives. Our individual concern needs to be primarily on our relationship with God.

God's protection (Gen. 4:15-16). Once again God was gracious and merciful. He responded to Cain's outburst of accusation and fear by promising a measure of protection, even though what he feared would have been entirely deserved. What God would do to anyone who harmed Cain would be far worse than what that person would have done. Here we see the first indication of God's later statement: "To me belongeth vengeance, and recompence; their foot shall slide in due time" (Deut. 32:35).

In order to visibly portray His promise to protect Cain and as a warning, God put a mark on him. Many ideas have been presented as to what this mark was, but since it is not explained in the text, we do best to just accept that it was some sort of visible sign. MacArthur noted that "it involved some sort of identifiable sign that he was under divine protection which was mercifully given." This should cause us to thank God for His mercy!

—Keith E. Eggert.

QUESTIONS

1. What do Eve's names for her sons indicate about her understanding of God?
2. What were the brothers' vocations, and how did these bear on what they brought to God as an offering?
3. What are some explanations for why God rejected Cain and his offering?
4. How did Cain react, and what did God ask him about that?
5. Despite His rejection of the sacrifice, what did God graciously make clear to Cain?
6. What warning did God give Cain about sin that we also need to hear?
7. Why did God ask Cain about his brother? How did he respond?
8. What was God's twofold curse pronounced upon Cain?
9. What was Cain's greatest fear regarding his punishment?
10. How did God promise to protect Cain as he wandered?

—Keith E. Eggert.

Preparing to Teach the Lesson

Little by little the wonderful world that God had created was getting tarnished by sin. This week we learn of the first murder.

TODAY'S AIM

Facts: to learn the facts about the first murder that was committed in history.

Principle: to see that because sin lies in wait to trip us up, we must always be ready for it.

Application: to acknowledge that God offers us His mercy in the midst of our sin and calls us to recognize it.

INTRODUCING THE LESSON

Almost everyone knows the story of young George Washington and the cherry tree. When asked whether he had chopped the tree down, the boy replied that he could not tell a lie and admitted to the deed. His father forgave him. The lesson for us in this legend is that we must not be afraid to do what is right even if we will suffer for it. In our lesson this week, we see how Abel was killed for doing the right thing. Cain blew his chance to confess his misdeed. God's just punishment was severe, but we also see His great mercy.

DEVELOPING THE LESSON

1. Two offerings (Gen. 4:1-5). Adam and Eve had their first two children. The first was named Cain, a name that means "gotten," or "acquired," reflecting Eve's recognition that he was given to her by God. The other son was named Abel, whose name means "breath," or "vanity," an odd name in that he is shown to be the virtuous one of the two. Abel became a shepherd, Cain was a farmer, and they both brought offerings to God. Abel's offering was accepted, while Cain's was rejected.

Why Cain's sacrifice was rejected has been debated for centuries, but it seems clear at least that he did not give God his best. It is important that we give Him our best in response to all that He has done for us.

2. Sin at the door (Gen. 4:6-9). It is here that we see the first example of jealousy, depression, anger, and murder in the world. Notice the sequence of those dark words. It is important to realize that we all need to seek God's approval in all that we do. But we are never to resort to violence even in our thoughts, for that can lead to greater sins like murder.

The Lord asked Cain why he was so depressed and then added that if he did not respond appropriately, he was in great danger, for sin was waiting at the door, ready to destroy him. It waits for us too. How we respond to negative situations matters to God. We are called to do what is right.

Far from doing right, Cain let his anger build, and murder followed. When the Lord questioned him about Abel, Cain's anger flared again. He implied sarcastically that looking after his brother was not his job.

It is important to learn from this lesson that sin will catch us off guard if we are not alert to the schemes of the evil one. We are to be prepared at all times. Sin can catch any one of us by surprise.

3. Punishment and mercy (Gen. 4:10-16). Our God, who is holy, has a holy hatred of sin and must punish it. In these verses we see the punishment that Cain received. Notice the reference to Abel's blood that was spilled. Blood in the Bible is the symbol for life. Leviticus 17:11 says, "For the life of the flesh is in the blood."

After Adam's sin, the earth was cursed. Now that Cain had defiled the earth with his brother's blood, Cain, the farmer, was cursed from the earth. No matter how hard he worked the ground, it would not produce for him.

Moreover, we see that Cain was banished from the comfort of his familiar home. He would wander as a fugitive on the earth. That was not all. He would also be a target for those who sought to kill him.

As we study this lesson, we need to ask ourselves, Have we become so comfortable with sin that we fail to foresee its consequences? Sin separates us from God. That is a lonely place to be.

We have seen God's severe punishment of Cain, and now we see His mercy. God promised to protect Cain—no one would kill him. Anyone who attempted that would receive the maximum punishment. The promise of sevenfold vengeance was essentially a declaration that such a person would receive the maximum punishment. This is astonishing. Cain had just committed murder, and God was showing him mercy and protection! This tells us volumes about our God—His love covers us despite our sin.

Then we read that God put a mark on Cain. We are not told what kind of mark it was. But it certainly identified him as a murderer, for he was a marked man with a target on his back. Yet the mark also served as the sign of God's protection on Cain, for God was ready to punish anyone who would kill him. When we sin, God sets His love on us to bring us back to Him, for He does not want any of us to perish. God's punishment and mercy go hand in hand.

ILLUSTRATING THE LESSON

Sin destroys all that it comes in contact with. But God's mercy will preserve those who are faithful to Him.

MERCY

IN THE MIDST OF TRAGEDY

CONCLUDING THE LESSON

This week we learned of the way in which Adam and Eve's family was again wrecked by the devastation of sin. Cain murdered his brother Abel. We have also learned that we are to be always prepared for the onslaught of the evil one who catches us when we are least prepared for it. God also sets His love upon us so that we might return to Him in repentance and for restoration. He puts us under His care and protection.

As we seek to follow our Lord Jesus this week, it is important for us to know that He protects us from the world and the evil one. We can trust Him fully. We are called to do what is right and to seek His approval as Abel did, even if it costs us our lives.

"Be strong in the Lord . . . that ye may be able to stand against the wiles of the devil" (Eph. 6:10-11).

ANTICIPATING THE NEXT LESSON

In our lesson next week, we will learn about a time, not much unlike ours, when the world was full of sin and wickedness. We will see God's extreme anger against sin. And once again, we will learn about the grace of God at such an evil time through the life of one faithful man named Noah.

—A. Koshy Muthalaly.

109

PRACTICAL POINTS

1. All life is precious, for God is the source of all life (Gen 4:1-2).
2. God honors our faith in Him as we give Him the best we have to offer (vss. 3-5).
3. We must be on guard at all times not to allow our emotions to leave us vulnerable to sin's control (vss. 6-7).
4. Nothing in our lives can be hidden from God (vss. 8-10).
5. Our life's work becomes fruitless and difficult as sin separates us from God (vss. 11-12).
6. God is merciful to protect us from the full weight of our sin (vss. 13-16).

—Cheryl Y. Powell.

RESEARCH AND DISCUSSION

1. What can believers learn about the value that God places on human life? In what ways do we see our society devalue human life?
2. What does this passage teach about what God expects from us? What kind of sacrifice pleases God (cf. I Sam. 15:22; Mic. 6:8)?
3. Have you ever sensed God's warning that your attitudes or motives were making you vulnerable to Satan's attack? What Scriptures or truths did God bring to your remembrance at such times?
4. How does it encourage you that God showed mercy to Cain after he had committed such a heinous act? What example is God setting for the church as we minister to those who may have committed heinous or violent crimes?

—Cheryl Y. Powell.

ILLUSTRATED HIGH POINTS

The Lord had respect unto Abel

God valued Abel's offering because of his faith (cf. Heb. 11:4). Cain brought a costly sacrifice, but it was based on his own works instead of faith and obedience to God.

Suppose there was a device that would measure the integrity of our hearts as we sit in service on Sunday. How would we fare?

One man told me he only went to church to ogle the women. As one pastor said, "Satan does not do his most subtle work in the saloon but in the sanctuary."

My brother's keeper

Cain imagined he had a clever answer to God's penetrating question. God was not impressed. He held Cain accountable for Abel's death.

I have missionary friends in Europe who have a ministry that seeks to rescue people enslaved in the sex-slave trade. It is a hard, dangerous ministry but rewarding when one responds.

Now art thou cursed

Cain refused to do well (cf. Gen. 4:7) and so compounded the consequences of his failure to offer a faith sacrifice (cf. Heb. 11:4).

A fellow who was living a dissolute life was asked whether he was still getting "a kick" out of life. His honest answer was, "A kick? I'm getting a kickback."

The kickback of sin is always there. Sin may give pleasure "for a season" (Heb. 11:25), but there is one truth to remember. The justice of God is inevitable and unavoidable. "God is not mocked: for whatsoever a man soweth, that shall he also reap. For he that soweth to his flesh shall of the flesh reap corruption" (Gal. 6:7-8).

—David A. Hamburg.

Golden Text Illuminated

"And [God] said, What hast thou done? the voice of thy brother's blood crieth unto me from the ground" (Genesis 4:10).

Most of us know what sibling rivalry is. As a child, I was not immune to it. Even though I had only one sibling, I found myself living in competition with him. There was a drive to score higher in school, to perform better in extracurricular activities, and even to get into more clubs. I found myself striving to be "the good kid" in my parents' eyes.

For children to involve themselves in this type of rivalry is not uncommon. Certainly we grow out of it, though, right? Wrong. Not always. As we grow older, we may continue to find ourselves in competition. We want to be the better worker, the cooler parent on the street, or even the more active church member. We unconsciously try to outdo the other. In our society, the person with the highest status or the most toys is the best. When someone else has that, even a sibling, we can fall prey to envy.

That was what happened between Cain and Abel. We have a scenario of one person's heart being right but the other one's not. Abel was considered righteous by God (Heb. 11:4) and sincerely strove to serve Him. What about Cain? We do not know how sincere his sacrifice was. What we do know is that he was doing evil in God's eyes (I John 3:12).

So when the two brothers brought their sacrifices, only Abel's was considered worthy. Cain's, on the other hand, was rejected. Can you imagine Cain's anger and frustration? I can almost hear him saying, "Of course God accepted Abel's gift! Everyone likes him. He has always been the better brother, the one everyone favors." Cain gave in to bitterness, and the end result was dreadful.

You may be thinking, Yes, but I have never done anything that drastic. That is an extreme. We may think that what we are doing is not that serious, but Jesus teaches otherwise. In Matthew 5:21-22, Christ's teaching about anger is plain. He tells us that anyone who has unrighteous anger has sinned dangerously. The only difference between Cain and ourselves is that Cain allowed himself to carry his anger and jealousy to extreme physical violence.

Cain was banished for his terrible sin. However, even in the midst of tragedy, God still demonstrated His grace. God placed a mark upon Cain to protect him (Gen. 4:15). Though the consequences were dire, Cain would still be able to live. God did not put Cain to death.

How many times have we said something out of anger or done something out of jealousy? I do not know about you, but there are words I have said and things I have done that I have lived to regret. We are told that envy leads to emptiness (cf. Eccles. 4:4) and that jealousy is even more dangerous than anger (Prov. 27:4), which is itself quite deadly.

Have you shown anger or envy toward someone? Jesus tells us that we need to resolve the issue with that person. We cannot expect our worship to be accepted before God if we do not (cf. Matt. 5:23-24). As believers, we are admonished to live peacefully (Rom. 12:18). That means not giving way to envy or anger. Instead, we must do everything we can to resist the temptation to follow Cain's downward path (I John 3:12), lest the consequences be terrible for us.

—*Jennifer Francis.*

Heart of the Lesson

One winter in the city where I live, more than a dozen tents lined the sidewalk under a particular freeway bridge. Shopping carts overflowed with clothing. I even spotted an easy chair on the sidewalk. Homeless people had set up a camp. Sheltered from the Northwest's constant winter rain, homeless people lived under the bridge until spring and then moved on. Life on the move without a real home is a harsh way to live. For Cain, Adam and Eve's son, life on the move was his punishment for murder.

1. Birth of two sons (Gen. 4:1-2). God had commanded Adam and Eve to fill the earth. After their expulsion from the garden, Eve became pregnant with Cain, her first child recorded in the Bible. She named a second son Abel. He became a shepherd; Cain was a farmer.

2. Offerings to God (Gen. 4:3-7). God apparently had given instructions to the first family about sacrifices to worship Him because both brothers brought offerings to God. Cain sacrificed crops from his harvest. Abel sacrificed several of his choicest firstborn lambs.

God accepted Abel's offering, but He was displeased with Cain's. Perhaps God wanted only blood sacrifices on this occasion. Perhaps God looked at the men's hearts. The New Testament says that Abel sacrificed in faith (Heb. 11:4).

Cain was furious with God for rejecting his sacrifice but accepting his brother's. God urged Cain to do the right thing—perhaps bring the right offering or have the right attitude. He would have further opportunity then to please God. God warned that like a wild beast, sin was crouching at Cain's door, ready to devour him.

3. Murder in the field (Gen. 4:8-10). Cain chose to reject God's warning. Filled with bitterness and rage, Cain lured his brother to a field, far from anyone who might see them or hear Abel cry for help. Then Cain attacked and killed his brother.

After Adam sinned, God asked him, "Where art thou?" (Gen. 3:9). Now God asked Cain a different question: "Where is Abel thy brother?" (4:9). Cain feigned ignorance and sought to evade responsibility. He asked if he was his brother's keeper. Was he supposed to constantly keep track of Abel's every move?

God said Abel's blood was crying out to Him from the ground. No human witnesses saw the murder, but God did. And God sees us today when we choose to disobey Him.

4. Consequences for Cain (Gen. 4:11-16). God proclaimed judgment on Cain. The ground would withhold crops from him, and he would be a fugitive and a wanderer on the earth.

Overwhelmed, Cain said this punishment was more than he could bear. He did not repent or ask for forgiveness. His concern was solely the punishment—he was being driven from his home and land, he said. God had hidden His face from him. Cain would never be able to settle down. And he feared a family member would avenge Abel's death and kill him.

God addressed only the last of Cain's concerns. God marked Cain in a way that would prevent retaliation. Then Cain went and lived in the region east of Eden.

When King David sinned, he confessed and begged God not to take His Holy Spirit from him. But there was no sign of repentance with Cain. He was angry and prideful. When we have these kinds of attitudes, we hurt others, and we move far away from God. If you see these tendencies in yourself, beware—sin is at your door.

—*Ann Staatz.*

World Missions

This will not be an easy story to write, nor an easy one to read. When I left for the mission field, I idealized missionaries as spiritual giants, heroes who were very strong spiritually with unwavering commitment.

But I did not become a spiritual hero when I got off the plane, and I was equally disappointed to discover that the other missionaries in my field, though great men and women of God, were also only frail and faulty humans just like me.

The truth is that missionaries are sinful and just as capable of giving in to temptation, deceit, and immorality as anyone else. Sometimes a given sin can overcome a person in ministry completely. A highly revered man on the mission board, in my own field, was revealed recently not only to have had affairs, but he had also deceived missionary moms in order to behave inappropriately with their daughters. He left a trail of victims who still suffer many years later.

The mission board, in trying to protect its reputation by keeping things hushed, damaged its honor in a massive way (now that the truth has been exposed) and has given the enemies of God cause to blaspheme (II Sam. 12:14).

The Bible tells us to give honor to whom it is due (Rom. 13:7), and certainly missionaries should be esteemed highly "for their work's sake" (I Thess. 5:13). However, we must never lift them above the reality that they are saved only by the power of God's grace. To assume they are on a higher spiritual plane does not protect them from sin, but rather leaves them more vulnerable to it. (More on that next week.)

It only took one generation to plummet from the perfection of Adam and Eve before the Fall, to murder. We must not assume that accepting God's call to service makes a person immune to the call of sin. In fact, we should expect that Satan will more heavily attack those in ministry than those who are not fighting against him. And if he can conquer them in a moral way, what a great victory, for it harms God's work around the world and diminishes their testimony.

One counselor stated, "For the last twenty years thousands of men from across America struggling with sexual sin have come to our intensive counseling workshop. Over half were pastors and missionaries."

The counselor also recounted how a seminary professor once said to him, "We no longer ask our entering students if they are struggling with pornography; we assume every student is struggling." He also said that within just one mission board "80% of their applicants voluntarily indicate a struggle with pornography, resulting in staff shortages on the field."

We have to recognize that sin, especially sexual sin, is tearing into kingdom work and kingdom workers. If we can recognize it, we can fight it. To turn away, to keep it secret, gives a dark and powerful tool to Satan.

Missionaries need God's grace every hour of every day, as we all do. Next week we will discuss practical ways to help, but for today, let us simply remember that sin crouches at the door for each of us (Gen. 4:7), even those we most revere. They need our prayers for victory, not just for their work, but for their own spiritual walk in the face of the powerful pull of the flesh.

—Kimberly Rae.

The Jewish Aspect

The birth of Cain (*qayin* in Hebrew) was a joyous occasion for his mother, Eve, who said, "I have gotten [*qanah*—to acquire] a man from the Lord" (Gen. 4:1). Note the similarity in sound. Of Abel the text simply says that Eve gave birth to him, without stating that she named him. However, the Hebrew noun translated as Abel means "vapor" or "breath," a term that described his subsequent fate of a short life cut off in its prime.

Cain and Abel worked as food producers for their family. Cain was a tiller of the soil (a crop farmer), and Abel was a keeper of sheep (shepherd). Both occupations were respectable and honorable trades. Cain brought some of his crop—the harvest of the soil—as an offering to the Lord. There was no blood sacrifice in his offering. Abel brought an offering from the choicest of the firstlings of his flock.

Abel's offering was acceptable because it involved blood and the sacrificing of an animal and was the very best of what he had. God Himself had killed an animal and made coats of skin to clothe Adam and Eve (Gen. 3:21). God rejected Cain's offerings but accepted Abel's (4:3-5). Abel brought his very best, whereas Cain was satisfied to bring the leftovers. In Rabbinic literature, Cain is viewed as greedy—only offering worthless portions, the remnants of his meal.

Rather than being repentant for his sinful disobedience, Cain was hostile toward God, whom he could not kill, and jealous of his brother, whom he could kill. God had given Cain the opportunity to do well, to make the right kind of sacrifice. If he did, he would find the same acceptance that Abel had. God warned, however, that if he did not, sin was lurking at the door. Cain rejected the wisdom spoken to him by God, rejected doing well, refused to repent, and treacherously murdered his brother Abel. When asked by God, "Where is Abel thy brother?" Cain sarcastically responded, "Am I my brother's keeper?" (Gen. 4:9).

Cain's sarcasm was a play on words, for Abel was the keeper of the sheep. The motives for Cain's murder of his brother were jealousy and anger at God's rejection of his offering while accepting Abel's. Cain killed Abel, committing the first murder. Cain was the first person born, and Abel was the first to die. Abel was the first murder victim and is sometimes seen as the first martyr, while Cain, the first murderer, is often seen as an ancestor of evil.

God told Cain that his brother's blood was crying out to Him from the ground. Now Cain himself was under a curse and would be driven from the land that had received his brother's blood from Cain's violent act. Because he had committed such a horrendous crime, Cain was sentenced to a life of vagrancy and homelessness, wandering aimlessly in the land of Nod (a name that itself means "wandering"), always looking over his shoulder in fear of dangers real and perceived.

Cain would move from place to place looking for a more productive field to plant on, but he would never find one. His crops would fail wherever he was. The blessings of God were revoked, and a curse was given instead.

Cain's punishment was far less severe than it could have been or that he deserved. To protect the murderer from being murdered by others, the Lord mercifully set a mark on him for divine protection from premature death. The mark, however, was also a lifelong sign of his shame.

—Deborah Markowitz Solan

Guiding the Superintendent

God's words that disobedience would bring death (cf. Gen. 2:17) came true all too soon. Mankind was barely out of the garden before the first murder was committed. Adam and Eve produced two children—Cain and Abel. Sibling rivalry raised its ugly head. As a result of different attitudes about worshipping God, murder entered the world. The wages of sin are surely death (Rom. 6:23).

DEVOTIONAL OUTLINE

1. The sacrifice of Cain (Gen. 4:1-5). Adam and Eve began filling the earth as commanded (1:28). Cain and his younger brother Abel joined the family. Cain was a farmer while Abel was a herdsman.

Mankind worshipped God. The two brothers brought the labor of their hands as their offerings. Cain was no atheist. He worshipped God but not from the right spirit. Hebrews 11:4 indicates that only Abel's sacrifice was by faith.

In response to God's rejection of his sacrifice, Cain grew very angry (Gen. 4:5). Something was wrong. Here was a person who desired to worship God but on his own terms. His reaction indicated what was in his heart.

2. The murder of Abel (Gen. 4:6-8). While it was necessary for Eve to be talked into sin (3:1-6), it was necessary to try to talk Cain out of sin (4:6-7).

God appeared to Cain and asked, "Why is thy countenance fallen?" (Gen. 4:6). God was telling Cain to deal with his anger that was demonstrated all over his face. God warned the angry brother that "sin lieth at the door" (vs. 7). The idea here is that sin was like a wild animal that was crouching at the door (cf. I Pet. 5:8).

Cain's rage boiled over. Instead of dealing with his anger, he went out into the field and killed his brother.

3. Sentence on Cain (Gen. 4:9-16). When confronted by God with their sin, Adam and Eve blamed others. When God confronted Cain, he pled ignorance, saying, "I know not." Sin had taken its toll on early man. Cain's answer reveals a definite hardening of attitude. He questioned whether he was his brother's keeper.

God's judgment fit the crime. Cain, the tiller of the ground, now had the ground cursed. In addition to having the ground cursed, God also prophesied that Cain would become "a fugitive and a vagabond" (Gen. 4:12) as he wandered the earth. He would find no rest or peace. He would never be satisfied.

Cain was more concerned about himself than what he had done to his brother. He feared that the avenging hand of man would kill him. There was little evidence of concern for God. In His grace, God extended mercy. Cain would be protected from being killed.

CHILDREN'S CORNER

text: **II Kings 2:1-12**
title: **A Heavenly Whirlwind**

God's ministers come and go, but God's ministry goes on. Time had now come for Elijah to depart the earth and for Elisha to inherit Elijah's ministry.

The succession took place in a most remarkable way. As Elijah and Elisha were talking, "a chariot of fire, and horses of fire" (II Kings 2:11) took Elijah up into heaven. Elisha was empowered with special divine abilities to work great miracles for God.

—*Martin R. Dahlquist.*

Scripture Lesson Text

GEN. 6:1 And it came to pass, when men began to multiply on the face of the earth, and daughters were born unto them,

2 That the sons of God saw the daughters of men that they were fair; and they took them wives of all which they chose.

3 And the LORD said, My spirit shall not always strive with man, for that he also is flesh: yet his days shall be an hundred and twenty years.

4 There were giants in the earth in those days; and also after that, when the sons of God came in unto the daughters of men, and they bare children to them, the same became mighty men which were of old, men of renown.

5 And God saw that the wickedness of man was great in the earth, and that every imagination of the thoughts of his heart was only evil continually.

6 And it repented the LORD that he had made man on the earth, and it grieved him at his heart.

7 And the LORD said, I will destroy man whom I have created from the face of the earth; both man, and beast, and the creeping thing, and the fowls of the air; for it repenteth me that I have made them.

8 But Noah found grace in the eyes of the LORD.

9 These are the generations of Noah: Noah was a just man and perfect in his generations, and Noah walked with God.

10 And Noah begat three sons, Shem, Ham, and Japheth.

NOTES

Worldwide Wickedness

Lesson Text: Genesis 6:1-10

Related Scriptures: Romans 1:21-32; 3:9-18; Psalm 37:34-40

TIME: unknown   PLACE: unknown

GOLDEN TEXT—"God saw that the wickedness of man was great in the earth, and that every imagination of the thoughts of his heart was only evil continually" (Genesis 6:5).

Introduction

Look at this interesting exchange recorded in Haggai: "Thus saith the Lord of hosts; Ask now the priests concerning the law, saying, If one bear holy flesh in the skirt of his garment, and with his skirt do touch bread, or pottage, or wine, or oil, or any meat, shall it be holy? And the priests answered and said, No. Then said Haggai, If one that is unclean by a dead body touch any of these, shall it be unclean? And the priests answered and said, It shall be unclean" (2:11-13).

In a basket filled with apples, one that is rotten spreads that rottenness to the others. It would never work to put one good apple into a basket filled with rotten ones and expect that good one to cause all the others to become good. A bad steak will make one next to it bad also, but a good steak will never make a bad one next to it good.

In the spiritual realm, sin has an automatic corrupting influence, making it possible for one sinful person to drag another down easily.

LESSON OUTLINE

I. MAN'S UNGODLINESS—
   Gen. 6:1-5

II. GOD'S RESPONSE—
   Gen. 6:6-10

Exposition: Verse by Verse

MAN'S UNGODLINESS

GEN. 6:1 And it came to pass, when men began to multiply on the face of the earth, and daughters were born unto them,

2 That the sons of God saw the daughters of men that they were fair; and they took them wives of all which they chose.

3 And the LORD said, My spirit shall not always strive with man, for that he also is flesh: yet his days shall be

an hundred and twenty years.

4 There were giants in the earth in those days; and also after that, when the sons of God came in unto the daughters of men, and they bare children to them, the same became mighty men which were of old, men of renown.

5 And God saw that the wickedness of man was great in the earth, and that every imagination of the thoughts of his heart was only evil continually.

Unholy intermarriage (Gen. 6:1-2). The chapter begins by mentioning the multiplication of people on earth. This could have happened quite rapidly, considering the longevity of lives up to that point. In the list of Adam's line through Noah, who lived 950 years, the oldest person lived 969 years and the youngest 777 years (5:1-31). These long lives could have easily caused extremely rapid growth in the population of the earth. Daughters are mentioned, but it is obvious that there were many sons being born at the same time.

One of the most debated statements in the entire Bible is found in Genesis 6:2: "The sons of God saw the daughters of men that they were fair; and they took them wives of all which they chose." The question is, who were the "sons of God" and the "daughters of men"? Each of us must read the various arguments promoting an answer and then decide individually which arguments are the strongest. There are three primary possibilities for this answer.

Some believe the sons were male descendants of Seth (righteous sons in Genesis 4:26) who married female descendants of Cain (daughters). If this is the case, it would be a unique use of the phrase "sons of God."

Some believe the statement is referring to dynastic rulers, or nobles, who

were married to common women. The Old Testament does occasionally refer to judges and other rulers as "gods" (Ps. 82:6; cf. John 10:34-36), but there would be no reason for these to be immoral relationships and for giants to come from them.

Some believe the sons of God were fallen angels who cohabited with human women. The objections to this view are that angels are sexless and do not reproduce, that angels cannot have the same bodily functions as men, and that this idea does not fit with our understanding of the real world. In support of this view is the fact that the Bible uses the phrase "sons of God" to refer to angels (Job 1:6; 2:1; 38:7). We also know from Genesis 18 and 19 that angels can take on human form.

We might also consider two New Testament passages that refer to a group of angels without specifically identifying them. Second Peter 2:4 says, "God spared not the angels that sinned, but cast them down to hell, and delivered them into chains of darkness, to be reserved unto judgment." Who are these angels, and what did they do?

Jude 1:6 says, "And the angels which kept not their first estate, but left their own habitation, he hath reserved in everlasting chains under darkness unto the judgment of the great day." The passage then continues about "Sodom and Gomorrha, and the cities about them in like manner, giving themselves over to fornication, and going after strange flesh, are set forth for an example, suffering the vengeance of eternal fire" (vs. 7).

Is it possible these sons of God in Genesis 6:2 are the ones that Jude describes as not keeping to their first domain, or proper sphere of authority? Is it also possible that the "locusts" in Revelation 9:1-11 are these angels who have been confined through all these years?

Perhaps Henry M. Morris summarized it best: "This seems to be such a grotesque situation that it does appear extremely doubtful that God would have allowed it at all, even if it were physiologically a realistic possibility. And yet, . . . it does violence to the actual text of the passage if we make it mean merely that the sons of Seth began to marry the daughters of Cain. (If this were what it meant, why did not the writer simply say so, and thus avoid all this confusion?)" (*The Genesis Record,* Baker).

An affront to God (Gen. 6:3-4). Apparently, one of the results of this combination was the presence of giants on the earth at that time. They appeared "when the sons of God came in unto the daughters of men, and they bare children to them," so the connection of their presence and the intermarriage already mentioned seems clear, although this is disputed by some Bible students. The translation "giants" comes from the Septuagint, which translated the Hebrew word *nephil* this way.

The Nephilim (meaning "fallen ones," "tyrants," or "mighty men of renown") in Numbers 13:31-33 were described by the spies as being so big the spies felt like grasshoppers in their presence (cf. Deut. 9:2). This tells us they existed long after the days of Genesis 6, so the question remains as to whether they were the result of those marriages or were already present. The Hebrew root *naphal* means "fallen." While people saw them as mighty leaders, God saw them as fallen.

This was the world of which God spoke His displeasure, promising that His Spirit would not continue to strive with man, for he was merely mortal. This is the second reference to the Holy Spirit (cf. Gen. 1:2). Through the example and preaching of Noah (cf. II Pet. 2:5) and perhaps Enoch (cf. Jude 1:14), God had been trying to reach mankind with His message of righteousness and warning. From the time of His statement in Genesis 6:3, He gave humanity 120 more years in which people could turn to Him. After that He would send the Great Flood.

What a patient God He is! To allow that much more time in the face of how wicked mankind had already become shows Him to be very merciful, gracious, and kind. He could have immediately wiped everybody out except Noah and his family (whom He could save in some miraculous way), but instead He gave an extended time during which people could turn to Him and begin living righteously.

Increasing wickedness (Gen. 6:5). This verse indicates the extent of the wickedness of mankind in those days. God had observed the deterioration of mankind throughout the years, but He finally took specific note of the depths they had fallen to and determined that it was time to act. The Hebrew word for "wickedness" is based on a root word often used for things that spoil, are broken into pieces, or are made good for nothing. In every way, physically, socially, and morally, mankind had become evil.

The statement that every inclination of the thoughts of people's hearts was nothing but continual evil is difficult to comprehend. However, we see the same thing in our society today. Matthew 24:37-39 partially describes what the time of Noah was like, with people focusing on sensuous and pleasure-seeking living with no thought of God. Romans 1:18-32 lays bare the utter debasement of mankind's thought processes when God is pushed aside and human desires are allowed to run rampant. Our world is filled with this.

It is now impossible to even watch decent programs on television without seeing violent or sensuous advertisements for other programs. It is impossible to stop at a magazine stand without seeing brazen celebrations of evil living. It is a constant challenge for us as children of God to maintain pure thoughts while we are relentlessly bombarded with worldly and godless promotions.

GOD'S RESPONSE

6 And it repented the LORD that he had made man on the earth, and it grieved him at his heart.

7 And the LORD said, I will destroy man whom I have created from the face of the earth; both man, and beast, and the creeping thing, and the fowls of the air; for it repenteth me that I have made them.

8 But Noah found grace in the eyes of the LORD.

9 These are the generations of Noah: Noah was a just man and perfect in his generations, and Noah walked with God.

10 And Noah begat three sons, Shem, Ham, and Japheth.

Grief and judgment (Gen. 6:6-7). "And it repented the Lord that he had made man on the earth, and it grieved him at his heart." "This is one of some thirty expressions in the Scriptures that express God's response using human emotions. God's creation had ceased to reflect His glory in almost every way (see Rev. 4:11), so he was no longer pleased or comforted by it" (Anders, ed., *Holman Old Testament Commentary,* B&H). How startling that God would reach the point where He regretted having made mankind in the first place!

God had carefully and thoughtfully made mankind just the way He wanted and with a specific purpose—to live in holy fellowship with Himself. Now as He observed His creation, He saw that mankind had perverted everything He had intended, and it pained His heart. The original root word translated "repented" means "to sigh heavily," usually in great sorrow. Those of us who have been through the kind of grief that causes such sighing can at least partially identify with what God was feeling.

Since God's attributes, responses, and emotions are typically described by the use of human terms (anthropomorphisms), we would be accurate in saying that God's heart was broken. A parent who has experienced a child's departure from godliness and moral standards, especially one who has seen that child ruin his or her life beyond repair, can identify with God's disappointment over mankind's change of direction. God was grieved, meaning He was deeply sorrowful over what He saw and decided there was but one solution.

He would have to destroy what He had created and begin again. He would completely get rid of His ruined creation except for the one godly man left. God felt so deeply grieved that He decided to make a clean sweep of everything, including the entire animal creation other than what He chose to spare. Such a drastic course of action indicates to us the depth of His disappointment. The word translated "destroy" means "to abolish," to "erase," or to "wipe out" completely.

We do not normally think of God in such human terms, for they do not seem to fit an exalted understanding of His greatness. This reminds us that while God is transcendent, that is, far above and beyond His entire creation, He is also immanent, that is, intimately involved in the details of His creation. God has a very personal concern for each of us, which is why He is "our refuge and strength, a very present help in trouble" (Ps. 46:1).

Grace (Gen. 6:8-10). In the midst of all the filthiness, darkness, despair, and disappointment was one bright light! An exception to the universal rejection of God appears in the record, and his name was Noah. Because of his lifestyle and commitment to God, he was an object of God's favor in the midst of all that disappointed Him. We are not given details of Noah's religious life or dedication to God. We have no idea how much he knew about God or how he served Him. We know only that God was pleased with him.

God had just determined judgment and destruction upon His creation, but Noah would be spared from that. Here was a righteous man who would be used by God for a new beginning. The reason is clear to see; Noah was a righteous man, blameless among the people of his era, and he walked with God. He was obedient to whatever he knew to be the law of God (which in written form was still future with Moses).

Noah was also morally and spiritually complete, that is, a man of integrity and truth. He was without spiritual or moral blemish; he was undefiled by the moral rot that surrounded him. This picture we are given is of a man with the highest of standards both morally and spiritually. We cannot help wondering how he maintained these in the midst of such corruption. Noah serves as an encouragement to each of us to aspire to the same reputation in the midst of the corrupt world we live in today.

In case we might be tempted to think this was an easy way for Noah to live, all we have to do is look ahead to Genesis 6:11-12 and read, "The earth also was corrupt before God, and the earth was filled with violence. And God looked upon the earth, and, behold, it was corrupt; for all flesh had corrupted his way upon the earth." We have already noted that Noah "walked with God" (vs. 9). He lived in daily fellowship with the Lord. This is the only way we too can be lights in a dark world.

"The important relation in which Noah stands both to sacred and universal history, arises from the fact, that he found mercy on account of his blameless walk with God; that in him the human race was kept from total destruction, and he was preserved from the all-destroying flood, to found in his sons a new beginning to the history of the world" (Keil and Delitzsch, *Commentary on the Old Testament,* Hendrickson). For this reason, we are introduced to Noah's three sons.

—*Keith E. Eggert.*

QUESTIONS

1. Why would the multiplication of people happen so easily before and during Noah's day?

2. What is your understanding of the phrases "sons of God" and "daughters of men"?

3. What are some of the objections against and reasons for fallen angelic involvement?

4. What did God say about His Spirit in those days?

5. What does the figure of 120 years in Genesis 6:3 refer to?

6. How did God describe the depth of wickedness on earth then?

7. What did God feel as He saw the way He had been rejected?

8. What did God decide He had to do to deal with this?

9. Who caught God's attention, and how is he described?

10. How is Noah an encouragement to us in our day?

—*Keith E. Eggert.*

Preparing to Teach the Lesson

Last week we learned that sin lurks at the door, waiting to destroy us. This week our lesson shows that sin quickly increased to the point of destroying all mankind.

TODAY'S AIM

Facts: to show the extent of man's great wickedness on the earth.

Principle: to understand that God's patience with sinners eventually reaches an end.

Application: to commit ourselves to deal with sin quickly, before it builds to a crisis.

INTRODUCING THE LESSON

It was Bob Pierce who is credited with the short prayer: "Let my heart be broken with the things that break the heart of God." If you and I were living in the days of Noah, this would have been a good prayer to pray because there was rampant worldwide wickedness, and God could not tolerate it any longer. Our lesson this week shows us a God whose patience and forbearance is not to be taken as a license to flout His holiness.

DEVELOPING THE LESSON

1. The multiplication of humanity (Gen. 6:1-4). These four verses contain some mysterious elements as well as plain facts. The straightforward truths are that in the centuries following Adam and Eve, humanity increased greatly in number on the earth. The mystery involves who some of these people were.

Some commentators say that the phrase "sons of God" in Genesis 6:2 and 4 is a reference to godly men who married women who were wicked, hence the phrase "daughters of men." Others claim they were fallen angelic beings. It is not likely that the "sons of God" were angels, for two simple reasons. The first is that angels do not have physical bodies (Heb. 1:14) and do not marry or reproduce (Matt. 22:30). Second, angels are not mentioned anywhere in the first five chapters of Genesis. There is nothing to connect them to the sons of God.

Genesis 6:4 also mentions two other mysterious classes of people: the "giants" and the "mighty men . . . of old." It is unclear exactly who the "giants" were and even whether they existed before the marriages mentioned in verse 2 took place or were the product of those marriages (or both). The Hebrew term is *nephilim,* which appears again only in Numbers 13:33, referring to the sons of Anak.

Those who did come from the marriages in question are termed "mighty men . . . men of renown" (Gen. 6:4). They were powerful and made a lasting name for themselves. But what they were known for does not appear to have been anything admirable or praiseworthy. This is clear from the divine assessment of mankind found in verse 3.

After only some sixteen hundred years since the creation of man, the Lord appears to have been already growing weary of the conflict with a rebellious and disobedient mankind. He declared that His Spirit would not strive with man forever. In fact, He set a time limit of one hundred twenty years. Some think this refers to a shortened human life span that would now take effect, but it more likely speaks of the time remaining before man's sin would be decisively judged.

2. The multiplication of evil (Gen. 6:5-7). What previously had been hinted at is now stated unambiguously and ominously. The text pauses to give the Lord's verdict on mankind, and it is a stark assessment. God took special note of the evil condition of man. Man's wickedness was very great, and his thoughts and imaginations were evil all the time. Evil had taken over.

The text here makes it clear that evil was and is not just a matter of outward acts. Our inward thoughts and attitudes are involved as well. And even though these can be hidden from others, they are laid bare before God.

Man had become so permeated with evil that the Lord felt sorry that He had created the world. It was not that He had made a mistake. The statement simply reveals that our God is a God of emotions and that He felt incredible sadness that mankind had pursued this horrible path. Nothing takes God by surprise, for He knows it all before it happens. He is all-knowing. But it breaks His heart when He sees us persist in doing what is wrong.

God made a very grim decision. The earth needed to be cleansed. He decided to destroy man, whom He had created, along with the animals, birds, and all creeping things. Sin had left its mark on all creation, and it had to be wiped out. Our holy God cannot tolerate sin's continued existence. Help the class understand that if we refuse to repent of sin, we can expect the punishment of God on our lives.

3. The righteousness of one (Gen. 6:8-10). In the midst of man's total degradation in sin and evil, one shining exception stood out. In our lesson this week, we see that Noah pleased God in that very evil time. Three things are said about Noah. He was truly righteous ("a just man"). He was blameless before God ("perfect in his generations"). And he walked faithfully with God, following His ways. Noah can be a role model in our evil day. Would it not be wonderful if we too could say that we walk daily with God? In fact, we can and should please God as Noah did.

ILLUSTRATING THE LESSON

Like a judge's gavel held aloft in restraint, God's judgment may be long in coming; but when sin is persisted in, it falls swiftly and decisively.

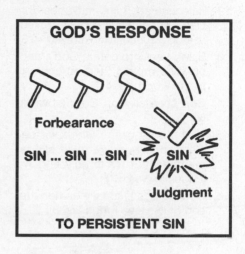

GOD'S RESPONSE

Forbearance

SIN ... SIN ... SIN ... SIN

Judgment

TO PERSISTENT SIN

CONCLUDING THE LESSON

Impress on your class the gravity of sin during Noah's day. Jesus Himself reminded us that the world will be the same when He returns. People will live life as if nothing were wrong, but evil will be rampant (Matt. 24:37). If sin during Noah's time was going to face the judgment of God, how can our world escape judgment? God has not changed; even in this age of grace, He will not tolerate sin. Persistent, unrepented sinful ways will always incur punishment.

ANTICIPATING THE NEXT LESSON

In our lesson next week, we will learn about God's plan for man after he sinned. Where there is sin, God's grace abounds. We will see how God prepared the way for deliverance from His punishment for all those who would receive it. It is important for us to see what a wonderful God we have! Even as He watches us sin, He is already preparing a way out for His children.

—A. Koshy Muthalaly.

PRACTICAL POINTS

1. Believers build families on a shared faith in God (Gen. 6:1-2).
2. Be encouraged and remember that God will not allow human wickedness to go unchecked forever (vs. 3).
3. Satan seeks to defeat God's people by tempting them to conform to the world (vs. 4).
4. God sees all, and God knows all (vs. 5).
5. In times of grace when we see God's patience, we must still remember that He is holy and will judge sin (vss. 6-7).
6. God's grace is a daily demonstration of His love for us (vs. 8).

—*Cheryl Y. Powell.*

RESEARCH AND DISCUSSION

1. In what ways was God's promise of a Messiah threatened by the intermarriage between the "sons of God" and the "daughters of men" (Gen. 6:2)?
2. What warning signs can alert Christians that they are falling into sin and away from God (cf. Rom. 1:21-32)?
3. How are Christians to respond to other Christians who may be involved in sinful lifestyles (cf. Gal. 6:1-3; Jude 1:20-23)? How are Christians to respond to nonbelievers involved in sinful lifestyles (cf. Rom. 3:9-20)?
4. What does it mean that "Noah walked with God" (Gen. 6:9)? Does this mean that he was perfect or without sin? Why or why not (cf. I Cor. 1:8; Heb. 11:7)?

—*Cheryl Y. Powell.*

ILLUSTRATED HIGH POINTS

The wickedness of man

It all started with Adam. In *Systematic Theology* (Kregel), Lewis Sperry Chafer pointed out that when Adam committed his first sin, he experienced a conversion downward. He became degenerate and depraved.

One time the distinguished journalist James Reston interviewed his own mother, who was ninety-four at the time. She said, "Progress is merely wickedness going faster" (www.nytimes.com, "On the Nobility of Old Age"). This was true in Reston's day, in Noah's day, as well as in ours.

Evil continually

England's great playwright, William Shakespeare, was an astute observer of human nature. He captured the truth of the sinfulness of man back in the days of Noah in *Titus Andronicus* (Act V, Scene 1) with these words:

"Tut! I have done a thousand dreadful things
As willingly as one would kill a fly,
And nothing grieves me heartily indeed
But that I cannot do ten thousand more."

But Noah found grace

"But" is a little word; however, it can make a huge difference.

There is a story of a diplomat who told his interpreter, "While a running translation is ample for my purpose, I want you to give me every word after the speaker says *but*." All that followed "but" was of supreme importance.

Just before the "but" in Genesis 6:8, God had declared that He intended to destroy "man whom [He had] created" (vs. 7). But one man would be spared because of his faith (cf. Heb. 11:7). And because Noah was spared, the world was repopulated. Thus you and I are here today because of God's grace and mercy.

—*David A. Hamburg.*

Golden Text Illuminated

"God saw that the wickedness of man was great in the earth, and that every imagination of the thoughts of his heart was only evil continually" (Genesis 6:5).

One of my least favorite tasks is disciplining the children in my life. Although it is a necessary part of molding them into godly people, I do not enjoy it. However, I know that when I allow bad behavior to slip by, I am not doing them any favors. There are times when their behavior is just downright inexcusable.

It hurts me most when their behavior is something they know Is wrong. When they know something is bad and do it anyway, punishing them is twice as painful. I grieve not only for their behavior but also for their wayward tendency. When they do something even though they know it is wrong, my heart grieves.

Knowing how I grieve, I can only wonder about how saddened God was in Noah's time. Generations after Eden, the world was a far cry from paradise. Apostasy was widespread, and people did not care about their sin. Their behavior was sinful to the point of being intolerable.

Remember that these were Adam and Eve's descendants. They were not necessarily people who were ignorant of right and wrong. Many of them had probably been raised with some understanding of God. Certainly they had a conscience to guide them. However, like wayward children, they chose to turn away from what they knew was right.

All of us have done something we know is wrong at some point in our lives. None of us can honestly say that we have never sinned. But there is a difference between us and the people of Noah's time, and it is an obvious one. While we who are believers generally attempt to live righteous lives, the people of Noah's time did not. Doing what was right in God's eyes was not at all important to them. They simply did not care about the absence of righteousness in their actions. These people were wicked to the core.

Scripture has much to say about people like this. We are told that wicked people have no future (Ps. 37:38). Such people are considered worthless because of their sinful path (cf. Rom. 3:12). Their behavior breaks God's heart (Gen. 6:6).

Our God is incredibly patient. Scripture tells us that He is not going back on His promise of Christ's return (II Pet. 3:3-10). He is rather giving ample time for every person to repent. He desires that people be saved, not destroyed.

However, God will reach the end of His patience. We learn that God will demonstrate anger toward those who are rebellious (Rom. 2:8). As we see in this week's lesson, unrepentant people face only judgment and destruction.

What happened was tragic, even more so because it was not inevitable. Had the earth's inhabitants repented, they would have been spared. Their choices broke God's heart and caused the destruction of what He once considered good (cf. Gen.1). God demolished the world and started fresh.

There is a valuable lesson here. We need to remember that we can only continue so far in rebellion before God will give us over to it. If we persist even after the Spirit's repeated warnings, we risk a potential hardening of soul. When we do that, we are in great danger. If there is something He is talking to you about, do not delay. Repent while there is still time.

—*Jennifer Francis.*

Heart of the Lesson

I enjoyed the drawing class I was taking at a community college until the professor announced the class would be drawing nude men and women. Later that week, I met the professor in his office and explained that as a Christian I could not in good conscience draw unclothed men and women. The professor agreed to give me a different assignment.

On nights when the class drew nudes, I drew a fully clothed person in a different classroom. I believed my actions pleased God, but I still felt a little odd and alone. In this week's lesson, Noah also knew the feeling of being alone in his culture.

1. A growing population (Gen. 6:1-2). The human population of the earth's opening millenias grew rapidly—and no wonder. With men and women living hundreds of years, they potentially could produce many offspring. Adam's descendents were fulfilling God's command to be fruitful, multiply, and fill the earth.

During this time, the "sons of God" (Gen. 6:2) saw the beautiful "daughters of men" and picked whomever they wished as wives. Some believe these sons of God were fallen angels, but Jesus taught that angels are asexual and do not marry. Quite possibly, the sons of God were descendents of Seth, Adam's third and godly son, and the daughters of men were descendents of unrighteous Cain.

2. God's judgment on wickedness (Gen. 6:3-7). God was displeased with these marriages because they joined believers with unbelievers. The result was a gradual watering down of Seth's godly line until the human race had become an ungodly, wicked, and violent society.

Not even a glimmer of goodness remained in the population. The people's only thought was about doing evil.

They were totally depraved in both thought and behavior.

As a result, God said He was not always going to strive with men. He would not tolerate them and let them live forever. He would give the human race another 120 years to repent, and then, if no change occurred, He would destroy everyone and everything, including animals and birds. He planned to destroy the creation He once had called good and very good.

God repented that He had made man. Did God, the Changeless One, change His mind? No, "the repentance of God is an anthropomorphic expression for the pain of divine love at the sin of man" (Keil and Delitzsch, *Commentary on the Old Testament,* Hendrickson). God's heart was broken over mankind's condition. He ached because of their sin.

3. A righteous remnant (Gen. 6:8-10). Out of the burgeoning population, only one man stood out. His name was Noah, and God looked upon him with favor. Noah was righteous. He had a relationship with God, and he behaved in a manner that pleased God. He was upright and undefiled in his generation.

Noah refrained from participating in the wickedness of the society around him and overcame the pressure to conform. He was one man going against his culture. No doubt he was an object of ridicule.

Just as past generations did, we as believers live in an evil world. But God has called us to be His holy people. We are to work, raise families, and live our lives in this world. But like Noah, we are to walk with God and separate from our culture's sin. God's Spirit will give us the power to consistently and lovingly live holy lives within our culture. Just ask Him for His sustaining power.

—Ann Staatz.

World Missions

We think to pray for protection for missionaries against outside wicked forces—against sickness or persecution or other impediments of the enemy that might damage a missionary's work. But what of the darkness within our own lives—the sin nature that tempts us all (Jas. 1:14)?

If we decide that missionaries (or any Christian workers) are above being snared, we cannot be the support system they need, and our putting them on spiritual pedestals actually makes them more vulnerable rather than less.

This article sets forth ways we can help missionaries battling a wicked world and their own fleshly nature.

1. Pray for them to be strengthened. Satan will attack them through any means possible, but if he can get a stronghold in their spiritual walk through secret sin, this is the greatest way to cause damage. We need to pray with the understanding that missionaries *will* encounter temptations.

2. Hold them accountable. Before I left for the field, I do not recall any church asking me what plans I had to resist temptation or maintain my spiritual walk with the Lord while on the field. They assumed I would be stronger than regular Christians, but the truth was that being on the mission field brought me face-to-face with my own weaknesses and besetting sins in ways I never would have in my own comfortable environment at home. (Regarding the story from last week, my mission board previously had no protocol in place for dealing with a missionary exposed as living in chosen, continued sin—something different than what the Bible says on how to deal with a one-time sin. Their lack of consideration given to this possibility led them to deal with it incorrectly.)

3. Make protective boundaries. My spouse and I have a rule that we will not ride in a car or be alone with a member of the opposite sex. This was a frustration on the field, as we had a single teammate, but that rule not only kept us above reproach, it also eliminated any room to give in during a moment of temptation. Boundaries protect; a lack of boundaries creates vulnerability. (Had such a rule been in place on my field, the man I mentioned last week would not have been able to molest young girls.)

4. Do not cover up sin to "protect" the ministry. The Bible never approves concealing sin for the sake of reputation, but rather the opposite (cf. Prov. 28:13; Eph. 5:11). Expose it and deal with it.

5. Allow them to be transparent about their struggles. If a missionary struggled with a temptation to view pornography, would he have anyone with whom he could share his struggle? If not, he will likely keep struggling in secret, feeling alone in his fight against it, and being more vulnerable to things like having Internet access in his bedroom—because everyone thinks he is above temptation. Again, regarding missionaries as spiritual giants leaves them more susceptible rather than stronger.

Our missionaries need our help. They need prayers against the onslaught of temptation the devil will surely send their way. Our understanding and prayers can help them continue with victory the work God has called them to for His name's sake.

—Kimberly Rae.

The Jewish Aspect

Genesis 6 records degradation so great in the Lord's sight that He came to the end of His patience. Long life spans were the norm, and there was a massive increase in the earth's population at this time. According to verse 2, "sons of God" were taking "daughters of men" as wives. There are different opinions regarding who these "sons of God" were. Some believe they were fallen angels who indwelt men. Others believe they were the godly lineage of Seth who intermarried with the ungodly lineage of Cain. Whatever the case, it seems the intent was to produce offspring who were opposed to God. Clearly, Satan wanted to ruin man, the only creature created in the image of God. As it happened, these spiritually mixed marriages—and the corruption and violence fomented on earth—brought the judgment of God.

With the words, "My spirit shall not always strive with man" (Gen. 6:3), the Lord gave mankind 120 years after His warning before the judgment fell. God set a specific time limit before any penalty would occur to give humans a chance to repent. This principle is seen again in the Bible, when Nineveh was given a period of forty days to repent before judgment was rendered (Jonah 3:9-10).

God saw that "every imagination of the thoughts of [man's] heart was only evil continually" (Gen. 6:5). Sin sorrowed God's heart to the point that He regretted making man (vss. 6-7). This does not imply that God had made a mistake in His dealings with man; it indicates a change in divine direction resulting from the actions of man. God promised total destruction when His patience ran out. "But the transgressors shall be destroyed together: the end of the wicked shall be cut off" (Ps. 37:38).

Noah, however, "found grace in the eyes of the Lord" (Gen. 6:8). The name Noah means "rest" and "comfort." This is the first time the word "grace" (which can mean "favor") is used in Scripture. In Hebrew it is *hen*.

Noah was a just man, blameless among the people of his time, and he walked with God. He lived by God's perfect standards and single-mindedly pursued righteousness. His characteristic of walking with God put him in a class with Enoch (Gen. 5:24). The root word for "just" in 6:9 indicates conformity to an ethical or moral standard. It is used of Noah, Daniel, and Job. "Perfect" has the idea of completeness, or that which is entirely in accord with truth and fact.

Noah separated himself from the wickedness of his contemporaries and followed the Lord. "Only Noah found grace in the eyes of G-d, and he was to be spared the fate of all the other living things, because he was the only pious person who had tried to arouse the conscience of the people and warn them of the punishment to come" (Isaacs, *Our People,* Kehot Publication Society).

Noah was blessed by God with three sons—Shem, Ham, and Japheth. Noah and his wife plus his three sons and their wives were saved from the Flood in order to repopulate the earth. The observation in Genesis 6:9 that Noah was perfect "in his generations" may imply that his sons were also considered righteous by the Lord. Eight people were saved from the Flood. "Eight . . . is symbolic of an entity that is one step above the natural order, higher than nature and its limitations" (Posner, "What is the Spiritual Significance of the Number Eight?" www.chabad.org.) The number eight in the Bible represents a new beginning, a new order or creation.

—Deborah Markowitz Solan.

Guiding the Superintendent

Just when you think it cannot get any worse, it does! The rapid spread of sin throughout early civilization was far beyond any easy comprehension. From the disobedience of eating the forbidden fruit (Gen. 3) to the first sibling murder (chap. 4) to the record of the deaths of early men (chap. 5), the reader comes to Genesis 6 wondering what more could possibly happen. And then we read, "God saw . . . that every imagination of the thoughts of [man's] heart was only evil continually" (vs. 5). The situation needed direct divine attention.

DEVOTIONAL OUTLINE

1. The problem (Gen. 6:1-4). After the Creation, the call to fill the earth (1:28) was being carried out by people of the early civilizations. Without hesitation (Matt. 24:37-39) there was intermarrying between "sons of God" (Gen. 6:2) and "daughters of men." The text seems to indicate that the wicked and righteous intermarried and produced a race of wicked people who turned on God completely.

God is very patient. He gave these people a long time (120 years) to change their direction (cf. II Pet. 3:9). But to no avail. The biological result of these mixed marriages was giants on the earth who were mighty in power (Gen. 6:4).

2. God's evaluation (Gen. 6:5-7). God's original evaluation of His entire creation was that "it was very good" (1:31). Centuries later, a second evaluation showed how mankind had changed. Man's evil heart caused God's heart to grieve (6:5-6).

The earth was not only full of people, but it was full of people with very evil imaginations and hearts. God had to deal with this. The Bible is very clear. God never changes His moral law or His Person (Mal. 3:6), but His procedures sometimes do. God announced His plans to destroy all mankind and all creation (Gen. 6:7).

3. God's solution (Gen. 6:8-10). In spite of the fact that the whole world was evil at heart, God saw there was one who had favor in His sight. After describing worldwide evil, the text describes this one person whom God would use in His renewal of creation.

The man was Noah, and he stood out from the crowd. He was just and perfect, that is, blameless, and he enjoyed being on God's side ("walked with God") (Gen. 6:9). God would honor this man by allowing him and his family to escape divine judgment on the earth (future lessons will describe many details about Noah's deliverance from the universal Flood).

CHILDREN'S CORNER

text: **II Kings 2:13-25**
title: **The Start of Elisha's Ministry**

Elijah was gone. A search party of fifty men spent three fruitless days looking for the "missing" Elijah. God replaced him with Elisha. To prove that Elisha was now God's man, God had him work several miracles. Elisha used Elijah's mantle, which fell from him when he ascended into heaven, to divide a river so that he could cross. He "healed" (II Kings 2:21) the water of an unnamed village. Then he defended his ministry by calling down punishment upon a group of young people who were mocking him. Young people must be careful to respect men of God; mocking them only courts terrible disaster!

—*Martin R. Dahlquist*

Scripture Lesson Text

GEN. 6:11 The earth also was corrupt before God, and the earth was filled with violence.

12 And God looked upon the earth, and, behold, it was corrupt; for all flesh had corrupted his way upon the earth.

13 And God said unto Noah, The end of all flesh is come before me; for the earth is filled with violence through them; and, behold, I will destroy them with the earth.

14 Make thee an ark of gopher wood; rooms shalt thou make in the ark, and shalt pitch it within and without with pitch.

15 And this is the fashion which thou shalt make it of: The length of the ark shall be three hundred cubits, the breadth of it fifty cubits, and the height of it thirty cubits.

16 A window shalt thou make to the ark, and in a cubit shalt thou finish it above; and the door of the ark shalt thou set in the side thereof; with lower, second, and third stories shalt thou make it.

17 And, behold, I, even I, do bring a flood of waters upon the earth, to destroy all flesh, wherein is the breath of life, from under heaven; and every thing that is in the earth shall die.

18 But with thee will I establish my covenant; and thou shalt come into the ark, thou, and thy sons, and thy wife, and thy sons' wives with thee.

19 And of every living thing of all flesh, two of every sort shalt thou bring into the ark, to keep them alive with thee; they shall be male and female.

20 Of fowls after their kind, and of cattle after their kind, of every creeping thing of the earth after his kind, two of every sort shall come unto thee, to keep them alive.

21 And take thou unto thee of all food that is eaten, and thou shalt gather it to thee; and it shall be for food for thee, and for them.

22 Thus did Noah; according to all that God commanded him, so did he.

NOTES

Preparation for Deliverance

Lesson Text: Genesis 6:11-22

Related Scriptures: Romans 9:22-24; Hebrews 11:6-7; I Peter 3:18-22

TIME: unknown   PLACE: unknown

GOLDEN TEXT—"Behold, I, even I, do bring a flood of waters upon the earth, to destroy all flesh, . . . But with thee will I establish my covenant" (Genesis 6:17-18).

Introduction

In October 2016 Hurricane Matthew headed toward the United States, threatening Florida, Georgia, and South Carolina. All the forecasts said it would then turn back into the Atlantic.

Hurricane Matthew came onshore in South Carolina but then stayed close by the shore and hit North Carolina with a vengeance. While the coastal cities were inundated with lots of wind and rain, the inland city of Lumberton, about an hour from the coast, took the force of a direct hit. In many parts of the city, the water rose until houses and businesses had several feet of water in them. Roads were closed all over the county, electrical power was lost, and the water and sewer systems shut down.

Since such a hit in that city was unexpected, preparations ahead of time were not adequate. In the story of Noah, however, God provided plenty of time and preparation for Noah and his family so that disaster for them was averted.

LESSON OUTLINE

I. COMING CATASTROPHE—
   Gen. 6:11-13

II. PREPARATION FOR
    CALAMITY—Gen. 6:14-22

Exposition: Verse by Verse

COMING CATASTROPHE

GEN. 6:11 The earth also was corrupt before God, and the earth was filled with violence.

12 And God looked upon the earth, and, behold, it was corrupt; for all flesh had corrupted his way upon the earth.

13 And God said unto Noah, The end of all flesh is come before me; for the earth is filled with violence through them; and, behold, I will destroy them with the earth.

Corruption and violence (Gen. 6:11-12). Cause and effect is a fundamental rule of logic used often in Scripture. In a multitude of passages, we are told that certain things happened because of what preceded those events. This is especially so concerning many of God's actions with His people. It was because of their sinful ways that God allowed them to be taken into captivity, the northern nation by Assyria and the southern nation by Babylon. These captivities could have been avoided.

The cause-and-effect relationship in this week's text is easy to spot. When God looked upon the earth He had created, He saw that it was corrupt and violent. This is what caused Him to determine that He would have to destroy His creation and have a new beginning with Noah and his family. It would be good for each of us to recognize this principle in our own lives. How many times have we gone through hard times because of how we have lived, especially when we have purposely ignored the teachings of God's Word?

Genesis 6:11 declares that the earth was "corrupt before God." "Corrupt" pictures for us an earth that was decayed and ruined. We noted last week how highly disappointed God was at the way things had gone. His perfect creation, including the garden where He had placed Adam and Eve, was ruined when sin entered the world. It did not take long for the effects of sin to grow and spread to many other regions. It had now reached the point where the entire creation was corrupt. "All flesh had corrupted his way upon the earth" (vs. 12).

The earth was, therefore, also filled with violence. People were destructive and injurious to one another instead of caring and loving. Violence is physical force used to injure or damage other people and things. Corruption and violence are the natural results of the depraved, sinful nature of mankind. During the days of the judges, corruption and violence dominated life, and the era is summarized tellingly: "In those days there was no king in Israel: every man did that which was right in his own eyes" (Judg. 21:25).

Judgment and destruction (Gen. 6:13). After taking note of the condition of His creation, God made an announcement to Noah. It must have been a startling thing for Noah to hear since there was no prior warning that it was coming. God said He was going to bring an end to all flesh. This would include human and animal flesh, so He was saying that in His judgment He was going to bring complete destruction to His creation. This was to be a complete interruption of what appeared to be normal life.

We cannot help thinking that it will be much like this when Jesus comes for His church. It will be a sudden interruption of all that is viewed as normal. First Thessalonians 4:16-17 says, "For the Lord himself shall descend from heaven with a shout, with the voice of the archangel, and with the trump of God: and the dead in Christ shall rise first: then we which are alive and remain shall be caught up together with them in the clouds, to meet the Lord in the air: and so shall we ever be with the Lord."

Noah was told that since the earth was filled with violence because of God's created people, God was going to destroy them from that earth. God was telling Noah this because he was going to be spared, along with a few other people and some of the animals. It was a drastic move on God's part, however; so His sudden announcement to Noah must have been puzzling.

PREPARATION FOR CALAMITY

14 Make thee an ark of gopher wood; rooms shalt thou make in the ark, and shalt pitch it within and without with pitch.

15 And this is the fashion which thou shalt make it of: The length of the ark shall be three hundred cu-

bits, the breadth of it fifty cubits, and the height of it thirty cubits.

16 A window shalt thou make to the ark, and in a cubit shalt thou finish it above; and the door of the ark shalt thou set in the side thereof; with lower, second, and third stories shalt thou make it.

17 And, behold, I, even I, do bring a flood of waters upon the earth, to destroy all flesh, wherein is the breath of life, from under heaven; and every thing that is in the earth shall die.

18 But with thee will I establish my covenant; and thou shalt come into the ark, thou, and thy sons, and thy wife, and thy sons' wives with thee.

19 And of every living thing of all flesh, two of every sort shalt thou bring into the ark, to keep them alive with thee; they shall be male and female.

20 Of fowls after their kind, and of cattle after their kind, of every creeping thing of the earth after his kind, two of every sort shall come unto thee, to keep them alive.

21 And take thou unto thee of all food that is eaten, and thou shalt gather it to thee; and it shall be for food for thee, and for them.

22 Thus did Noah; according to all that God commanded him, so did he.

Command to build (Gen. 6:14-16). Instead of immediately telling Noah how He was going to destroy all flesh, God moves next to a surprising command—to build an ark—accompanied by detailed instructions on how to build it. This ark was to be made of gopher wood, a term not used today but probably referring to cypress, which is known for its durability even in water. The ark was to be built with rooms in it and was to be waterproofed both inside and out with pitch. This was probably a dark, sticky substance similar to our asphalt.

Using what is the most normally accepted length for a cubit (18 inches), the dimensions of the ark were to be 450 feet long, 75 feet wide, and 45 feet high. It was to have three stories on the inside, with an 18-inch window near the top and a door in the side. These dimensions are so perfect in proportion that modern-day ships are usually built in exactly the same way in order to make them seaworthy. Noah's ark, however, probably looked like a huge rectangular box designed for flotation.

Dr. Charles Ryrie estimated that the ark had "a displacement of about 20,000 tons and gross tonnage of about 14,000 tons. Its carrying capacity equaled that of 522 standard railroad stock cars (each of which can hold 240 sheep). Only 188 cars would be required to hold 45,000 sheep-sized animals, leaving three trains of 104 cars each for food" (*The Ryrie Study Bible,* Moody). Noah probably collected young and small representatives of the various animals, thus having plenty of room for all of them.

This ark was to be the means of salvation for those God chose in His mercy and grace. It is clearly a type of our Saviour, Jesus. As the ark had just one door leading into it, Jesus is the only means of salvation and guarantee of heaven. He Himself said, "I am the door: by me if any man enter in, he shall be saved, and shall go in and out, and find pasture" (John 10:9).

Reason to build (Gen. 6:17). Now Noah was to learn both how God was going to destroy all flesh and why he was to build an ark. The word "behold" is often used to get the attention of those who were about to receive an announcement. In order to emphasize His own direct action in what was coming, God began with the phrase "I, even I." He Himself would bring a flood upon the earth. The flood was to be a deluge. God was planning to bring such a deluge of water upon the earth that everything living would be drowned. It would affect everything that had "the breath of life."

This description was meant to convey the extensiveness of the flood that was coming. There has been much discussion as to whether it was a universal or a local flood. If it had been local, it would have been limited to the area of Mesopotamia. The wording of the text throughout the account, however, indicates much more than that. It was going to destroy everything under heaven that breathed air; all life on earth would die.

The *Holman Old Testament Commentary* (Anders, ed., B&H) also adds, "The universal interpretation is further substantiated by the laws of physics. Water seeks its own level. So if 'all the high mountains under the entire heavens were covered' (Gen. 7:19) for a period of almost a year, then the world would have been under water."

Referring to last-day scoffers, Peter wrote, "For this they willingly are ignorant of, that by the word of God the heavens were of old, and the earth standing out of the water and in the water: whereby the world that then was, being overflowed with water, perished" (II Pet. 3:5-6). A literal interpretation of these descriptions tells us that it was a universal flood that affected the world.

A special covenant of deliverance (Gen. 6:18). Noah and his family, along with representatives of the entire animal kingdom, were to be exceptions to this coming universal destruction. It was only after giving the warning that God informed Noah of the special relationship He was establishing with him and his family. This turned things back to the days of Adam, from whom all human generations came. Now Noah was to be the new beginning of all humanity.

This is the first time we read of a covenant in the Old Testament. At this point, the covenant is stated only in broad outline, but further details would be given to Noah after the Flood. There were two different kinds of covenants in the ancient Near East. A parity covenant was an agreement made between equals. A suzerainty covenant was an agreement made between a superior and one or more inferiors. The covenant God made with Noah was the latter; as Creator and Sovereign, God was going to bestow upon Noah and his family special benefits.

God made certain that Noah knew this covenant included him and his entire family—his wife, his three sons, and their three wives. This was surely a gracious act on God's part, for we have no indication that any of them shared Noah's understanding of and relationship with God. We hope they did, but we cannot be certain of it. It might be that they were saved from the Flood simply on the basis of their relationship with Noah. We know that eternal salvation is not determined this way; each individual must receive Jesus as Saviour.

Preservation of all life (Gen. 6:19-20). God also directed that animals were to be saved with Noah and his family. Noah was to bring pairs of every living thing into the ark. God said it was for the purpose of keeping the animal kingdom alive. He left no details out of His instructions to Noah, now specifying the various creatures to be included.

All these creatures would be included in the covenant, as explained later: "And I, behold, I establish my covenant with you, and with your seed after you; and with every living creature that is with you, of the fowl, of the cattle, and of every beast of the earth with you; from all that go out of the ark, to every beast of the earth" (Gen. 9:9-10).

The three categories of living things cover everything in the animal world.

Fowls were the creatures with wings and feathers. Cattle were large quadrupeds, but this would certainly include all those with four legs and feet. The Hebrew word refers to beasts, domestic as well as wild. The intention of God would reach further than this word implies, however. Creeping things were animals that glided or crawled as their means of getting around.

We like to joke about this by asking why God allowed Noah to take things like mosquitoes and flies into the ark. The reality is that God cares about all His creatures. This should be a reminder to us of the importance of not being cruel to animals in any way or at any time. (That will probably not deter us from swatting mosquitoes, however!) Regarding how animals can teach us, Isaiah wrote, "The ox knoweth his owner, and the ass his master's crib: but Israel doth not know, my people doth not consider" (Isa. 1:3).

Provision of food (Gen. 6:21). Noah's final instruction was to prepare food supplies for all the people and all the animals. This was no doubt a huge task, but the size of the ark made it entirely possible.

Noah's complete obedience (Gen. 6:22). What an example of faith Noah is to us! When we think of the immensity of the task God had just laid out for him, we realize that it could have been immensely daunting. Many of us would simply want to walk away and ignore it. Imagine the amount of material that had to be collected to build something the size of this ark. Imagine how much work would be necessary to accomplish the building (verse 3 implies that it took 120 years). Then imagine the work of gathering enough food for the occupants of the ark, and it would have to be enough for an entire year!

We have no indication that Noah even gave a second thought to doing anything other than what God said.

The statement in Genesis 6:22 is both simple and profound: "Thus did Noah; according to all that God commanded him, so did he." Perhaps the reason God included so much detail in the text about dimensions and other necessary information was more to help us recognize the extent of Noah's obedience than to have us marvel over the size and capacity of the ark.

Noah was the only person left on earth of whom it is recorded that he found grace in God's eyes (Gen. 6:8). Talk about standing alone! It is possible to stand for and walk with God in the midst of a wicked world. Noah serves as an example for us as we see today's world forgetting and rejecting God.

—*Keith E. Eggert.*

QUESTIONS

1. What cause-and-effect relationship is presented to us in this text?
2. What two realities describe the earth in those days?
3. What did God tell Noah that He was about to do?
4. What command did God give Noah, and why might this have been puzzling to him?
5. What were the dimensions of the ark Noah was to build, and what features were included?
6. In what way is the ark a type of Jesus Christ?
7. What did God finally explain He was going to do, and what would this accomplish?
8. Who and what was going to be spared when the Flood came?
9. How was Noah to preserve animal life on earth?
10. How did Noah exemplify faith?

—*Keith E. Eggert.*

Preparing to Teach the Lesson

This week in our lesson we learn that even as mankind plunged ever deeper into sin, God was already preparing a way of redemption.

TODAY'S AIM

Facts: to show how God established a covenant with Noah for redemption even as mankind persisted in sin.

Principle: to remember that God loves us so much that He has prepared a way for our deliverance from sin.

Application: to make sure that we have taken refuge in His covenant.

INTRODUCING THE LESSON

For those of us who are parents, how often have we used the term "grounded" in punishing our children? They know what that means. It means a lockdown, no freedom, and retribution for what they did wrong that day. But many parents already have a plan of redemption for their children even as the punishment is doled out. After children are seen to be remorseful and have learned the intended lesson, parents usually restore the lost privileges.

This is akin to what God does with us in our world today. He is a loving Heavenly Father who does not want to see anyone destroyed by sin. But He will punish those who persist in going the wrong way. Yet he has provided a way of redemption. Our lesson this week shows us the heart of God as He makes a covenant with a good man named Noah.

DEVELOPING THE LESSON

1. God's decision to destroy the earth (Gen. 6:11-13). God looked at the earth that He had created and saw all the wickedness of man. The earth was now filled with violence, depravity, and corruption. This certainly was not what God had intended for His world. But there was one man who stood out in that sinful world. It was Noah.

Noah walked with God. It is fitting, then, that God opened His heart to Noah and told him what He was about to do. We might wish God would do that with us, but He has fully shared His heart with us in His Word. And we too can walk with God.

God told Noah that He was going to destroy the whole earth because of mankind's entrenched and pervasive sin. The earth was filled with violence and needed to be thoroughly cleansed. Discuss this with the class. Was God being too harsh here? Talk with them about the holiness of God and the proper response to continual sin.

2. God's instructions for deliverance (Gen. 6:14-16). Here we truly see the heart of God. Even in His anger, we see mercy toward any who will follow Him. God told Noah to build a boat.

It was not to be just any boat. God gave instructions with specific measurements. We find them in the form of Hebrew cubits, and we get a full sense of the vessel's size when we remember that a cubit is about eighteen inches. The ark, or boat, had to be of gopher wood, which was almost indestructible. Some have suggested that the term refers to cypress. There were to be rooms in the ark. The ark itself was to be 450 feet long, 75 feet wide, and 45 feet in height.

God also told Noah to put a window, or opening, in the ark. The window was to go all the way around the ark just eighteen inches under the roof line. The ark was to have one door and three stories within. Discuss with the class the nature of such detail in His instructions. Does God talk with us today with such clarity? What do we need to do to more accurately understand His Word and follow what He is telling us there?

It must also be noted that before Noah's time, there was no rain (cf. Gen. 2:5); so it must have taken great faith for Noah to trust God that a flood was coming when he had never seen rain.

3. God's covenant with Noah (Gen. 6:17-22). Here we see the first mention that God was going to use a flood to destroy all the earth and everything that lives. Nothing was going to escape the wrath of God. But even in the midst of this declaration of punishment against the world that God had created, we see His compassionate heart, for He made a covenant with Noah.

Genesis 6:18 draws a sharp contrast between the judgment on all mankind and what God had in mind for Noah. The statement "But with thee will I establish my covenant" signifies a special relationship. There is a lesson for us here. When we walk with God, He will surely bless us. In times of crisis, He will be our shelter. He promises this for us as His children.

The purpose of the covenant with righteous Noah was one of safety and protection in an evil time. While the whole world was about to perish in the Flood, Noah would be safe in the ark.

It is important to note that even though God was about to bring total destruction on the whole earth, Noah and his family were promised safety. The animals and birds and other living creatures were to be brought in two by two, male and female, for procreation. God had planned everything to the very last detail. Even in the midst of severe judgment, there is always mercy with our God if we come to Him in faith (cf. Ps. 103:8).

Noah obeyed God in everything that he was asked to do and took with him all the food that his family needed for themselves and for all the living creatures in the ark—just as God had commanded. God knows the future, and if we obey Him, we will be OK through all kinds of circumstances.

ILLUSTRATING THE LESSON

God has already covenanted with us for our eternal safety. When we follow Him, we will experience His blessing and protection.

GOD'S COVENANT

God's Covenant

KEEPS US SAFE

CONCLUDING THE LESSON

Leave the class with the understanding that God loves us so much that He has every detail covered for our safety. Look at all the planning that went into the building of the ark so that Noah and his family would be safe through the calamity of the Flood. We can put complete trust in how much God cares for our safety from sin and the bad things that happen in this world. Obedience to God is the key to being sure of that safety.

ANTICIPATING THE NEXT LESSON

Next week we will learn how Noah and his family were invited into the ark for safety during the Flood. We learn that we too can be sheltered from the storms of life through God's covenant with us, for He is our Protector.

—A. Koshy Muthalaly.

PRACTICAL POINTS

1. Corruption results when man turns away from God (Gen. 6:11-12).
2. In a corrupt world, believers must remain confident that God is in control (vs. 13).
3. God is the Master Builder—always trust His blueprint (vss. 14-16).
4. God's holiness requires that He judge and punish sin (vs. 17).
5. God is faithful to His covenant people, and we can trust His promises (vs. 18).
6. God's power in nature allows all mankind to see His work and believe (vss. 19-20).
7. No detail escapes God's attention when it comes to His care for His own (vss. 21-22).

—*Cheryl Y. Powell.*

RESEARCH AND DISCUSSION

1. What steps should we as Christians take today to prevent becoming overwhelmed or defeated by the corruption and violence in our world?
2. Have you ever sensed God giving you specific directions for a task? What was the outcome?
3. How does the term "covenant" help believers to understand our relationship with God?
4. How do you think Noah's nonbelieving neighbors reacted to Noah's work and God's gathering of the animals? How do neighbors respond to us when they see our work in the world today?

—*Cheryl Y. Powell.*

ILLUSTRATED HIGH POINTS

Corrupt before God

We are aware that Mexico is the source of much drug trafficking. Along with it comes corruption and violence. As one social activist and grieving father of one victim of the war on drugs said, "I don't know where the state ends and organized crime begins."

An article on this subject went on to say that while Mexican politics have long been corrupt, the level of violence and brutality has never been higher. We wonder how long it will be before the Lord makes an end of it all.

Make thee an ark

Artists of Sunday school literature probably mean well but all too often give children the wrong idea of Noah's ark. It was not a cruise liner, but it was far more than a cute houseboat.

In July 2016, a replica of the ark was opened to the public in a Christian theme park in Williamstown, Kentucky. This huge structure is 510 feet long, 85 feet wide, and 51 feet high containing over 120,000 square feet of space.

These dimensions demonstrate how it was possible for Noah, his wife, three sons, and their wives, along with the multitude of animals, to survive the flood.

A flood of waters

When the sky clouds up, your local TV station will usually break into the program to give a report. They often mention the possibility of flash floods.

You can be knocked down in just six inches of fast-moving water. A car can be swept away in two feet of flowing water.

Noah's Flood was far more than a local flash flood. It was even more than a one hundred-year flood. It rained for forty days, eliminating all the high ground. There was no escape.

—*David A. Hamburg.*

Golden Text Illuminated

"Behold, I, even I, do bring a flood of waters upon the earth, to destroy all flesh, . . . But with thee will I establish my covenant" (Genesis 6:17-18).

When I was a child, one of my favorite songs in Sunday school had to do with Noah and the ark. Starting with God's message to Noah, it basically outlined the entire story of the Great Flood. It had a catchy little chorus that reminded us to give glory to God in our lives.

What I liked about this song was how easy the story was to remember. When that little tune got stuck in my head, I had no problem recalling it. I could just sing the story if I wanted to remember.

As an adult, I have caught on to a few nuances that I did not understand as a child. What strikes me now about Noah's history is the precise nature of the task Noah was asked to undertake. I think we tend to overlook that.

Noah's task was not simple at all. Noah was given detailed instructions on everything from the type of wood to use for the ark (Gen. 6:14), its dimensions, and even how to waterproof it. God told Noah how many doors to build and how many decks to make. Then He told Noah exactly how many of the animals should go into it (6:19-20; 7:2-3). Nothing was left unclear in the directions.

We see this happening often with God. When He chooses to deliver His children from something, He usually gives specific instructions. It happened in Exodus 12 when the Israelites left Egypt, and again when they were given victory over Jericho (Josh. 6:1-5). We begin to see a pattern of clear direction given by God just before He provides deliverance for His children.

What is our part in all this? We are expected to obey. In every instance I have mentioned, obedience brought about blessing. There have also been instances when someone did not pay attention to God's instructions (cf. Exod. 16:19-20; Num. 20:8-12). When that happened, those individuals suffered severe consequences.

What if Mary had not consented to bear our Saviour or Paul had not chosen to listen when God told him to spread the gospel? God will raise up individuals whose hearts are turned toward Him. Following Him requires complete obedience. There is to be nothing halfhearted about it.

Noah could have chosen to build the ark with any dimensions, yet he chose to follow God's instructions down to the last detail. He spent years of preparation paying attention to every minor detail. During those years, he no doubt was mocked; yet he was diligent in his obedience. Because of this, his family alone received God's blessing of salvation.

We need to be intentional about our obedience. When God gives us clear directions, we should not dispute them. Even when they do not make sense, we need to be obedient to the last detail. God may not always give us precise instructions, but we need to follow those He does give. Remember that they may be a preparation for something to come. If you disobey, you may not experience His full blessing and deliverance in the situation.

Is there an area where God is giving you instruction? If there is, God may be asking you to prepare for something. Choose to obey His instruction and receive the blessing He will bring.

—Jennifer Francis.

Heart of the Lesson

My family camped one night at a New Jersey state park. We parked our tent trailer along a ten-foot-wide stream that tumbled down a hillside. By the time we had eaten and crawled into bed, a light rain was falling.

Sometime after midnight, someone pounded on our trailer door and woke us up. A park ranger stood there. "You need to move to higher ground," he said. "The creek's rising, and this whole area will soon be flooded."

Wearing our pajamas, we piled into the station wagon and pulled the trailer up the hill to the nearest vacant campsite. We were thankful for the warning and gladly heeded it. But the people of Noah's day ignored Noah's message of impending judgment as he built the ark, a refuge from the Flood God had said was coming.

1. The coming judgment (Gen. 6:11-13). The earth had become corrupt. Violence was everywhere. Today we hear about outbreaks of violence in our country. But imagine a society in which riots, murders, rapes, robberies, angry looting mobs, and fights were daily occurrences in every neighborhood—and everyone participated! This was the state of society in Noah's day.

The people were living according to the flesh and had sunk to the lowest level of depravity. Noah was the exception to this violent population, the one man who followed God. God told Noah that He intended to destroy all living creatures on the earth except him and his family.

2. Blueprint for an ark (Gen. 6:14-18). God instructed Noah to build an ark—a floating, rudderless box—from gopher wood, which was probably cypress. The ark was to have three decks divided into rooms. Noah was to line the inside and outside of the ark with pitch to make the craft waterproof. The size of the ark—450 feet long, 75 feet wide, and 45 feet high—matched the proportions of ships today. This boat was much longer than a football field!

Noah was to include a window about eighteen inches below the roof. This window opening probably ran all the way around the boat, providing light and ventilation. A single door was to open on the side of the ark. After the ark's completion, Noah, his wife, his sons, and his daughters-in-law were to enter the ark; they alone would survive the Flood.

God promised that He would establish His covenant with Noah. Noah would be the father of a new line of humanity that would repopulate the earth after the Flood. God was preserving a righteous remnant to start over again on the earth.

3. Menagerie in the making (Gen. 6:19-22). Noah's responsibility included preserving animal life by housing two of every living animal and bird—male and female—in the ark. Lawrence O. Richards noted that Noah only needed to take a prototype of each animal kind. "A single pair of cattle contained the genes that provide for the wide variation within this animal class that we see in the Brahma, the Longhorns, and other cattle" (*The Bible Reader's Companion,* Cook). Variation within a species does not counter biblical teaching on Creation.

Noah did not have to round up the animals. They came to him through God's supernatural intervention. To feed these animals during the Flood, he was to store up food for them.

Noah's faith resulted in obedience. He began building the ark and warning about the coming Flood. We also should be warning our friends and family of the judgment to come and of salvation through Jesus' work on the cross.

—Ann Staatz.

World Missions

In II Peter the Word of God indicates that Noah was a preacher of righteousness. He had one hundred years to warn people of the coming judgment.

From an earthly perspective, his mission work was a horrible failure, for not one person outside his own family heeded his message.

However, in missions and any kingdom work, God's eternal perspective is far different from the world's (Isa. 55:8-9). For Noah's generation, none could say they had not been given the truth before the judgment came. God revealed His divine will through the preaching of Noah during those years. Noah's obedience mattered in an eternal way, regardless of how his efforts appeared to have failed or succeeded.

God's definition of success in ministry can be very different from our own. When fifty thousand Syrian soldiers forced themselves into Beirut and began tearing it apart, one believer named Samuel wept tears of anger before God. "Lord, what are You doing?"

Life was going wrong, and Samuel's world was out of control. Then he said it was as if God told him, "For all these years, you have been complaining that Syria has shut its doors and will not allow missionaries to enter . . . I answer by sending 50,000 Syrians to you. And you are still complaining" (Zacharias, "But they're so Different . . . ," christianitytoday.com).

In North Korea, a family struggled through years of persecution and hardship for the sake of the gospel. Finally, they were able to make a plan to escape. The middle-aged couple went through horrible trials, but finally made it to freedom. They waited for news of their parents, the "old ones." A good earthly story would end with the parents also finding freedom and ending their years in peace and comfortable retirement. However, the family learned that the parents were captured and sent to a camp where they would likely die.

The eternal perspective? The family said God loved those prisoners in the camp so much, He sent their parents to share the good news of the gospel with them.

We all naturally want lives devoid of suffering. When we hear of things getting worse in the world, we pray for God to take away the problems. We ask for a world where we can live free as believers.

There is nothing wrong with such prayers (I Tim. 2:2), but God granting us comfort should not be the focus of our lives. To have an eternal perspective means we care more about the kingdom than ourselves, more about what God wants for eternity rather than what we feel right now.

It means we are willing to suffer here in this life so that others can come to Christ for eternity. This is opposite the world's perspective and often contrary to many of our prayers. Few of us would pray, as some Vietnamese Christians did, that they would be arrested so they could witness to their interrogators!

Yet God calls us into a life seeking first the kingdom of God (Matt. 6:33). Because we know God's perspective is higher and better than our own, we need not fear encroaching darkness or difficulty. We may not be able to see it, but He has an eternal purpose for our lives within the framework of the nations and kingdoms of this earth. We are not required to understand the purpose, only to obey His leading.

How is He leading you?

—Kimberly Rae.

The Jewish Aspect

The Genesis Flood was God's way of giving the earth a chance to start over after the extreme wickedness that man had brought upon it. God chose the Flood as the instrument of destruction in a reversal of Creation. Noah, a righteous and pious man, could not change the evil ways of the people around him, despite God's warnings. Only Noah found grace in the eyes of God, and Noah and his family were spared.

God ordered Noah to build an ark. He did it slowly, completing it in one hundred and twenty years. By the end of that time, the people still had not repented. The evil was so great that God carried through with His plan to destroy all life by a universal deluge. All men and beasts (except those in the ark) would perish so that no trace of the wicked age would remain (Isaacs, "Noah and the Flood," www.chabad.org).

"Orthodox Judaism, stressing that the whole of the Pentateuch (the Five Books of Moses) is the very word of God, accepts the narrative as factually true in all its details; although Chief Rabbi J. H. Hertz is prepared to admit that the Pentateuchal narrative is paralleled in the Babylonian myth. Hertz's view is that the narrative is factual. There really was a flood of universal proportions and Noah is a historical figure, both the Babylonian myth and the Genesis narrative being no more than different versions of the same facts" (Jacobs, "Noah's Flood," www.myjewishlearning.com).

God "told Noah to build his ark in public and to tell everyone its purpose: that it would save him from the coming Flood. The Ark was to be three hundred cubits in length, fifty in width, and thirty in height, and was to consist of three stories, divided into small rooms to hold people, animals, and food" (Isaacs).

According to Rabbinic literature, "When Noah was four hundred and eighty years old all the righteous sons of men were dead, except Methuselah and Noah himself. At God's command they both announced that one hundred and twenty years would be given to men for repentance; if in that time they had not mended their evil ways, the earth would be destroyed. But their plea was in vain; even while Noah was engaged in building the ark the wicked made sport of him and his work, saying: 'If the Flood should come, it could not harm us. We are too tall; and, moreover, we could close up with our feet [which were of monstrous size] the springs from below'" (Flood, The, www.jewishencyclopedia.com).

God then established His covenant with Noah. This was the first explicitly designated covenant God made with man, afterward called the Noahic covenant. The specific promise of this covenant was that God would never destroy the world again by water. The Noahic covenant is an unconditional covenant because it does not depend on anything Noah or his descendants had to do to fulfill it. "The conception of religion as a covenant concluded by God with man is peculiarly Jewish . . . In Rabbinical Literature . . . the intimacy existing between God and Israel as the descendants of the 'fathers' was shown in the form of a covenant when Israel received the Torah" ("Covenant," www.jewishencyclopedia.com).

The Hebrew word for covenant is *berith,* meaning "pact" or "treaty." It is one of the most frequently used words in Hebrew Scripture, appearing over 260 times. The other four covenants established by God were the Abrahamic (Gen. 17:7); priestly (Num. 25:10-13); Davidic (II Samuel 7:5-16; 23:5); and the New (Jer. 31:31-34; 32:40).

—*Deborah Markowitz Solan.*

Guiding the Superintendent

It was not long into human history before "every imagination of the thoughts of [man's] heart was only evil continually" (Gen. 6:5). God decided to destroy this wickedness with a great flood. But God is also merciful (Hab. 3:2). Even though all other life would be destroyed, God would save eight people and two of every animal in a large boat.

DEVOTIONAL OUTLINE

1. God's observation (Gen. 6:11-12). The spiritual cause for the Flood is stated here. Mankind had been commissioned to fill the earth, but God saw they had filled it with corruption and violence.

While people had forgotten about God, He had not forgotten them. He grieved over the corruption that filled the earth.

2. God's plan (Gen. 6:13-16). God told Noah His plan. Because His creation was so polluted with violence, He was planning to destroy all that was on the earth.

Noah was instructed to build a large boat, called an ark, in which he, his family, and some animals would be preserved throughout the coming Flood.

Specific instructions were given. The ark would be made of gopher wood. This was probably some particularly water-resistant wood. The ark was to be made watertight with pitch.

The ark was more like a box that was intended for floating than for speed or navigation. It was to contain rooms for the animals.

Nothing was left to chance. Noah was given very specific dimensions for the ark. While the exact length cannot be precisely known in current measurement, suffice it to say it was longer than a modern football field. It was to contain three decks, with a window (probably for light and ventilation) that ran around the top of the boat. There was also to be a door in the side of the ark.

3. God's provisions (Gen. 6:17-22). Noah was specifically told that God intended to destroy all life (all that had "breath of life"). However, God covenanted with Noah to deliver him and his family, a total of eight people—wife, sons, and daughters-in-law.

In addition to Noah's family, God would use the ark to save a male and female of every animal—bird, cattle, and "creeping thing" (Gen. 6:20).

Noah was also instructed to bring along food provisions for all on the ark. Unlike the rest of the earth's people, Noah listened to all that God commanded and did it.

In the provision of the ark, a great biblical principle was established. While God sees evil and will eventually and severely punish it (cf. II Pet. 3:5-6), He is also a God of mercy and extends salvation to those who are His.

CHILDREN'S CORNER

text: **II Kings 4:1-7**
title: **God's Plentiful Supply**

This lesson discusses another miracle. The widow of one of Elisha's fellow prophets found herself in a desperate situation. She was down to her last little bit of oil, and creditors were threatening to take her sons into debtor slavery.

Elisha told her to gather as many vessels (jars) as possible and fill them with the little oil that she had left. She filled every vessel she had and sold them to take care of her needs.

—*Martin R. Dahlquist.*

Scripture Lesson Text

GEN. 7:1 And the LORD said unto Noah, Come thou and all thy house into the ark; for thee have I seen righteous before me in this generation.

2 Of every clean beast thou shalt take to thee by sevens, the male and his female: and of beasts that are not clean by two, the male and his female.

3 Of fowls also of the air by sevens, the male and the female; to keep seed alive upon the face of all the earth.

4 For yet seven days, and I will cause it to rain upon the earth forty days and forty nights; and every living substance that I have made will I destroy from off the face of the earth.

5 And Noah did according unto all that the LORD commanded him.

6 And Noah was six hundred years old when the flood of waters was upon the earth.

7 And Noah went in, and his sons, and his wife, and his sons' wives with him, into the ark, because of the waters of the flood.

8 Of clean beasts, and of beasts that are not clean, and of fowls, and of every thing that creepeth upon the earth,

9 There went in two and two unto Noah into the ark, the male and the female, as God had commanded Noah.

10 And it came to pass after seven days, that the waters of the flood were upon the earth.

NOTES

Safety in the Ark

Lesson Text: Genesis 7:1-10

Related Scriptures: Psalm 91:1-10; Matthew 7:24-27;
Luke 13:23-30; II Peter 2:4-9

TIME: unknown

PLACE: unknown

GOLDEN TEXT—"The Lord said unto Noah, Come thou and all thy house into the ark; for thee have I seen righteous before me in this generation" (Genesis 7:1).

Introduction

Everyone wants to be safe in a storm. The Prophet Jonah was commanded by God to go to Nineveh and warn them of coming judgment (Jonah 1:2). Because Jonah did not want them to be warned and perhaps escape judgment, he headed as fast as he could for a ship sailing in the opposite direction. Twice we read in verse 3 that he was attempting to flee "from the presence of the Lord." When God hurled a strong storm onto the sea, Jonah was down in the hold taking a nap.

Apparently, Jonah felt safe in his hiding place, but we know it is a ridiculous idea to think a person can actually escape God's presence. Jonah was not safe, even while doing his best to hide from God or even the sailors on that ship!

On the other hand our greatest place of safety is being exactly where God wants us. Noah was there.

LESSON OUTLINE

I. PREPARATIONS COMPLETED—
Gen. 7:1-4

II. READY FOR THE STORM—
Gen. 7:5-10

Exposition: Verse by Verse

PREPARATIONS COMPLETED

GEN. 7:1 And the LORD said unto Noah, Come thou and all thy house into the ark; for thee have I seen righteous before me in this generation.

2 Of every clean beast thou shalt take to thee by sevens, the male and his female: and of beasts that are not clean by two, the male and his female.

3 Of fowls also of the air by sevens, the male and the female; to keep seed alive upon the face of all the earth.

4 For yet seven days, and I will cause it to rain upon the earth forty

days and forty nights; and every living substance that I have made will I destroy from off the face of the earth.

God's invitation (Gen. 7:1). "God had spoken to Noah nearly one hundred years earlier giving instructions concerning the Ark and the animals, . . .There had been no further word from heaven, but Noah had proceeded steadily and faithfully with his unique mission and ministry, obeying God's commandments without question. With all the urgency possible, he preached the coming judgment, year after year, but to no avail, so far as converts were concerned" (Morris, *The Genesis Flood,* Baker).

Here is an example of a faithful servant of God. The 120 years God had said He would wait were now about over as Noah put the finishing touches on his ark. During all those years, he had probably answered thousands of questions as to what he was doing, giving him multiple opportunities to warn people of what was coming. No one had listened and responded, however; so when the time came for Noah to enter the ark, no one but his family had the privilege of going in.

Genesis 6:8 tells us that Noah found grace in God's eyes, and the next verse explains that it was because he walked with God, that is, lived a life of consistency in his relationship with Him. Another word is now used in 7:1 to describe Noah. God said he and his house should enter the ark because he was "righteous" before Him in the midst of a depraved generation of people. This is the first time this word is used in Scripture, and it is descriptive of the character of this man who had so consistently walked with God.

God had taken the initiative in calling Noah to build this ark and now took the initiative to invite him into it. It is interesting that He said to *come* instead of *go.* God was going to be in that ark with him and the others, giving further assurance of their safety.

Directions for the animals (Gen. 7:2-3). In telling Noah to gather the animals for which the ark had also been prepared, God gave a distinction that He had not mentioned previously. After telling Noah that He was establishing a special covenant with him and his family (6:18), God had also told him to plan to take one pair of every kind of animal into the ark (vss. 19-20). Each pair was to be one male and one female. Now for the first time in the biblical record, God specified a difference between clean and unclean animals.

We are not told at this point in the Bible what the distinctions were; these would be spelled out in detail when the Law of Moses was given. Evidently, however, the basic difference had already ben made known. After the Flood, Noah knew which animals were clean and acceptable as sacrifices to God (Gen. 8:20). Of the clean animals, he was to take seven pairs into the ark and of the unclean, one pair. He was also to take seven pairs of all the fowls. The purpose was "to keep seed alive upon the face of all the earth" (7:3).

This stated purpose adds to the evidence for a universal flood. The clear implication is that if these animals were not spared by having a male and female in the ark, their kind would come to an end. It is interesting to note that while the beasts were separated into clean and unclean and birds were included in the seven pairs, there is no mention at all of the creeping things. This automatically left them as unclean. There was also no mention of sea creatures for obvious reasons.

We can be quite certain that Noah did not scramble around the earth herding these creatures into his ark. Although it is not detailed to us, surely God saw to it that they came; after all, it was His concern to save them.

Promise of rain (Gen. 7:4). God now explained in detail exactly what He was about to do. He gave Noah a one-week notice that rain was coming and that it would last for forty days and forty nights. Genesis 2:5 states that after the Creation, "the Lord God had not caused it to rain upon the earth." Verse 6 adds, "There went up a mist from the earth, and watered the whole face of the ground." It is possible that this condition remained true until the time of the Flood, so no one living would have known rain.

That would make rain an entirely new and unknown phenomenon to Noah and everyone else. Imagine how that would have further stimulated the mockery in Noah's day. One day when Jesus was asked by the Pharisees when the kingdom of God would come, He pointed to the spiritual indifference of Noah's day. People "did eat, they drank, they married wives, they were given in marriage, until the day that Noe entered into the ark, and the flood came, and destroyed them all" (Luke 17:27). It is clear that no one believed Noah.

Whether or not Noah understood the concept of rain right then, God made it clear that it would be the main cause of destruction for everything living on the face of the earth. The destruction would be total because the rain was going to continue for forty days and forty nights. Those of us who have been in downpours of rain that lasted for several hours or a few days realize that continuous rain for this amount of time would be totally destructive. Tropical storms and hurricanes cause serious flooding in shorter time than this.

The Hebrew word translated "destroy" in Genesis 7:4 means to "wipe out," "blot out," or "erase." All creatures that lived on the surface of the earth were going to be completely wiped out.

READY FOR THE STORM

5 And Noah did according unto all that the LORD commanded him.

6 And Noah was six hundred years old when the flood of waters was upon the earth.

7 And Noah went in, and his sons, and his wife, and his sons' wives with him, into the ark, because of the waters of the flood.

8 Of clean beasts, and of beasts that are not clean, and of fowls, and of every thing that creepeth upon the earth,

9 There went in two and two unto Noah into the ark, the male and the female, as God had commanded Noah.

10 And it came to pass after seven days, that the waters of the flood were upon the earth.

The faith of Noah (Gen. 7:5-6). Verse 5 is probably the highest commendation of Noah possible: "And Noah did according unto all that the Lord commanded him." We can think of many reasons for Noah to doubt. There had never been rain, so there had never been a reason for anyone to make a floating shelter. The notion of the destruction of every living thing on earth was almost unbelievable. The fact that Noah had spent over one hundred years in construction of an ark undeniably made him a figure of ridicule in many minds.

In spite of the apparent unlikeliness of the danger, however, Noah persisted in all that God had commanded. This was an exercise in faith that ranks him among the greatest saints in all of Scripture. Noah had already embarked on a journey never before encountered by mankind, and now with the completion of the ark and the entrance of the people and animals into it, that journey was about to take another leap forward.

On top of everything else that made

this entire venture unlikely, Noah was six hundred years old. At the end of the genealogies in Genesis 5, we are told that "Noah was five hundred years old: and Noah begat Shem, Ham, and Japheth" (vs. 32). It was now one hundred years later, and the Flood was coming.

In Genesis 7, more details are given: "In the six hundredth year of Noah's life, in the second month, the seventeenth day of the month, the same day were all the fountains of the great deep broken up, and the windows of heaven were opened. And the rain was upon the earth forty days and forty nights" (vss. 11-12).

The boarding of the ark (Gen. 7:7). Noah is mentioned first as the obvious head of this family and the one to whom God had continually given instructions about this event. The mention of everyone else in a methodical format indicates that all preparations had now been completed, so one by one the family members entered the ark. Noah's three sons followed him. They were named for us at the end of chapter 5: Shem, Ham, and Japheth, but we cannot tell their order of entrance.

Noah's sons are not listed in the order of their birth. Genesis 9:24 says that after Noah's later episode of drunkenness, "Noah awoke from his wine, and knew what his younger son had done unto him," indicating that Ham was the youngest of the three. Chapter 10 lists the genealogies, with Japheth's list first, Ham's second, and Shem's last. In each instance where all three are named together (5:32; 6:10; 10:1), it is likely that Shem is listed first because it was from his line that the family of Abraham would appear, leading eventually to the Messiah.

Listed next in Genesis 7:7 is Noah's wife in accordance with the normal perspective of the Old Testament world concerning women. In that time, men were considered to be, for the most part, the leaders and prominent ones in society. That is what makes women like Deborah, Esther, Ruth, and others so significant—they rose to prominence in a male-dominated culture. Finally, mention is made of the sons' wives, again in accord with the ancient perspective of the younger ones following the older.

Whether or not the family actually entered the ark in this precise order cannot be known for certain, of course. It seems likely that they entered as couples even though the biblical list names them in the above-noted order.

After the list, the reason given for all this is stated. It was to escape the coming floodwaters. This is a summary of why they were entering the ark and also an anticipation of what was about to happen.

The procession of the animals (Gen. 7:8-9). There is a fourfold division mentioned here: clean animals, unclean animals, fowls, and creeping things. The term "beasts" probably refers to all large, quadruped animals, some of which were considered clean and some unclean. Smaller quadrupeds are not specified, with some probably being in each category. The word translated "fowls" refers to everything with feathers. The word translated "creepeth" refers to everything that glides, crawls, or takes short steps.

Once again we are given the detail that the animals entered in pairs—male and female. Although it is not the point being made here, it is significant to note that in God's eyes, His creation has been male and female from the beginning; modern-day attempts of using Scripture to validate same-sex marriage do not work. God has always seen marriage as being one man and one woman, and the Old Testament goes as far as stating that same-sex relationships are an abomination (Lev.

18:22; 20:13; cf. Rom. 1:26-27).

The entrance of both the people and the animals occurred according to God's command to Noah. Noah stuck to the project for over one hundred years and accomplished God's will in doing so. Here was a man who stood alone in his generation as a God-fearer and who was determined to do nothing but what God wanted. He stands, therefore, as a prime example for us today.

We too now live in a world that has departed far from God's ways. Although there are still millions of believers scattered around the world, we live in societies that are becoming increasingly godless and under leaders who ignore or actively oppose the holy standards once adhered to. We must, therefore, determine that we will stand firm in our culture. As Paul described to Timothy, the last days are going to become more and more wicked (II Tim. 3:1-7).

The coming of the deluge (Gen. 7:10). After the week following God's warning had passed, the waters came. It had probably taken all of that week to get everybody and everything settled into place inside the ark. The number of animals coming in, the number of cages being occupied, and the preparation for care and feeding would have kept Noah and his sons scrambling the whole time. Was there a big sigh of relief on that last day when everything was in place and they were completely ready for the storm to come?

Matthew Henry made this observation: "The brute creatures readily went in with him. The same hand that at first brought them to Adam to be named now brought them to Noah to be preserved. The ox now knew his owner, and the ass his protector's crib, nay, even the wildest creatures flocked to it; but man had become more brutish than the brutes themselves, and did

not know, did not consider, Isa. 1:3" (*Matthew Henry's Commentary on the Whole Bible,* Hendrickson). The obedience of both man and animals led to this moment when the floodwaters came.

Noah, his family, and the animals were safe. We too can know such safety in stormy times. "He that dwelleth in the secret place of the most High shall abide under the shadow of the Almighty. I will say of the Lord, He is my refuge and my fortress: my God; in him will I trust" (Ps. 91:1-2).

—Keith E. Eggert.

QUESTIONS

1. How is Noah a prime example of a person who lives by faith?

2. What does Genesis 7:1 say about Noah that led to God's protection of him through the Flood?

3. What new details did God give at this time about the animals to be taken on the ark?

4. What is the stated purpose for sparing the animals?

5. How much advance notice did God give before the rain began, and how long would it last?

6. Why would rain have been an unknown concept to Noah and the people of that time?

7. How old was Noah when the time came to enter the ark?

8. Why are Noah's sons listed ahead of his wife in the boarding of the ark?

9. What fourfold division of the animals is mentioned?

10. How does Noah's obedience make him an example for us today?

—Keith E. Eggert.

Preparing to Teach the Lesson

In our lesson this week, we learn that destruction will come to all who turn away from God, but those who obey Him will dwell in safety. But our obedience must be in faith, which is the gift of God (Eph. 2:8-9).

TODAY'S AIM

Facts: to show through the life of Noah and his family that all who trust God will be safe.

Principle: to understand that those who obey God will be safe.

Application: to obey God even under difficult circumstances, for God will take care of us and keep us safe.

INTRODUCING THE LESSON

As we look at our world today, there is no question that we live in days of uncertainty and fear. Our country is threatened by hostile forces. Many people fear for their safety as they go about their daily business. Many air travelers wonder whether they will reach their destination. Many parents fear for their children when they send them to school. Too many people seem to be looking over their shoulder all the time, not knowing what will happen next.

In our lesson this week, we learn about safety and being secure in our relationship with God as we take steps to obey Him. Obedience by faith is the secret to true safety.

We learn of one family who obeyed God and how God kept them safe from disaster when the whole world around them was being punished. It is important to note that one person in a family can lead everyone in it to safety through obedience to God even when it is hard to understand what is happening.

DEVELOPING THE LESSON

1. Summons to enter the ark (Gen. 7:1-4). As we glean from Genesis 6:3, it had been 120 years since Noah started building the ark. Now it was ready. God told Noah and his family to go into the ark, and with them came seven of each of the clean animals and birds for sacrifice. Explain to the class that even though this was long before the Mosaic Law, God was setting some things in place for that time. The other animals were to be in pairs, male and female, for procreation.

God made the devastating declaration that after exactly one week, it would rain for forty days and forty nights. God stated that He would wipe out everything that He had created. Again, you might ask your class, Was God being too harsh? The truth is that a holy God has to punish sin and disobedience. The better question to ask might be, Why is God so gracious as to allow sin to continue so long before He lets the hammer fall in judgment? Where would we be if this were not so?

2. Noah's complete obedience (Gen. 7:5-9). Put yourself in Noah's shoes. Would you have obeyed God if He commanded you to do what He told Noah? But here we see Noah obeying God even though he did not quite understand it all. Remember that Noah had never seen rain before, let alone a flood! We read that he obeyed God to the very last letter. Scripture tells us that Noah was six hundred years old when the Flood came upon the earth. He may have felt that everything was stacked against him, but he chose to obey God.

The ark was provided for safety, and Noah, his wife, and his three sons and their wives walked into the vessel. It had not been built for travel but only for flotation and protection. It may have taken Noah and his family the entire week to get all the animals on board—the clean animals, the unclean animals, all kinds of birds, and other creeping things. We are told that the animals came into the ark two by two, male and female.

If the question arises, point out that there is no contradiction in the fact that the animals are described as entering two by two in Genesis 7:9 and by sevens in verses 2-3. The latter number refers specifically to the clean animals. What is important to note in this section is that Noah obeyed God to the very last letter, and safety was provided for him and his family. We learn that with obedience to God alone comes safety and protection, even when we do not have all the details clearly spelled out for us.

3. Onset of the Flood (Gen.7:10). In verse 4 we read that God had told Noah that after he had come into the safety of the ark with his family, He would flood the earth after seven days. Now we read that the Flood came just as God had promised Noah. Here is something to think about. What would have happened if Noah had ignored God's instructions and warnings? Safety in this world comes through obeying God alone. God's Word can be trusted.

Remind the class again that whatever God says will always come to pass. In our lesson this week, we read that God said it would rain, and it did. It is worth contemplating what those seven days in the ark might have been like for Noah before the rain finally came. But God kept His word.

ILLUSTRATING THE LESSON

God invites all who would come to take safety in Him. When we trust Jesus as Saviour, we will be safe with Him.

GOD CALLS US

God

TO EXPERIENCE HIS SAFETY

CONCLUDING THE LESSON

This week we learned that obedience to God equals safety. God loves us so much that despite our sin, He is making provision for our safety and our deliverance. He knows that we will sin, for that is the nature of fallen mankind. God has made provision for our safety and salvation today by sending Jesus to die in our stead and be punished for our sins on the cross. We cannot fully fathom a love that would do this, but we are nonetheless called to trust the God who has already planned for our safety.

Leave the class with the sobering thought that we will always be safe when we trust the God who has already prepared for our safety and knows how much we need His protection in this sinful world we live in. Like Noah, we are called to be His holy people in our time.

We have many advantages over Noah in our call to be holy before a wicked world—the Holy Spirit living in us and the gospel's power to save!

ANTICIPATING THE NEXT LESSON

In our next lesson, we will learn how Noah and his family survived the devastation of the Great Flood while every living thing was totally destroyed just as God had promised.

—A. Koshy Muthalaly.

PRACTICAL POINTS

1. God always provides for those who will obey Him (Gen. 7:1-2).
2. Even as we see God's love in His provision, we recognize His holiness in His judgment (vss. 3-4).
3. The obedient find peace and safety in God's care (vs. 5).
4. Obedience to God displays our faith to the world.
5. No one can ever claim to be too old to do God's work (vs. 6).
6. When God gives us a plan, we must follow through (vs. 7).
7. In grace and in judgment, believers can count on God to keep His Word (vss. 8-10).

—Cheryl Y. Powell.

RESEARCH AND DISCUSSION

1. Why is it often more difficult to share God's Word with our families? What resources and tools can a believer use at those times?
2. What are examples of clean animals that God approved for eating and sacrifice? What are examples of unclean animals? Why do you think God declared some animals "clean" and others as "unclean" when He created them all (Lev. 11:1-47; Deut. 14:1-21)?
3. How can you describe the relationship between faith and obedience (cf. Heb. 11:1-40; Jas. 2:14-26)?
4. How does Noah's experience challenge those who may think they are too old or too young to be actively involved in God's work? How should the church help in those cases?

—Cheryl Y. Powell.

ILLUSTRATED HIGH POINTS

Come . . . into the ark

The mix of divine judgment and grace seen in Noah's story is also seen in the destruction of Sodom and Gomorrah in Genisis 18 and 19. Those people had tried God's patience.

Knowing that his nephew Lot lived in Sodom, Abraham pleaded with God to show mercy if there were godly people there. Since there were not even ten, the destruction proceeded.

God did, however, rescue Lot and his little family, but they had to be almost forced to leave (Gen. 19:15-16). Noah and his family responded to the gracious invitation of "come," which reminds us of Matthew 11:28-29.

Noah did . . . all

Noah was industrious and patient since it took 120 years to build the ark (cf. Gen. 6:3). It is hard to imagine the work it must have taken to cut the trees, trim the branches, haul them to the site, saw them to the appropriate width and length, and then peg them together to form the ark of 300 by 50 by 30 cubits (450 by 75 by 45 feet).

We are not told whether he hired other workers, but even so it was a prodigious accomplishment.

There went in two and two

How many animals did Noah have with him on the ark? We are not given a number. Popular authors in this field give estimates that range from two thousand to thirty-five thousand species of animals today.

How could this be? First, the ark was huge. Second, only land-based, air-breathing animals were included. Third, many were small and probably young. Fourth, some suggest the animals may have gone into a type of dormancy.

—David A. Hamburg.

Golden Text Illuminated

"The Lord said unto Noah, Come thou and all thy house into the ark; for thee have I seen righteous before me in this generation" (Genesis 7:1).

One night when my husband and I were traveling, the rain was pouring down in sheets. The windshield wipers could hardly keep up with the deluge. We could barely see the taillights of the car in front of us.

When I glanced at my husband, I could see the tight set of his jaw. We were driving through the mountains of Pennsylvania with a heavy load on the back of the semi. I could tell he was having a time keeping the machine safely on the road. I have rarely been so elated to pull over at a truck stop for the night. When we pulled into the spot, both of us looked up and thanked God for safety.

We often take God's protection for granted. We go through our days without even thinking about the many times that we are saved from danger. Most of the time, we are probably oblivious to those occasions. It is only when we meet with something extreme that we are truly aware of His protection.

That day in Pennsylvania, I could not help but think about Noah and his family. I pictured them standing on the deck of the ark, watching the rain come down. They could no doubt hear the screams of people who were drowning as they watched the ground disappear underwater. When the ark slipped its moorings and they felt it riding on the waves, what thoughts and emotions must have gone through them!

I imagined that they were much like mine that night as I watched the other drivers continue down the highway. Although we were safe at the truck stop, they had not found refuge. While we found freedom from worry and the ter-rible storm, they continued to face it. We had rest; they would have to fight the weariness of their struggle.

We often find ourselves facing storms in life. There may be a job loss, an unexpected illness, or perhaps a broken relationship. Suddenly the rains are swirling around us, and we cannot see clearly. We cry out in fear.

We do not have to do that. As God's children, we are already protected. Scripture tells us that we dwell safely with God as our confidence (Prov. 3:23-26). He will preserve us when threatening things happen. Like Noah and his family, we will be carried through the floods in our lives.

Unfortunately, there are many people who do not follow Jesus. If they do not turn to Him, they will not find protection; instead, He will cast them out (Luke 13:24-27). When that happens, they will be swept away eternally. There will be no second chances. Like those outside the ark, they will beg for rescue and not find it. They will meet with eternal destruction.

Do you know people who need to be rescued? Perhaps they are unaware of their desperate need. As a believer, you have the opportunity to show them the way. If they turn to Christ, you will know that they too are safe inside God's refuge. Would that not be wonderful?

Those of us already in Christ's refuge can give praise that we are safely sustained by His grace. Because of this, we, like Noah, can watch the floodwaters rise and not fear. With Jesus as Saviour, we are secure. We are not only protected on this earth but into eternity. How wonderful that is!

—Jennifer Francis.

Heart of the Lesson

My family traveled from Washington state by way of Portland, Maine, to visit our Kansas grandparents one summer. We camped during the six-week trip. In preparation, my mother made clothes for hot weather for herself, my sister, and me. She aired out the trailer, bought groceries, and stocked the cupboards with dishes.

Meanwhile, my dad changed the oil in the car, checked the tires, washed the trailer, filled the propane tank, and mapped out the trip. Peachy, our little dog, needed bedding, a travel box, and food. Although my brother, sister, and I helped our parents, they were tired before the vacation even began.

Just imagine Noah's preparation for a year-long stay in an ark filled with thousands of animals and birds!

1. Invitation to enter the ark (Gen. 7:1-3). After Noah's years of building and preparing, the ark was finished, and the grace period for humanity had ended. God told Noah and his family to go into the ark. God invited them to enter the place of safety. He reminded Noah why He had singled him out to be on the ark—Noah was righteous. He had faith in God.

God refined his earlier instructions regarding the pairs of animals that would enter the ark. Seven pairs of male and female clean animals and just one pair of unclean animals were to be on board.

Clean animals chewed the cud and had split hooves. They included cattle, sheep, and goats. These were the animals Noah would sacrifice, and these were the animals he and his family would eat after disembarking from the ark. So they needed to take more clean animals than unclean.

Keil and Delitzsch noted that the idea of clean and unclean animals did not originate with Moses. Rather, God confirmed this division to Moses. It was "a long-established custom" (*Commentary on the Old Testament,* Hendrickson).

2. The coming Flood (Gen. 7:4). God told Noah that in one week the rains would start, bringing the Flood that would destroy every living thing on the earth except for those creatures and people in the ark.

3. Noah's obedience (Gen. 7:5-10). Noah's neighbors had watched him build the ark. They had heard him preach about the coming Flood and the need for repentance. They had watched him stock the ark with food and all the household goods he and his family would need to begin a new civilization.

Now they watched as God brought a parade of animals to the ark in male-female pairs. There were elephants, sheep, giraffes, rabbits, lizards, spiders, and birds. One estimate is that as many as 45,000 animals could have fit in the ark (Barton, ed., *Life Application Study Bible,* Tyndale). A week passed, and none of Noah's neighbors asked to join him.

Noah was six hundred years old when he and his family entered the ark. The family no doubt shared Noah's faith or they would have mockingly stayed behind as Lot's sons-in-law did when God destroyed Sodom and Gomorrah. Noah was the spiritual leader of his family. And one week after God told them to go on board, rain began to fall.

Like Noah, are you a spiritual leader in your family? Is your life a godly example for those under your influence? Does your life reflect God's love to your family—both immediate and extended? If you are a parent, the most important thing you can do in life is do your best to make sure your children are "on the boat" with you.

—Ann Staatz.

World Missions

At times it may seem that our world is as bad as in Noah's time, and there is no hope for the next generation. But there are still those who seek to honor the Lord with their lives. We can be encouraged by teens like RJ, who is already serving God and changing his world for good.

RJ Kopituk lives in Morristown, Tennessee. He is seventeen years old and is homeschooled. RJ is active in his church and youth group and says, "I am always looking for a way to help others and serve God in any way He directs me."

RJ learned about the "epidemic of human trafficking" at a youth rally. He says, "It really stuck out to me that there were so many people in pain while I lived my normal life. I did more research and really became aware of how serious this problem was." Later, when planning a Youth Sunday, where the youth themselves lead the service, RJ chose to share about human trafficking.

"While planning and researching for the service and what to present," RJ continues, "I wanted to come up with something the congregation could do and also to remind them that slavery exists. This is when I came across Red Thread Movement . . . an organization that rescues girls who are being trafficked at the border of Nepal and India. They bring them to safe houses and teach them how to make bracelets along with other clothing items. Now Red Thread lets people order a large amount of bracelets and sell them for the girls. Once a girl has recovered and made enough money, they will return back home and start a new life."

When asked if his faith was part of his decision to get involved in fighting trafficking, RJ's answer was clear.

"From the very beginning I relied on God to show me which direction to take and what He wanted me to present. This path is the one He has showed me."

RJ read Proverbs 31:8-9 in the service. "Open thy mouth for the dumb in the cause of all such as are appointed to destruction. Open thy mouth, judge righteously, and plead the cause of the poor and needy."

"This verse spoke to me," he says, "and showed me that this is what I needed to be doing. I needed to stand up for all those in bondage who can't speak up and defend themselves. It has been amazing to see how God has worked through this mission."

RJ was asked what he would say to other teens who want to make a difference. He answered, "I was fifteen when I began working on this, and there are stories of little kids wanting to make a difference; there is no age too young or old to take action. This problem may seem bigger than we can conquer but nothing is too big for God, and it takes people like you to make a difference. We may not be able to save everyone but it makes a difference to the people we can save. Deuteronomy 31:6 says, 'Be strong and of a good courage, fear not, nor be afraid of them: for the Lord thy God, he it is that doth go with thee; he will not fail thee, nor forsake thee.'"

To think that a problem like trafficking is hopeless shows a lack of faith in God, with whom all things are possible.

God is at work in this next generation. Let us find more young people like RJ and do all we can to help them change the world for Christ.

—Kimberly Rae.

The Jewish Aspect

In the midst of the unparalleled wickedness, evil, and violence that consumed the whole earth, the Lord found Noah alone righteous among all people of his generation. It was this righteousness that allowed Noah and his family to be saved from the Flood that destroyed the whole earth. "Judaism alone has placed the story [of the Flood] in the context of the struggle between good and evil. Noah was selected to renew the world because he was the most righteous man in his generation. The Torah describes him as someone who 'walked with God' and was blameless, or, in the Torah's words, 'righteous and whole-hearted in his generation'" (Bayer, "Noah and the Difference Between Blameless and Righteous," www.myjewishlearning.com).

Righteousness is an attribute of a person who is leading a life pleasing to God. Righteousness is not an abstract notion in Judaism; it simply consists of doing what is just and right in all relationships. In the Hebrew Bible, "righteousness bears a distinctly legal character; the righteous man is the innocent party, while the wicked man is the guilty one. . . . Righteousness requires not merely abstention from evil, but a constant pursuit of justice and the performance of positive deeds" ("Righteousness," jewishvirtuallibrary.org).

"Zaddik, 'righteous man' . . . is found throughout rabbinic literature denoting the good man, the man free from sin, the one who carries out his obligation to God by obeying the precepts of the Torah [the first five books of the Hebrew Scriptures]" ("Righteousness," louisjacobs.org).

In its earliest use among Hebrews, the term "righteousness" has a moral intention. The ethical aspect of righteousness is made fully clear in the Prophets. In the book of Amos, "'righteousness' and 'justice' are urged as higher and nobler and more pleasing [to God] than ritual religiousness" ("Right and Righteousness," jewishencyclopedia.com). Hosea, Isaiah, and Jeremiah spoke of righteousness as true religion with Israel expected to be devoted to it. In the book of Job, Job is described as being perfect in righteousness. "The conquest of the 'yezer ha-ra' (i.e., of the inclination toward immorality) marks the righteous" ("Right and Righteousness").

The righteous man is often described as being godlike. This is not surprising since righteousness is one of God's chief attributes. Righteousness marks God's judgments. Abraham knew this, as seen in his question before the judgment on Sodom: "Shall not the Judge of all the earth do right?" (Gen. 18:25).

It is because of God's righteousness that He brought judgment upon the earth during the days of Noah. It was also as a result of righteousness (God's and Noah's) that Noah was spared. God instructed Noah to build an ark to be saved from the Flood. The ark was the vessel by which God spared Noah, his family, and a remnant of the world's animals from the Flood. The same Hebrew word for the "ark"—teba—is also used for the floating basket that saved the infant Moses from Pharaoh's wrath (Exod. 2:3).

Although it is not stated explicitly in our passage, we know from the testimony of later Scripture that Noah's righteousness was not his own. His own righteousness would not have sufficed to make him acceptable in God's sight. Like Abraham's (Gen. 15:6), Noah's righteousness was a righteousness of faith. He trusted God and walked with Him by faith. It is the same righteousness that we are offered in Christ and can live out by faith in Him.

—Deborah Markowitz Solan.

Guiding the Superintendent

In 2004, a gigantic tsunami wave towering up to one hundred feet high struck fourteen Indian Ocean beachfront countries. In a matter of moments, over two hundred thousand people were killed or missing. It is considered one of the worst natural disasters in human history. However, it pales in comparison to the Flood of Noah's day that destroyed all the world population except Noah and his little band of family and animals. The lesson this week describes details of the beginning of the greatest flood in the earth's history.

DEVOTIONAL OUTLINE

1. The Flood promised (Gen. 7:1-5). In contrast to the world's disobedience, Noah obeyed all that God had commanded. God commanded Noah and his family to enter into the ark. Noah was "righteous" in God's sight.

In addition to one pair of male/female unclean animals, God also instructed Noah to take seven pairs of clean animals. This is the first time in the Bible that the idea of clean and unclean animals is introduced. God had probably told Noah beforehand about the difference between clean and unclean. However, these details are never recorded in the Bible. It is usually assumed that the seven pairs of clean animals were intended for sacrifice after the Flood.

Noah was then told that the Flood would begin in seven days. Forty days and nights of rain would wipe from the earth every living creature. In Genesis 2:5, the reader is told that God's plan for watering the earth was with groundwater. Now water from the sky would be used by God as an additional water source to accomplish His plans for destroying the earth.

2. The Flood begins (Gen. 7:6-10). With the seven-day advance notice, Noah, his wife, sons, and daughters-in-law entered the ark to escape the coming Flood. This was the only way they could escape. It was obvious that this would be a universal flood. If it were only a local flood, all Noah would have had to do was relocate. No special boat loaded with animals would be necessary.

Some more details are added for the reader's knowledge. Noah was six hundred years old at the time. And the pairs of clean and unclean animals came to Noah and then entered the ark.

After Noah, his family, and the animals were safely in the ark and the seven days were over, rain started to fall on the earth. The Flood had now begun.

CHILDREN'S CORNER

text: **II Kings 5:1-8**
title: **Naaman's Need For Healing**

This lesson discusses a most "honorable"commander of the army of Syria, which is located at Israel's northern border and was their major enemy at the time. But there was a problem. This commander named Naaman was a leper. Leprosy is similar to the HIV of our day in that the disease was usually incurable and often ultimately terminal.

An Israelite servant girl of Naaman's wife told the family about a prophet in Israel who could heal her master. The desperate king of Syria sent a letter to Israel's king requesting help. At first the request was greeted with suspicion. But when Elisha heard about the strange request, he declared that he was God's prophet, meaning he could cure the diseased commander.

—*Martin R. Dahlquist.*

Scripture Lesson Text

GEN. 7:11 In the six hundredth year of Noah's life, in the second month, the seventeenth day of the month, the same day were all the fountains of the great deep broken up, and the windows of heaven were opened.

12 And the rain was upon the earth forty days and forty nights.

13 In the selfsame day entered Noah, and Shem, and Ham, and Japheth, the sons of Noah, and Noah's wife, and the three wives of his sons with them, into the ark;

14 They, and every beast after his kind, and all the cattle after their kind, and every creeping thing that creepeth upon the earth after his kind, and every fowl after his kind, every bird of every sort.

15 And they went in unto Noah into the ark, two and two of all flesh, wherein is the breath of life.

16 And they that went in, went in male and female of all flesh, as God had commanded him: and the Lord shut him in.

17 And the flood was forty days upon the earth; and the waters increased, and bare up the ark, and it was lift up above the earth.

18 And the waters prevailed, and were increased greatly upon the earth; and the ark went upon the face of the waters.

19 And the waters prevailed exceedingly upon the earth; and all the high hills, that were under the whole heaven, were covered.

20 Fifteen cubits upward did the waters prevail; and the mountains were covered.

21 And all flesh died that moved upon the earth, both of fowl, and of cattle, and of beast, and of every creeping thing that creepeth upon the earth, and every man:

22 All in whose nostrils was the breath of life, of all that was in the dry land, died.

23 And every living substance was destroyed which was upon the face of the ground, both man, and cattle, and the creeping things, and the fowl of the heaven; and they were destroyed from the earth: and Noah only remained alive, and they that were with him in the ark.

24 And the waters prevailed upon the earth an hundred and fifty days.

NOTES

The Great Flood

Lesson Text: Genesis 7:11-24

Related Scriptures: Exodus 14:27-31; Isaiah 24:1-3;
Matthew 24:34-42; II Peter 3:3-7

TIME: unknown

PLACE: unknown

GOLDEN TEXT—"Every living substance was destroyed which was upon the face of the ground, . . . and Noah only remained alive, and they that were with him in the ark" (Genesis 7:23).

Introduction

A recent news report showed the devastating approach and passing of a tsunami in Japan. It was filmed by someone standing on a high balcony in a city close to the ocean shore. People were shown one minute going about their business on a city street and the next minute fleeing for their lives as a huge wave suddenly bore down on them.

It is different to have rain that gradually causes an accumulation of water. A woman who lived through the flooding of a hurricane described how she noticed water in her front yard early one morning, then went back to sleep, only to be awakened by a friend calling to alert her to danger around her house. Water was four inches from her doorstep, and she ended up losing everything she owned.

LESSON OUTLINE

I. COMING OF THE FLOOD—
Gen. 7:11-16

II. DEVASTATION OF THE FLOOD—
Gen. 7:17-24

Exposition: Verse by Verse

COMING OF THE FLOOD

GEN. 7:11 In the six hundredth year of Noah's life, in the second month, the seventeenth day of the month, the same day were all the fountains of the great deep broken up, and the windows of heaven were opened.

12 And the rain was upon the earth forty days and forty nights.

13 In the selfsame day entered Noah, and Shem, and Ham, and Japheth, the sons of Noah, and Noah's wife, and the three wives of his sons with them, into the ark;

14 They, and every beast after his kind, and all the cattle after their kind, and every creeping thing that creepeth upon the earth after his kind, and every fowl after his kind, every bird of every sort.

15 And they went in unto Noah into the ark, two and two of all flesh, wherein is the breath of life.

16 And they that went in, went in male and female of all flesh, as God had commanded him: and the LORD shut him in.

Onslaught of water (Gen. 7:11-12).

The Flood of Noah's day might have been a fascinating combination of these two scenarios because of the two sources of water involved. It was in Noah's six hundredth year—on the seventeenth day of the second month of the year—that "all the fountains of the great deep [were] broken up, and the windows of heaven were opened." All at once two things began to happen at the same time, with water appearing from both above and below the earth's surface.

The phrase "fountains of the great deep" indicates that waters came gushing up like springs from a huge subterranean abyss. The *Believer's Study Bible* notes, "The 'fountains of the great deep' refers to 'springs,' while 'deep' is the same word as the vast and almost infinite 'deep' at creation (1:2). The word for 'broken up' could also be translated 'split,' 'ripped open'" (Criswell, ed., Nelson). This was an unexpected eruption never before witnessed by mankind.

At the same time the windows of the heavens were opened, indicating torrential rains. Many believe God had placed a canopy of water around His creation ("the waters which were above the firmament" in Genesis 1:7), protecting the earth in a greenhouse type of environment and contributing to the longevity of people prior to the Flood. It was at this point in time that God opened that canopy and dumped the

water onto the earth. What makes this a probability is the fact that lifespans were significantly reduced after the Flood.

This deluge of water continued for forty days and forty nights. We will see in a few more verses what the extent of coverage was from all this. Everything about this explanation points to a universal flood covering the entire surface area of the earth.

Safety in the ark (Gen. 7:13-14).

The tremendous importance of this event is emphasized by the degree of repetition of the information related to it. Verse 13 begins with the phrase "in the selfsame day," which is a repeat of the information in verse 11: "In the six hundredth year of Noah's life, in the second month, the seventeenth day of the month, the same day were all the fountains of the great deep broken up, and the windows of heaven were opened." After this there is a repeat of what is found in verse 7.

Once again we are told that on a certain specific day Noah and his family entered the ark. Unlike in the previous instance, however, this time the sons are named. Neither Noah's wife nor his sons' wives are ever named even though they were obviously being cared for by God just as much as the men were. This again points to the male-dominated culture in the ancient world, but in no way does it make the women any less important or valuable in God's eyes. The New Testament clearly shows Christianity elevating women.

It is encouraging to see that God was and is concerned about the entire family. This is also emphasized in the New Testament, seen in passages like Ephesians 5:22–6:4, where God gave specific instructions through Paul about the conduct of family relationships. It is also implied in Paul's respectful mention of Timothy's godly grandmother and mother (II Tim. 1:5).

We are also informed again of the

entrance of the animals into the ark (Gen. 7:14). All of them are included in the terms "beast," "cattle," "creeping thing," "fowl," and "bird of every sort." These terms include wild and domesticated animals along with everything that crawls and everything that flies.

God's command and protection (Gen. 7:15-16). We noted in an earlier lesson that Noah would not have had to scamper all over the earth chasing these animals toward the ark; God would have directed them there. That is clearly brought out here, for the text says that "they went in unto Noah into the ark." Verse 15 states that they were in pairs ("two and two"), and verse 16 specifies that they were male and female. God made provision for the continuation of all life even while destroying it.

The pairs of animals represented all creatures that had the breath of life in them. This is a reminder that bodies are lifeless without breath and that all breath comes from God. It takes us back to the creation of Adam in Genesis 2:7, where we are given the details of the process that took place. First, "the Lord God formed man of the dust of the ground," after which He "breathed into his nostrils the breath of life." As a result, "man became a living soul."

Life has great value because it is a gift from God that we should never take lightly. This is especially true of human life, but we should recognize it also in the animal kingdom. Proverbs 12:10 states, "A righteous man regardeth the life of his beast: but the tender mercies of the wicked are cruel." There is no more excuse for the abuse of animals than there is the murder of a fellow human being.

Genesis 7:16 notes that the animals entered the ark "as God had commanded" Noah, giving him credit for it. This is appropriate, for he was the one who made provision for them. After all of them were safely inside, God shut the door of the ark, again emphasizing Noah's role ("shut him in").

DEVASTATION OF THE FLOOD

17 And the flood was forty days upon the earth; and the waters increased, and bare up the ark, and it was lift up above the earth.

18 And the waters prevailed, and were increased greatly upon the earth; and the ark went upon the face of the waters.

19 And the waters prevailed exceedingly upon the earth; and all the high hills, that were under the whole heaven, were covered.

20 Fifteen cubits upward did the waters prevail; and the mountains were covered.

21 And all flesh died that moved upon the earth, both of fowl, and of cattle, and of beast, and of every creeping thing that creepeth upon the earth, and every man:

22 All in whose nostrils was the breath of life, of all that was in the dry land, died.

23 And every living substance was destroyed which was upon the face of the ground, both man, and cattle, and the creeping things, and the fowl of the heaven; and they were destroyed from the earth: and Noah only remained alive, and they that were with him in the ark.

24 And the waters prevailed upon the earth an hundred and fifty days.

Increasing waters (Gen. 7:17-18). Imagine nonstop pouring rain for forty days in a row! Gradually, all ponds and lakes would overflow, followed by cresting rivers. Before long oceans would reach beyond their boundaries and spread until all of earth's surface was covered. That, however, would just be the beginning as the water continued to get deeper and deeper. People and animals alike would seek higher ground, going farther and farther up into the hills and some climbing the mountains.

We can only imagine the panic that began to grow in the hearts of the people, getting worse and worse as the rain continued and the water rose higher and higher. It is probable that those in the vicinity of the ark desperately cried out and clawed at the structure with hopes of getting inside. It was too late for them, of course; so they were all left to the deepening waters. Here is a portrait of the hopelessness that will accompany those in eternity without Jesus as their Saviour.

When the water became deep enough, the ark started to float. It would have taken some time because of its size and weight, but eventually it began to sway and lift off the surface of the earth. Before long it was fully afloat and moving in the water. The fact that the ark floated safely on the surface of the water tells us that what Noah had built was completely seaworthy with no danger of capsizing or sinking. God had given him the perfect proportions of length, width, and height for staying afloat.

The day Noah had warned about for over one hundred years finally arrived. God always fulfills His word, but He always allows time for repentance before the punishment. An even greater destruction is coming in the future for those who do not know Him. It would be wise for any who have not received Jesus to pay attention to His warnings.

Prevailing waters (Gen. 7:19-20). We are told in verse 18 that as the waters increased, they "prevailed." In verse 19 this reality is emphasized. The word translated "prevailed" is the Hebrew word *gabar,* meaning to "be mighty" or "have strength." A related form designates a "mighty man of valour" (Judg. 6:12; 11:1; I Kings 11:28), a person who prevails in battle or in spiritual endeavors in the strength of the Lord. Used of the floodwaters, the verb

vividly pictures an unstoppable force overwhelming everything in its path.

We saw in Genesis 7:18 that the waters "were increased greatly upon the earth," while in verse 19, the statement is made that they "prevailed exceedingly upon the earth" until "all the high hills, that were under the whole heaven, were covered." This is confirmed in verse 20: "Fifteen cubits upward did the waters prevail; and the mountains were covered." Twenty-two feet of water covered the highest mountain peaks, easily allowing the ark to float over them.

"The author implies that the highest waters covered the Ararat mountain range, the height of which is approximately 16,000 ft. (8:4). Surely a flood more than 3 miles in depth could not be confined to any portion of the earth. The Hebrew word *kol,* used twice in the verse (translated 'all' and 'the whole') adds to the impression that the Flood was a universal phenomenon. No one could have escaped the catastrophe except those in the ark" (Criswell).

Total destruction (Gen. 7:21-23a). Here is a summary of the extent of death caused by the Flood. Outside of marine life, every living thing died. The emphasis here is on everything that lived on the earth, all creatures that had the breath of life, and everything that normally existed on dry land. The repeated absolutes—"all flesh died," "all in whose nostrils was the breath of life," "all that was in the dry land," and "every living substance"—leave no exceptions.

If any person or animal tried to survive at the beginning of the rain by clinging to a piece of floating debris, and if by some outside chance some pocket of air was discovered somewhere in a cave, the hope of safety soon disappeared and was replaced with destruction. Water covering everything to the point of being high above the highest mountain peaks would run into everything that might provide temporary safety. There was absolutely no escape for anything living on the face of the earth.

There is a parallel here with the day when unsaved people appear before the Great White Throne. In the book of Revelation, John described that day: "And I saw the dead, small and great, stand before God; and the books were opened: and another book was opened, which is the book of life: and the dead were judged out of those things which were written in the books, according to their works. . . . And whosoever was not found written in the book of life was cast into the lake of fire" (20:12,15).

It is impossible to overemphasize the importance being ready to meet God. Our lives are not meant merely for personal enjoyment and achievement. Throughout life we are given the opportunity to receive Jesus as personal Saviour, and that is the only guarantee of heaven. As often as we might hear that and as trite as it might begin to sound, it is the truth we must accept.

Preservation amid the cataclysm (Gen. 7:23b-24). A final emphatic point of comparison is made in the statement that Noah and those with him in the ark remained alive. It is a stark contrast— everything outside the ark on the face of the earth died, but those inside the safety of the ark remained alive. Once again we see a type of Christ presented by this ark. Though there are many who tell us that all religions lead to heaven, this is not the truth presented in the Scriptures. Jesus is the only way to eternal life in heaven.

One day, Jesus explained to His disciples that His Father's house had many dwelling places in it and that He was going there to prepare it for them (John 14:2). Thomas said, "Lord, we know not whither thou goest; and how can we know the way?" (vs. 5). Jesus answered, "I am the way, the truth, and the life: no man cometh unto the Fa-

ther, but by me" (vs. 6). The risk in ignoring this statement has eternal consequences just as the ignoring of Noah's warnings for so many years did in his day.

Genesis 7:24 closes our lesson with the observation that "the waters prevailed upon the earth an hundred and fifty days." For five months, the waters continued to rage and rise higher until they covered everything. According to Genesis 8:3-4, they must have then begun to slowly recede. Noah had entered the ark in the second month of his six hundredth year (7:11), and the ark did not come to rest until the seventh month (8:4).

—Keith E. Eggert.

QUESTIONS

1. What two sources of water brought about the Flood?

2. In which year of Noah's life did the rains begin, and how long did they continue?

3. What might the repetition of information on who entered the ark be telling us?

4. What categories of animals were included in the ark, and how did they get there?

5. Why is Noah given credit for gathering all the animals?

6. What happened to the ark as the waters began to rise?

7. How are the waters portrayed in the word "prevailed" (Gen. 7:19)?

8. How high above the mountain peaks did the water rise?

9. What strong contrast is underscored in verse 23?

10. How is the ark a type of Christ, and what is the warning for today?

—Keith E. Eggert.

Preparing to Teach the Lesson

This week in our lesson, we learn about the total devastation brought upon the whole earth by the Flood. It is possible that some of your students may be skeptical that such a world-wide flood occurred. But the biblical narrative is very clear in its precise detail and very convincingly true.

TODAY'S AIM

Facts: to show the devastation that came upon the earth from the Great Flood during Noah's time.

Principle: to remember that what God tells us will always come to pass.

Application: to know that when God shows us something that is coming, we had better listen to Him or face the consequences of being unprepared.

INTRODUCING THE LESSON

The Bible warns us of several things that will happen to the world in the end times. Some of them can be frightening. Some who read this lesson may be skeptical. But the Bible is not written to scare us or to frighten us away but to give us hope and confidence so that we will trust God. He prepares us for what is coming. When we study the narrative of Noah and the Flood, we ought to be reminded that God eventually punishes sin and disobedience. He also promises safety to those who listen to Him and obey.

DEVELOPING THE LESSON

1. The coming of the Flood (Gen. 7:11-16). How do we know we can trust God? We cannot see or hear Him, but He has told us many things in His Word. Noah did not see Him either, but the Flood he was told about certainly came to pass. Noah had the moral integrity to trust the God who had warned Him that

such a calamity was coming. He obeyed God to the very last detail. Scripture tells us that he was six hundred years old at this time. Would we be able to trust God as Noah did?

It is instructive to note the specific historical detail that the Genesis account provides for us in this section. It says that the rains fell when Noah was six hundred years old in the seventeenth day of the second month of that year. This helps to corroborate the fact that the Flood happened in real time.

Noah got on board the ark with his wife and three sons, Shem, Ham, and Japheth. The description of the Flood reveals a terrifying sequence of events for the people on the earth. The fountains of the deep and the windows in the heavens opened up and flooded the earth. In other words, there were torrents of water from above and floods below. It was something that no one had ever seen or experienced before. The rains poured for forty days and forty nights without a break.

Remind the class that the eight people who were protected that day—Noah, his wife, their three sons and their wives—enjoyed that protection because they trusted and obeyed God. Together with them, all the animals, two by two, male and female, were preserved—all kinds of birds, cattle, insects, and creeping things. They were to be the source of all life after the Flood. God had a specific plan in mind to preserve His creation.

After Noah, his family, and all the animals were safely inside the ark, the Lord shut them in. Make the point that there was a time when the invitation to safety was open to all who would come in. Now God Himself shut the door. There is an abrupt stamp of finality about this action on the part of God. Only those who had chosen to obey Him and come into safety were kept safe. The others would face destruction.

It is important to see that the ark is a picture of what is to come in our world, and now God calls us to come to Him for safety. Those who disobey and reject Him face destruction. All people everywhere must step into the safety of His covenant by trusting Christ before the door is finally shut for good. And the time to do that is now.

2. The extent of the destruction (Gen. 7:17-24). We read again that it rained for forty days and forty nights. That is a really long period of time for nonstop rain. The waters did not recede, so the ark started to float above the land. The waters continued to rise until they covered the highest mountains. The water level rose to more than twenty feet (fifteen cubits) above the highest peak at that time. The whole earth was covered with water. It was utter devastation.

The text specifies the destruction in the starkest terms. All living animals and birds and every creeping thing on the earth died. Genesis 7:22 reads, "All in whose nostrils was the breath of life." This is the Hebrew way of expressing everything that was alive and breathing. Life is characterized by breath. Every human being on earth at that time was overtaken by this destruction. Noah and his family were the sole exceptions.

We read a lot about the anger of God in the Bible. We also read of His great patience and grace—He is a God who is slow to anger. Both His great forbearance and His decisive anger are prominently displayed in the story of Noah. This is both a warning and a comfort for us today.

We are told that the waters began to recede after five months. This could be a picture that God's anger lingers but not forever. When we read about the Flood, we know God was very angry about the stubborn disobedience of

man. But the floodwaters subsided, and the earth was renewed. Show the class that there is hope for us in this. God will save and restore all those who repent, but His anger is not to be trifled with.

ILLUSTRATING THE LESSON

We can be certain that what God says will happen.

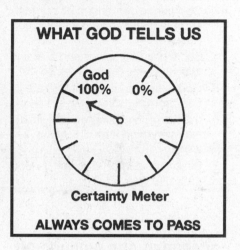

WHAT GOD TELLS US

God 100% 0%

Certainty Meter

ALWAYS COMES TO PASS

CONCLUDING THE LESSON

Our lesson this week is a serious reminder that we cannot toy with God. When He gives directions, He is serious about what He wants us to do. When we obey Him, we will be safe. When we ignore Him, we face the danger of being unprepared and vulnerable to harm, whether physical or spiritual. It is good that we ask ourselves what it would take to get us to pay attention to what God says.

ANTICIPATING THE NEXT LESSON

In the very last lesson of this quarter, we will see Noah's gratitude to God for keeping him and his family safe during the Flood. We will also see God make a promise to Noah that is still in force today. Our God can be trusted to keep His word.

—A. Koshy Muthalaly.

PRACTICAL POINTS

1. God allows men and women time to repent because he is gracious (Gen. 7:11).
2. God places limits on the severity of His judgment because He is gracious (vs. 12).
3. Obedience demonstrates our faith and places us in God's protection (vss. 13-14).
4. God's hand preserves and sustains that which He creates (vss. 15-16).
5. God is holy and cannot tolerate or compromise with sin (vss. 17-20).
6. If a man does not repent, his sin ruins everything it touches (vss. 21-22).
7. Sin brings death, while faith in God gives life (vss. 23-24).

—*Cheryl Y. Powell.*

RESEARCH AND DISCUSSION

1. What encouragement is found in Genesis 7 for the Christian who is troubled and anxious over the apparent prevalence of sin in our world (cf. II Pet. 3:8-9)?
2. How are Christians often challenged by those who choose not to hear God's Word (cf. II Pet. 3:3-7)? What example does Noah provide for believers today?
3. How is the number forty significant in Scripture (cf. Exod. 24:18; Num. 14:33; Ezek. 4:6; Matt. 4:1-2)?
4. How is it significant that God shut the door to the ark? How is that fact important for us in sharing the gospel with our families, communities, and the world today?

—*Cheryl Y. Powell.*

ILLUSTRATED HIGH POINTS

The six hundredth year

We note that the same water that caused destruction on earth also caused the ark to float, which preserved life. God's judgment and mercy are seen at the same time.

It reminds us that the same sun that melts wax also hardens clay. The difference is in the material. In Noah's day (and it is true today), there were two types of people—those who believed God and those who did not.

The Lord shut him in

Noah's faith and commitment to God in building the ark and being "a preacher of righteousness" for 120 years (II Pet. 2:5) remind us of the hymn "I Have Decided To Follow Jesus" (Singh).

This song came from the testimony of a nineteenth-century Christian in India who was challenged to renounce his faith in Christ. He declared, "I have decided to follow Jesus!" Even though they killed his wife, he continued, "Though no one join me, still I will follow." And then as he was killed, he sang, "The cross before me, the world behind me."

Noah did not die, but his faith stood firm.

Noah only remained alive

Noah spent a year and ten days in the ark. Have you ever wondered what occupied his time? Here are some possibilities.

Of course he would have cared for the animals by feeding and cleaning up after them. Did he keep a daily log? Day one: rain; day two: rain; day three, well, you get the idea.

He may have told funny stories, but soon his family would remind him that he had told that one before. And they must have spent time simply being thankful for life.

—*David A. Hamburg.*

Golden Text Illuminated

"Every living substance was destroyed which was upon the face of the ground, . . . and Noah only remained alive, and they that were with him in the ark" (Genesis 7:23).

There was no possible way of salvaging it. No matter how much glue I used, my cup could not be put back together. The shattered pieces were in too many fragments. All I could do was sweep it up, put it into a bag, and throw it into the trash.

The ceramic piece was something I had painted. The paint job was terribly splotchy. For years, it had stood on top of my dresser. When it came crashing to the floor, though, I was dismayed. It was just a ceramic cup, but it was something special to me. I knew the cup was irretrievably lost.

My dismay that day was real. I recognize, though, that it was no doubt only a fraction of the dismay God felt as He flooded the earth. From His throne He watched its inhabitants perish as earth's surface was swallowed up in the downpour. He heard the cries as people and animals vainly sought to be spared. The world and its inhabitants were beyond repair. It was time to start fresh.

This could not have been easy for God. He had lovingly molded the earth, paying attention to every detail. Now His beautiful creation was a soggy mess. Watching His creation being reduced to ruins must have been heartrending for God.

There was hope, though. Deep inside the ark, life still stirred. Riding on the waves was the seed for God's renewed world. The ark's precious cargo carried the seed for earth's renewal.

To protect the good that God intended, He destroyed the bad. When Noah walked out of that ark, it would be into a purified land. It would be a fresh start.

There are times when we think that our world is being torn apart. Turmoil swirls around us in our communities and in our nations. Perhaps the world has already fallen apart in some respects.

There is one thing we need to remember, though. God always preserves a seed of hope and renewal for each believer. Psalm 91 tells us that "a thousand shall fall at [our] side, . . . but it shall not come nigh [us]" (vs.7).

We may not always see the reason for the flood times in our lives. We may think that God is inattentive to our cries. In fact, what He is doing may well be an act of cleansing, helping us to shed something that hinders us in our walk with Him.

We cannot always discern the things in our lives that are causing destruction. There are times when we choose not to see. That is often when our loving Father allows the rains to fall. While we may hope to be like King David and yearn for purification (Ps. 51:7), we still may be tempted to complain. Instead, we need to accept the cleansing with the understanding that God will preserve what is truly important in our lives.

Are you seeking God's cleansing today? Is there an area of your life that you know needs it, but you are hesitant to ask for God's power to deal with it? Do not fear. Call out to God today, for He loves you and seeks only to sanctify you. You can trust Him to preserve you and to cleanse you of all unrighteousness (I John 1:9). When cleansing comes, welcome it. It is always followed with God's freshness.

—*Jennifer Francis.*

Heart of the Lesson

I chaperoned the teenagers in my church who were attending a youth convention in Florida one summer. One afternoon, the teens asked me to drive them to a doughnut shop. On our return to the convention center, a pounding rain began to fall. My windshield looked as if someone were dumping buckets of water over it.

Because I could see nothing but torrential rain, I pulled into a bank parking lot to wait out the squall. I imagine that rain must have been something like what Noah experienced when God opened the windows of heaven at the time of the Great Flood.

1. Beginning of the end (Gen. 7:11-12). As he wrote Genesis, Moses gave a precise date for the Flood's start: the seventeenth day of the second month in Noah's six hundredth year. On that day, the fountains of the deep burst open and began pouring onto the earth's surface. And sheets of rain fell from the sky. This continued for forty days and forty nights. After 120 years of warning, God's judgment had begun.

2. Safety in the ark (Gen. 7:13-16). God had given Noah a week to load the animals onto the ark, along with his family, before the Flood began. Pairs of animals and birds—male and female—had come to Noah and were now secure in the ark.

Noah, his wife, his three sons, and his three daughters-in-law had said any last good-byes they were led to have. Perhaps they made final pleas to friends and family to repent and join them. Noah and his family acted in faith, going into the ark even though they had yet seen no evidence of a flood. The eight of them were safe in the ark when the floodwaters began.

In loving protection, God Himself closed the ark's sole door. It was as if He was setting His seal on this voyage, promising He would be with them. God shut the door on their old life; when the door opened again, it would open to a new life and a fresh start for humanity.

3. Rising waters (Gen. 7:17-20). At first, the ark was sitting in puddles. But gradually the water rose until the ark was floating. Water covered trees, houses, and low hills. Eventually, the mountaintops were submerged twenty feet under water. This was no local flood.

4. God's judgment on evil (Gen. 7:21-23a). As the waters rose, places of refuge dwindled for living creatures and people outside the ark. Soon no high ground remained. Every living thing on the earth drowned.

A harsh punishment? Yes. But mankind had had a warning through Noah's preaching as he built the ark. Humanity had disregarded Noah's message and continued its violence, partying, and living daily without God. Then the waters came. "God is the moral Ruler of this universe, who has and who will exercise His obligation to judge sin" (Richards, *The Bible Reader's Companion*, Cook).

5. Survivors afloat (Gen. 7:23b, 24). Only Noah, his family, and his precious cargo of animals and birds survived the Flood. After the floodwaters rose on the earth, the water remained for many months more. Noah and his family stayed in the ark, caring for the animals and for their own needs.

Like Noah, are you on the boat? Have you placed your faith in Jesus, who died on the cross for your sins? Like Noah, do you obey God in faith even when you do not see the immediate fulfillment of God's promises? God's commands are for our good. He can be trusted.

—*Ann Staatz.*

World Missions

Zombies killing millions or nuclear warfare wiping out nations—the movies and books popular in society reveal that people fear destruction on a large scale. Humanity's fear of apocalyptic horror is sourced in the spiritual, for Judgment Day is coming.

Muslims are very aware of the coming Judgment Day. This is used as a tool by the missionaries who developed the "Any 3" method of presenting the gospel to them.

Anyone. Anywhere. Anytime.

Their approach has been extremely successful, and many, many Muslims have come to Christ.

It begins with natural, curious conversation. Derek asks Hasan about his religion and guides the talk to the fact that mankind has a sin problem. "Yes, we're all sinners," Hasan agrees.

Derek asks Hasan what he is doing to get his sins forgiven. Hasan mentions some of the things he does, but admits, "My sins aren't forgiven yet.— On the Judgment Day, I can only hope my sins will be forgiven."

Speaking of himself, Derek politely tells Hasan that he knows his sins are forgiven. He shares about Jesus, the Lamb of God, and His sacrifice.

Hasan that night puts his faith in Christ, and his life is changed.

This method can also be quite effective in our own culture. If we were to ask a lost person the typical question, "If you died today, do you know if you would go to heaven?" the response may also be a typical one. However, if we ask an atypical question such as, "What are you doing to get your sins forgiven?" people must think in order to answer. A few more well-placed questions can lead the lost person to recognize his own sin problem and come to the conclusion on his own that he needs a Saviour.

Here is a summary of the Any 3 method, taken from the book *Any 3* by Mike Shipman:

1. Get Connected. Get to know them. Ask curious questions about who they are. Be friendly.

Transition 1: Find out what religion they are.

2. Get to God. "Most religions are alike, aren't they?" you ask. "We are all trying to please God so that we can go to heaven someday. But we all sin, don't we? Even good people sin. Sinning is easy, but paying off our sin debt to God is much more difficult, isn't it?"

Transition 2: What are you doing to get your sins forgiven?

3. Get to Lostness. Listen to their answers then ask, "Are your sins paid off yet? On Judgment Day, do you know that your sin debt will be paid?"

Transition 3: What I believe is different.

4. Get to the Gospel. Tell about Jesus, His sacrifice, and how your sins are forgiven.

Transition 4: This forgiveness is also offered to you.

5. Get to a Decision. After you've explained the gospel, ask, "That makes sense, doesn't it?" Then, "Do you believe what I have told you: that Jesus died for our sins and was raised again?"

Through genuine questions such as "Why do you think people care about religion?" "In your opinion, what is God like?" or "What do you think is the way to heaven?" we can learn about the lost, get to know their hearts, and reveal their need of salvation to them in a powerful way, through their own answers.

—Kimberly Rae.

The Jewish Aspect

The Hebrew word *mabul,* meaning "deluge," is used to describe the floodwaters during the days of Noah. The Flood has been likened to a cosmic cataclysm. "The same day were all the fountains of the great deep broken up, and the windows of heaven were opened," (Gen. 7:11). "The 'deep' in Scripture usually refers to the ocean . . . the 'great deep' which was 'broken up' evidently speaks of the great subterranean reservoirs or chambers deep inside the earth" (Morris, "All the fountains of the Deep," www.icr.org).

The windows of heaven were also opened, which meant that "the celestial waters in the canopy encircling the globe were dumped on the earth and joined with the terrestrial and the subterranean waters. . . . The sequence in this verse [indicates] that the earth's crust breaks up first, then the heavens drop their water" ("Genesis Chapter 7 Explained," www.bible-studys.org). The word "broken up" is the same word used in Numbers 16:30-33, which describes "the supernatural opening up of a great pit into which the rebellious Korah and his followers and their families fell" (Morris).

There are more than 270 flood stories from cultures throughout the world, and all of them owe their origin to this one global event. In Jewish teaching, water has the power to purify, restore, and replenish. The mikvah, a ritual bath for women, is the ultimate Jewish symbol of spiritual renewal. One Jewish scholar made this connection: "The world's natural bodies of water—its oceans, rivers, wells and spring-fed lakes—are *mikvahs* in their most primal form" (Slonim, "The Mikvah," www.chabad.org).

It could be said that through the waters of the Flood, God purified His creation, the world that had been so thoroughly corrupted. The waters prevailed, covering all the hills and mountains on the earth, thus ensuring that the cleansing was complete. No location was allowed to escape the violent scouring of the floodwaters; no place of refuge was to be found except inside the ark.

It is no accident that the rains lasted for forty days and forty nights. On a Jewish question-and-answer site, a rabbi expounded on the great significance of the number throughout the Hebrew Scriptures. Forty represents transition or change, the concept of renewal, a new beginning. Moses was on Mount Sinai for forty days. God led the Jewish people in the wilderness for forty years. According to the Talmud, it takes forty days for an embryo to be formed in its mother's womb. The Talmud also states that at age forty, a person transitions from one level of wisdom to the next ("The Number 40," www.aish.com).

The rabbi also noted that there are forty days between the first day of the month of Elul when the shofar is blown to prepare for Rosh Hashanah (the Jewish New Year) until Yom Kippur (the Day of Atonement), the end of the repentance period. These forty days are considered the most important time for personal growth and renewal. The number forty has the power to lift a spiritual state. A mikvah is filled with 40 se'ahs of water. "Just as a person leaves a mikveh pure, so too when the waters of the flood subsided, the world was purified from the licentiousness which had corrupted it" ("The Number 40").

All the men, women, and children and all animal and vegetable life outside the ark perished during the Flood. But the Lord secured Noah, his family, and the animals inside. God preserved them all; the whole work was the Lord's, from first to last.

—Deborah Markowitz Solan.

Guiding the Superintendent

Because miracles are so hard to grasp, many have tried to explain the Noahic Flood as simply a natural one hundred-year flood somewhere in Mesopotamia that destroyed much life and property. But the passage for this week makes it very clear that this flood was not local but universal. From the duration of it, to the height of the floodwaters, to the personal accounts of it, the Genesis Flood can only be understood as universal.

DEVOTIONAL OUTLINE

1. The Flood began (Gen. 7:11-12). This was no typical flood. The biblical account gives the specific date it all began. The biblical dating is given in such a way that the Flood's magnitude is clearly set forth.

If the floodwaters covered the entire earth, where did they all come from? All this water came from two specific sources: the "fountains of the great deep" and the "windows of heaven" (vs. 11). Water from below and above the earth poured onto the earth for forty days.

2. Entrance to the ark (Gen. 7:13-16). The events of the entrance into the ark are now reviewed. Following Noah and his small family, matched pairs of all wild animals, livestock, ground creatures, and birds entered the ark.

The reader is reminded that all of this was by divine grace. God brought in the animals and then shut the door.

3. Forty days of rain (Gen. 7:17-24). The biblical accounts emphasize three great aspects that indicate that this Flood was no everyday flood— the duration, the height of the floodwaters, and the loss of all life except that in the ark.

The flood of subterranean and atmospheric water continued for forty days. There was so much water that the ark floated very freely. And there was so much water that the highest mountains were covered to a depth of about twenty feet ("fifteen cubits" [vs. 20]). This could not have been an ordinary flood. All life on the earth perished. Only Noah, his wife, his family, and a collection of animals and birds survived.

The waters "prevailed upon the earth an hundred and fifty days" (vs. 24). The amount of water involved, the height of the water, and the duration of the Flood all indicate that this Flood was indeed universal in nature.

The Scripture text indicates that Noah entered the ark and was saved because he obeyed God. "Noah did according unto all that the Lord commanded him" (vs. 5).

CHILDREN'S CORNER

text: **II Kings 5:9-19**
title: **Naaman Healed of Leprosy**

A great commander from Israel's northern neighbor of Syria, Naaman, approached the Israelite king to seek a cure for his leprosy. When the Prophet Elisha heard about the situation, he called for the commander to come to him for healing. To clearly convey that the healing was from God, Elisha requested that the commander bathe in the Jordan River. At first the proud commander refused to bathe in the dirty river, but his servants prevailed on him. To everyone's surprise, his flesh was restored to that of a child. To emphasize that this was God's doing, the prophet refused any money for his actions.

—*Martin R. Dahlquist.*

Scripture Lesson Text

GEN. 8:15 And God spake unto Noah, saying,

16 Go forth of the ark, thou, and thy wife, and thy sons, and thy sons' wives with thee.

17 Bring forth with thee every living thing that is with thee, of all flesh, both of fowl, and of cattle, and of every creeping thing that creepeth upon the earth; that they may breed abundantly in the earth, and be fruitful, and multiply upon the earth.

18 And Noah went forth, and his sons, and his wife, and his sons' wives with him:

19 Every beast, every creeping thing, and every fowl, and whatsoever creepeth upon the earth, after their kinds, went forth out of the ark.

20 And Noah builded an altar unto the Lord; and took of every clean beast, and of every clean fowl, and offered burnt offerings on the altar.

21 And the Lord smelled a sweet savour; and the Lord said in his heart, I will not again curse the ground any more for man's sake; for the imagination of man's heart is evil from his youth; neither will I again smite any more every thing living, as I have done.

22 While the earth remaineth, seedtime and harvest, and cold and heat, and summer and winter, and day and night shall not cease.

NOTES

Thanksgiving and a Promise

Lesson Text: Genesis 8:15-22

Related Scriptures: Isaiah 54:6-10; Philippians 4:15-18

TIME: unknown   PLACE: unknown

GOLDEN TEXT—"Noah builded an altar unto the Lord; and took of every clean beast, and of every clean fowl, and offered burnt offerings on the altar" (Genesis 8:20).

Introduction

"God remembered Noah," Genesis 8:1 tells us, and a good thing that proved to be! When used of God, the word "remember" does not imply recalling to mind something that had been forgotten. It speaks of intentionally directing His thoughts toward someone with a view to action.

As a result, God did several things for Noah. The first was to send a wind over the earth to cause the waters to abate. After this had gone on for a while, the water was low enough for the ark to settle on the mountains of Ararat (vs. 4).

Forty days later, Noah opened the ark's window (vs. 6) and sent out a series of birds to see how things were drying out on earth. The raven flew constantly until it could find a place to land. The doves did not have that kind of stamina, however; so the first one returned soon after being sent out, and the second one returned with a fresh olive leaf that showed progress was being made in the drying process. Finally, the cover of the ark was removed, and the ground was seen to be dry (vs. 13).

LESSON OUTLINE

I. LEAVING THE ARK—
   Gen. 8:15-19

II. WORSHIPPING GOD—
   Gen. 8:20-22

Exposition: Verse by Verse

LEAVING THE ARK

GEN. 8:15 And God spake unto Noah, saying,

16 Go forth of the ark, thou, and thy wife, and thy sons, and thy sons' wives with thee.

17 Bring forth with thee every living thing that is with thee, of all flesh, both of fowl, and of cattle, and of every creeping thing that creepeth upon the earth; that they may breed abundantly in the earth, and be fruit-

ful, and multiply upon the earth.

18 And Noah went forth, and his sons, and his wife, and his sons' wives with him:

19 Every beast, every creeping thing, and every fowl, and whatsoever creepeth upon the earth, after their kinds, went forth out of the ark.

God's liberating command (Gen. 8:15-17). According to verse 13, the surface of the ground was dried by Noah's "six hundredth and first year, in the first month, the first day." By the twenty-seventh day of the second month, it was dry enough to be walked on (vs. 14), and God told him to exit the ark. So how long had he and his family been in there altogether?

The "fountains of the great deep" and the "windows of heaven" had burst forth on the seventeenth day of the second month of Noah's six hundredth year (Gen. 7:11). There had been a one-week wait on the ark before this happened (vs. 10). The ancient calendar had 30 days per month, so one year would have been 360 days. By adding the 7 days ahead of the Flood and the 10 days afterward before they exited, we arrive at a total of 377 days on the ark, amounting to one year and 17 days. On that day, God spoke to Noah, telling him to exit with his wife, sons, their wives, and all the animals, described as "every living thing that is with thee" (8:17).

God added His purpose in having saved all those animals. He wanted them to breed and reproduce abundantly on the earth, to increase rapidly in numbers. At that point in time, there were no other living creatures besides the ones exiting the ark, so this was God's reminder that He intended to repopulate the earth with every type of animal. This was a new beginning.

God would later threaten to destroy the nation of Israel and start over again with Moses (Exod. 32:7-10). Moses interceded with God, and this never happened. God did have a new beginning with Abraham when He called him out of Ur of the Chaldees and told him to leave his country and go to a new place (Gen. 12:1). Noah and Abraham, therefore, both represent new beginnings in the course of human history.

Noah's eager obedience (Gen. 8:18-19). These verses simply state that everyone and everything left the ark just as God had commanded. We should note that Noah and all with him did not even attempt to exit the ark until God commanded them to do so. He relied totally on God's perfect timing for this next move. Noah had removed the covering of the ark several weeks earlier (vs. 13), but he made no attempt to leave at that time. If he had, he would have found the ground dry on the surface but unstable underneath and not safe to navigate. Only God knew when the dry surface was accompanied by dry and solid ground underneath it.

We do not know whether Noah was feeling any sense of frustration over having to wait what seemed like extra time; if he was, he did not give in to the temptation to run ahead of God. Waiting on God is often difficult for us, especially when we think about something that needs to be done immediately. Every evidence shows that Noah waited patiently until he received God's assurance (implied in the command to leave) that the ground was safe for him, his family, and all the animals.

At this time, God gave some new regulations for mankind, in effect delegating some of His authority to man. The Lord laid down guidelines people were to continue to obey. At the same time, they were to obey human authorities that He would place over them.

Those guidelines are specified in the Noahic covenant in Genesis 9. The first major change was to permit the eating of certain animals under certain regulations (vss. 1-4). Prior to this, the diet had been strictly vegetarian for both man and beast. The second major change was related to the shedding of blood. No flesh was ever to be eaten with the blood (vs. 4), but God extended the principle to the shedding of the blood of people by other people (vss. 5-6). Transgressors would be held accountable by a strict penalty: "At the hand of every man's brother will I require the life of man. Whoso sheddeth man's blood, by man shall his blood be shed: for in the image of God made he man."

Here we see the establishment of human government and the delegation of some of God's authority to man. This is the beginning of what Paul would later explain in Romans 13:1-7, where he wrote that we are to be subject to those in authority over us. Jesus also spoke of this in Matthew 22:21.

WORSHIPPING GOD

20 And Noah builded an altar unto the Lord; and took of every clean beast, and of every clean fowl, and offered burnt offerings on the altar.

21 And the Lord smelled a sweet savour; and the Lord said in his heart, I will not again curse the ground any more for man's sake; for the imagination of man's heart is evil from his youth; neither will I again smite any more every thing living, as I have done.

22 While the earth remaineth, seedtime and harvest, and cold and heat, and summer and winter, and day and night shall not cease.

An altar (Gen. 8:20). This is the first altar mentioned in the Bible, and the fact that Noah offered burnt offerings on it indicates an act of worship. Many of the Old Testament saints built altars, so this was the beginning of what became a regular worship practice from then on. There is no record that God instructed Noah to do this, but it seems likely that some kind of instruction had been given for this worship practice, and it might well be that the information was verbally passed on to later saints.

Early altars were probably made with stones supporting an elevated flat top on which offerings were placed and sacrifices were made. Archaeologists have discovered altars used by pagan religions, showing that it eventually developing into a universal practice after Noah's time.

Abraham also built altars to the Lord. Concerning his first one, Genesis 12:7 says, "And the Lord appeared unto Abram, and said, Unto thy seed will I give this land: and there builded he an altar unto the Lord, who appeared unto him." A short time later, he built another altar. "And he removed from thence unto a mountain on the east of Bethel, and pitched his tent, having Bethel on the west, and Hai on the east: and there he builded an altar unto the Lord, and called upon the name of the Lord" (vs. 8). His most difficult one to build, however, was the one on which he thought he was going to sacrifice his son Isaac. "Abraham built an altar there, and laid the wood in order, and bound Isaac his son, and laid him on the altar upon the wood" (22:9).

One of the most notable accounts of an altar concerned the one Jacob built to offer sacrifices while on his way to Egypt (Gen. 46:1). God responded by reassuring him that it was His will for him to go to that foreign land. This incident reveals that through the use of an altar, these men were connecting directly with God in their worship. At Mount Sinai God gave specific and detailed instructions about the building of altars and their use.

After Noah built his altar, he offered burnt offerings of all the clean animals and birds. It is not until Leviticus 1 that we read the instructions for burnt offerings; how much Noah had been instructed about the practice we are not told. Neither are we told how he knew which creatures were clean and which were not. Noah's relationship with God evidently was so close and meaningful that somehow he knew what was pleasing to Him.

A soothing aroma (Gen. 8:21). The statement "the Lord smelled a sweet savour" indicates that God took notice, was pleased with Noah and his offering, and fully accepted his attention and worship. This act of worship on Noah's part was an expression of gratitude to God for the way He had taken care of them. God's response, therefore, was not simply acceptance of Noah's act of sacrificing but pleasure in his heart's attitude, which was even more important.

God will always be pleased with our worship. We should note, however, that Noah offered him the best that he had, and this should remind us to do the same. When God established the sacrificial system later with Moses, He saw to it that those who served Him received the best the people had to offer. They were to offer to the Levites the best from their crops and animals, who in turn gave a tenth of the best of those offerings to the priests, who in turn gave a tenth of the best of those offerings to the high priest.

God always deserves our best, not our leftovers. That is one reason we are taught to give the first of our income to Him before spending it on other things. It is also why we are to see that His servants are well cared for. Have you ever noticed that the churches that receive the richest blessings from God seem to be the ones that take the best care of their pastors and missionaries? When we care for His servants, we are offering God our best; He in turn responds as He smells the sweet savor of our sacrifices.

God was so moved in His heart by Noah's offerings that He made a promise to Himself: "I will not again curse the ground any more for man's sake; for the imagination of man's heart is evil from his youth; neither will I again smite any more every thing living, as I have done" (Gen. 8:21). Perhaps the most amazing part of this promise is that He would never again totally destroy mankind even though He knows his heart is continuously evil! That is great mercy in action.

God had cursed the ground when Adam sinned and again indirectly when Cain sinned and was cursed by God (Gen. 3:17-19; 4:12). His promise here not to curse the ground again probably refers to not destroying it again with water. Genesis 9:11 specifically states, "Neither shall all flesh be cut off any more by the waters of a flood; neither shall there any more be a flood to destroy the earth." In later days, God punished His people for their sins, but He has never again used a universal flood to do so.

Natural catastrophes do happen today, making us wonder whether they are not sometimes God's chastening. Ever since the Flood, "length of life was decreased; oceans were more extensive and therefore habitable land was reduced; there was a greater variation in climate; the crust of the earth was now unstable and subject to seismic activity; hurricanes, tornadoes, and thunderstorms would now buffet the earth; and local floods and ocean surfs would also cause destruction" (Anders, ed., *Holman Old Testament Commentary,* B&H).

A covenantal promise (Gen. 8:22). In spite of the recurrence of various natural disasters, no flood has ever again destroyed mankind. In fact, God accompanied His thoughts with the assurance that as long as the earth remains, there will continue to be cycles in which there will be planting and harvesting, cold and heat, winter and summer, and day and night. After the Flood, major changes occurred, but God was not going to allow them to destroy mankind.

This statement is in the form of a poem (somewhat similar to Genesis 12:1-3) and might have become a song in later days. Since the Flood had totally disrupted everything normal about life, this reassurance that it was not going to happen again was a guarantee that mankind would continue and would be able to survive.

Warren Wiersbe encourages us with these words: "The guarantee in Genesis 8:22 gives us hope and courage as we face an unknown future. Each time we go to bed for the night, or turn the calendar to a new month, we should be reminded that God is concerned about Planet Earth and its inhabitants. With the invention of the electric light and modern means of transportation and communication, our world has moved away from living by the cycles of nature established by God.

"We no longer go to bed at sundown and get up at sunrise; and if we don't like the weather where we are, we can quickly travel to a different climate. But if God were to dim the sun, rearrange the seasons, or tilt the earth at a different angle, our lives would be in jeopardy" (*The Bible Ex-position Commentary,* Cook). Even in natural hardships around us, we can trust our God to care for us without fail.

In closing, hear the words of Isaiah: "For this is as the waters of Noah unto me: for as I have sworn that the waters of Noah should no more go over the earth; so have I sworn that I would not be wroth with thee, nor rebuke thee. For the mountains shall depart, and the hills be removed; but my kindness shall not depart from thee, neither shall the covenant of my peace be removed, saith the Lord that hath mercy on thee" (Isa. 54:9-10).

—*Keith E. Eggert.*

QUESTIONS

1. How old was Noah when the Flood began, and how old was he when it ended?

2. How long had Noah and his companions been in the ark?

3. Who besides Noah represents a new beginning in history?

4. Why was it important not to exit the ark before God gave the command to do so?

5. What can we learn from the fact that Noah patiently waited for God's command?

6. Why did Noah build an altar, and what did he do with it?

7. What did Noah offer to God on his altar?

8. How did God respond to Noah's offerings?

9. What did God promise Himself upon seeing Noah's offerings?

10. What assurance did God make regarding man's future?

—*Keith E. Eggert.*

Preparing to Teach the Lesson

In our lesson this week, we learn how Noah remembered to thank God for bringing him and his family safely through the floods. We also learn that God responded with a promise to the whole world that is still true today. Study the lesson to find out more.

TODAY'S AIM

Facts: to show that righteous Noah was also a grateful man. In addition, we see God make a promise to the whole world that is still valid today.

Principle: to realize that God's goodness to us demands a response of gratitude.

Application: to turn to God in gratitude when we experience His goodness.

INTRODUCING THE LESSON

Have you done something for someone else, especially something that demanded a sacrifice on your part? You probably felt good about that. But when the person on the receiving end did not even say a word of thanks, you no doubt felt hurt and disappointed. Gratitude is a big part of our normal human response to good things that happen to us. This week we see a grateful Noah giving thanks to God for His protection and goodness.

DEVELOPING THE LESSON

1. God's command to exit the ark (Gen. 8:15-19). After spending more than a year in the ark, Noah received the go-ahead from God to leave, along with his wife and family. He was to release all the animals and birds so that they could roam freely and breed abundantly. The command "be fruitful, and multiply," first given to Adam and Eve (1:28), was now applied to the an-

imals. It would soon be repeated to Noah and his sons (9:1). God was giving mankind another chance to begin again.

Emphasize to your students that even in God's anger against sin, He showed His grace. He did not allow humanity to perish. He saw to mankind's survival and welfare.

Noah went out of the ark with his wife, his sons, and their wives, along with all the birds and animals and other living things that had taken refuge inside. They came out in their family groups, each with their own kind. Note the clear sense of order here, so characteristic of our God and the way He does things in our world. Encourage the class to visualize the parade that marched out and the sense of freedom that must have been felt. It was indeed a new beginning for all life on earth.

2. Noah's sacrifice of gratitude (Gen.8:20). During a crisis, it is natural for us to cry out to God. It is not as natural or common for us to thank God after a crisis. Immediately after leaving the ark, Noah—whom we have seen designated a righteous man—took one of every clean animal and bird and offered them to God on an altar that he constructed. It was not an afterthought for Noah. It was a deliberate first action. He remembered to thank God for his safety.

Discuss with the class the importance of giving thanks to God for all that He has done for us. Make sure to highlight how Noah gave all the credit to God for their safety during the Flood. How often do we remember to thank God for what He has done in our lives? Emphasize that Noah's show of gratitude by way of his sacrifice was the first thing he did upon stepping onto dry land after the Flood.

3. God's response to Noah (Gen. 8:21-22). God loves thankful people. Thankful people are humble people—they credit their circumstances to the God who keeps them safe. When Noah offered the sacrifice, the fire and smoke it produced must have been awesome. We read that the Lord "smelled a sweet savour." Some would say that Noah's action amounted to an utter waste of resources. But Noah saw that an offering to God is never a waste. In making the sacrifice, he merely sought to honor his Lord.

Discuss with the class the sacrifices we make every day to honor our God and whether He is pleased with what we do in response to His goodness to us.

In response to Noah's offering, we read that the Lord made a promise to Himself. He affirmed that even though man's thoughts and actions are evil from the day that he is born, He would never again curse the earth or destroy the earth as He had done at that time. It is true that we do see floods today, but they are never worldwide like the Great Flood of Noah's time. That is God's promise. It is also a mark of His grace that He does not destroy the human race even though He knows that our ways are evil.

Keeping your student's attention on our place among humanity in general, discuss how God knows our thoughts and our ways yet chooses to show us His mercy by not destroying us completely. Instead, He gives us His promises to stand on. He can be trusted to protect us if we choose to take shelter in His grace and trust our lives to Christ.

Then we read that God adds a second part to His decision. It was the sign of a new beginning for the earth.

God said that as long as the earth remains, there would be seedtime and harvest, cold and heat, summer and winter, and day and night. It is interesting that we take all of these for granted. We often forget that God put these in place so that we can enjoy His renewed earth. We get to rest, and we get to work. God provides us with the seasons to meet our daily needs. Our dependence is on Him alone, for He set these things in place to sustain us on His earth.

ILLUSTRATING THE LESSON

God's goodness demands our response of thanksgiving to Him.

GOD IS GOOD

GIVE THANKS

CONCLUDING THE LESSON

We learn from Noah's life that our safety comes from God. He is the one who sustains us through all the crises of life that come our way. It is through His promises, however, that we are sustained. These promises are found in His Word, and they have been written down for our learning and for our benefit. We must always remember to thank our God for His protection.

ANTICIPATING THE NEXT LESSON.

Next week begins a new quarter. It is titled "God Comes to Earth." The quarter will look at Christ's coming, His mission, and His authority. The first lesson will focus on Isaiah 7:1-4, 7-16.

—A. Koshy Muthalaly.

PRACTICAL POINTS

1. Waiting is difficult, but we trust God, who knows the road ahead (Gen. 8:15).
2. Caring for God's creation honors Him (vs. 16).
3. Only God can restore what sin has destroyed (vs. 17).
4. God protects us as we follow His direction and submit to His timing (vss. 18-19).
5. As the One who delivers us from our trials, God deserves our worship (vs. 20).
6. Worship leads us to see our sins in the light of God's holiness, grace, and glory (vs. 21).
7. God shows faithfulness to mankind, and believers respond to Him with praise and worship (vs. 22).

—Cheryl Y. Powell.

RESEARCH AND DISCUSSION

1. How is it significant that Noah and his family remained on the ark until God gave the command to leave?
2. Why is waiting so difficult?
3. What does it mean to worship God? What are some common misunderstandings about worship?
4. In what ways are worship and thanksgiving crucial steps in the process of being restored after we have gone through a trial?
5. What is the difference between a covenant and a contract?
6. How do you know that God is faithful?

—Cheryl Y. Powell.

ILLUSTRATED HIGH POINTS

Noah builded an altar

Prayer highly laced with praise and thanksgiving must have been a daily experience for Noah during his time on the ark. As he disembarked on dry land, he intensified his gratitude with burnt offerings.

Our church's tradition at our Thanksgiving eve service is to invite the congregation to give testimonies of God's goodness. Many bring an object to illustrate their gratitude—a family picture, a diploma, car keys, a baby toy—something associated with their thanksgiving. The words are always good, but the objects add an impact just as Noah's offerings magnified his thankfulness.

I will

Some time ago a toy company in the United Stated offered a new toy. It was an action figure called Invisible Jim. Why was it called that? Because all you got was an empty package. There was no Jim because he was invisible. Evidently, people actually paid money to buy nothing.

Sadly, the same thing has been going on for a long time as people buy into the empty promises of Satan.

God is ever faithful to His promises. He never again will destroy the world with a flood.

Man's heart is evil

A Christian father claimed he was moving his family to a new area because of the present negative influences on his son. It should not be shocking that it was not much different in the new location.

Noah and his family faced a new beginning without the corrupting influences of an evil society. But they were still sinners by nature.

—David A. Hamburg.

Golden Text Illuminated

"Noah builded an altar unto the Lord; and took of every clean beast, and of every clean fowl, and offered burnt offerings on the altar" (Genesis 8:20).

In our area of Ohio, we get some pretty nasty summer storms. We are then subject to high winds, driving rain, and lightning. These are normal, and we are usually not unduly alarmed by them.

I was driving home after one of these storms one day and happened to glance up into the sky. There above me was something so beautiful that it took my breath away. I was awed at the sight of a perfectly formed double rainbow. I pulled into my driveway and sat in my car a moment, gazing as it gently faded.

In our world, we tend to overlook the wonder of a rainbow. We take it for granted, glancing at it and then going on with our lives.

Place yourself in Noah's shoes. You have spent many days on a ship, surrounded by animals needing your attention. Perhaps tempers are flaring as your family members start to irritate one another. Finally, the ark reaches ground.

Walking down the gangplank, you realize that the world you left behind is gone. Familiar people and familiar towns no longer exist. As the animals leave your lifeboat, you know you are starting over. More than that, the world you are stepping into has been purified, freed (for now at least) from the troubles of ages past.

These truths could elicit only one response from Noah. Before he did anything else, he built an altar and offered praise to God for His mercy.

While Noah praised God, he looked up to the sky. He must have marveled at a sight he had not seen before. As he looked at the colors splashing across the heavens, he heard God speaking once more of a covenant (Gen. 9:12-17).

Even though we tend to forget it, that covenant endures to this day. Because our God does not change His mind (cf. Num. 23:19), that promise remains true. As a wedding ring is a symbol of a promise, so the rainbow is also symbolic of God's promise from long ago.

As we have said, however, it is easy to forget about this promise. When I saw the double rainbow, it made me wonder, *Is this a promise that God has remembered His original promise? Is He reassuring me that He has not forgotten?* I think that we need reassurance at times.

When was the last time you thought about God's rainbow promise from long ago? We may put it into the back of our minds as something given to someone in history. In fact, it applies to us as a great demonstration of God's mercy.

When we see the rainbow, it is often after the strongest rains. It appears to remind us that God has sealed His promise and will keep it (cf. Gen. 9:13). This was a reason for Noah to rejoice.

We sometimes face the storms of life. When the deluge threatens to engulf us, it is easy to feel overwhelmed. We need to remember that Christ has gained victory for us (Col. 2:15). Because of this, we need not fear (John 14:27). His death and resurrection seals the victory of His people.

The next time you look at a rainbow, what will you remember? How about the cross? Both the rainbow and the cross are symbols of God's promises that still ring true. His promises give us reasons to offer Him praise.

—*Jennifer Francis.*

Heart of the Lesson

When my maternal grandparents died, my mother sorted through their possessions, which had accumulated over sixty-five years, as she settled their estate. When cleaning out a closet one day, Mom found a stack of envelopes, which she later gave to me.

For more than twenty-five years, Grandma had been saving letters and cards from me. Many were thank-you cards I had written in response to Christmas gifts from her and Grandpa. Apparently, my expressions of gratitude had meant much to them.

1. Disembarking from the ark (Gen. 8:15-19). After Noah had spent more than a year on the ark, the floodwaters had receded. God finally told Noah to move his family and the animals out of the ark. No doubt Noah and his family had longed for this day. The animals and birds were to multiply and repopulate the earth, and Noah would be the father of all future generations of humanity.

Again Noah and his family obeyed God. After so long a time on the ark, standing on firm ground must have felt strange but wonderful. They had landed in the mountains of Ararat in modern-day Turkey. But did they recognize the world around them? Did any vegetation look familiar? Where would they live? I wonder whether Noah and his family felt a twinge of sadness as they watched the pairs of clean and unclean animals leave the ark forever to find new homes and raise families.

2. Offering thanks to God (Gen. 8:20). Noah was a righteous man, and he also was a grateful man. The first thing he did after leaving the ark was to build an altar to God. There he sacrificed as a burnt offering one animal from each kind of clean animal on the ark.

Keil and Delitzsch note that a burnt offering's flame reduced the essence of the animal to a vapor. "When man presented a sacrifice in his own stead, his inmost being, his spirit, and his heart ascended to God in the vapour, and the sacrifice brought the feeling of his heart before God" (*Commentary on the Old Testament,* Eerdmans).

In this act of worship and thanksgiving, Noah was thanking God for preserving his family's lives on the ark and expressing his trust in God as he and his family repopulated the earth.

3. Promising a future for humanity (Gen. 8:21-22). As the smoke rose, what God sensed most was Noah's trust and love in making the sacrifice. God declared that He would never again destroy all living creatures as He just had done—even though man's heart is evil from his youth. Then God uttered this beautiful, poetic promise: "While the earth remaineth, seedtime and harvest, and cold and heat, and summer and winter, and day and night shall not cease." There would be no cataclysmic event on a planetary scale until Christ returns and God creates the new heavens and new earth.

This passage emphasizes Noah's thankfulness and God's acceptance of his worship, which resulted in a promise to all future generations. Today we no longer offer burnt offerings; Jesus' death on the cross fulfilled and ended the Old Testament sacrificial system. But God still delights when we thank Him. Our prayers rise like incense around His throne. Our gifts to God of our time and treasure waft upward like the aroma of Noah's offering. Take time each day to thank God for what He is doing in your life. Share your praise with others. Jot down His blessings to help you see His work in your life.

—*Ann Staatz.*

World Missions

If I were to give an offering of thanks for God's deliverance from evil, my thanks would be for Leyla (name changed for safety). My husband and I served in a Muslim country for several years, but disease brought us permanently back to the United States. We wondered why God had allowed this. Why all those years of studying language and culture and Islam? How could that be useful for our new life in small-town North Carolina?

God led us to a wonderful ministry called Search for Jesus (www.search-forjesus.net), where over 500 volunteers answer questions from seekers around the world. We were chosen to be sent the questions from Muslims. What a gift! This was a ministry I could do despite my disease.

And then God sent me Leyla. Leyla lives in the very country we served. When English gets difficult for her, she writes in her language, the only language besides English I know.

Leyla lives in a Muslim village in a Muslim family. She accepted Christ, and she is the only person in her village who is Christian.

"If my husband knows he will leave me. So till today I hide my faith to my family. . . . I'm so glad you help me."

She asked questions about living in Christ. What are the rules about wearing head coverings? What is the meaning of the Sabbath? What does the Bible mean when it says to love our enemies?

"I'm so happy today," she wrote. "I feel no fear like before because I commit my life for Him. I believe He will never leave me."

"Here is no Christian. I just can pray everytime to make me strong."

When Leyla's family found out about her faith in Christ, they threatened to kick her out of the village and told her she would never be allowed to see her seven-year-old son again. They brought in the Muslim religious leader, who pressured her to return to Islam. Leyla was aware that in Islam, people who convert away from it are to be killed. The religious leader affirmed that this is what Islam teaches.

After that, people from her village came to try to convince her to give up her faith in Christ.

"You know my sister try to find out about Jesus Christ," she wrote. "I showed her actions of Muhammad and compared to actions of Jesus Christ." Leyla loves how Jesus values women and teaches husbands to love their wives. Leyla's husband threatens to abandon her if she continues to profess Christ. He was scheduled to return home last month. I have not heard from Leyla in several weeks. It is possible something has happened to her. I continue to pray.

My last message from Leyla said this: "I wanna live in holy life like you. I don't wanna waste my time. Pray for me God always guides me in holy life. . . . Lots of love from your friend."

I give thanks to God for sending me the treasure of knowing Leyla, and am in awe of the God who reached into that fully Muslim village and called out one woman to know Him. That is the hope of missions. That is the hope of the gospel of Jesus Christ.

Wherever Leyla is now, whatever has happened to her, I know I will see her in heaven, and we will give thanks together to the God who adopted both of us as His own.

—Kimberly Rae.

The Jewish Aspect

When the waters of the Flood receded and the earth was dry, God told Noah to leave the ark with every living thing that was with him. In the process of replenishing the created order that He had judged with destruction, God repeated His earlier words of blessing on mankind: "Be fruitful, and multiply, and replenish the earth" (Gen.9:1; cf. 1:22). Noah, with a heart full of thankfulness, then obeyed God's command to "go forth of the ark" (8:16).

After Noah and his family and every living thing left the ark, one of the first things that he did was build an altar and offer a sacrifice of every clean animal that was on the ark. The Hebrew word for altar is *mizbeah.* It is related to the verb to "slaughter" or "sacrifice." Noah's altar is the first altar mentioned in the Bible. The English word "altar" signifies a high place—the altar was commonly a raised structure or mound of earth or stones.

The type of sacrifice that Noah offered was later called a "freewill offering" in the Mosaic Law (Lev. 22:17-25). In building this altar, Noah determined to consecrate the earth to God, who had been the object of the worship of his family. By doing so, he provided for future generations a central spot and sanctuary. The dominant thought of Noah's freewill offering was to consecrate his life to God by commencing it with worship. Noah renewed the worship of God, preserved it by his example, and thanked God for the fact that He had preserved him and his family.

A freewill offering was an offering of thanksgiving voluntarily given to God. Freewill offerings of clean animals in the Mosaic Law could be made at any time and were usually offered around God's holy days to give thanks for a specific blessing. These burnt offerings are sometimes spoken of as ascending to God, a reference to the ascension of the smoke of the sacrifice to heaven.

Noah offered burnt offerings of every clean beast and every clean fowl (Gen. 8:20), and God accepted Noah's offering. The sacrifice greatly pleased God. Noah received blessings for himself and for all mankind. The Lord's heart was touched by this unselfish act. The sacrifice that Noah made reconciled God to man. The Lord regarded this offerings as a "sweet savour" (vs. 21), a sweet smell, or "a smell of satisfaction."

How can the burning of sacrifices be pleasant to God, who does not literally smell aromas in the first place? The phrase is obviously metaphorical, referring to God's pleasure in the offered worship. In this instance there may also be a play on words between the name of Noah and the similar-sounding word for "sweet savour." "Noah" means "rest," and with the Flood now past, perhaps "God felt rest, peace and pleasure because the Noah that He loved felt rest, peace and pleasure" ("Word Study—Sweet Savor," www.chaimbentorah.com).

God said that "the imagination of man's heart is evil from his youth" but promised, "neither will I again smite any more every thing living, as I have done" (Gen. 8:21). And in verse 22, He further promised that the seasons would continue as long as the earth remained. He would not engage the world in global catastrophe by flood again. "In a little wrath I hid my face from thee for a moment; but with everlasting kindness will I have mercy on thee, saith the Lord thy Redeemer" (Isa. 54:8).

—*Deborah Markowitz Solan.*

Guiding the Superintendent

For over a year (Gen. 8:13); Noah, his family, and the animals were confined to the ark. However, nothing on earth lasts forever—and that included even the Noahic Flood. Eventually, it was time for them to exit the ark. Noah was very grateful to God for His deliverance.

DEVOTIONAL OUTLINE

1. God's command (Gen. 8:15-19). God had commanded all to enter the ark (7:1-4), and now He commanded all to leave the ark. Noah was told to bring forth the animals on the ark so that they might repopulate the earth. This command is reminiscent of the original mandate to fill the earth that was given at Creation (Gen. 1:20-28). In obedience to God's command, every one left the ark (8:18-19).

2. God's promise (Gen. 8:20-22). One of the first things that Noah did after leaving the ark was to offer a sacrifice to God out of thanks and gratitude. The additional clean animals seem to have been intended for this very purpose (7:2). In Romans the apostle Paul reminds us that mankind's walk away from God started with a lack of gratitude to Him (1:21).

Using the sacrifice language of Leviticus, the writer informs us that God "smelled a sweet savour" (Gen. 8:21) in Noah's sacrifice. This is the language of acceptance. God was pleased with the offering.

God then said in His heart that He would never again curse the ground; that is, He would never again use floodwaters to deal with man's evil heart—"neither will I again smite any more every thing living" (Gen. 8:21). God was never under the illusion that evil would not find its way into the human heart (Ps. 51:5). God would send His Son to deal once and for all with man's evil heart (Heb. 9:28).

The promise that there will never again be a universal flood continues with God's pledge that the cycle of seasons will continue (Gen. 8:22). As long as the earth remains, there will be "seedtime and harvest, and cold and heat, and summer and winter, and day and night shall not cease."

CHILDREN'S CORNER

text: **II Kings 6:8-23**
title: **Faith Without Fear**

Every attempt by Syria to raid its neighbor was met by a prepared Israelite army, for Elisha was telling the Israelite king every word the Syrian king spoke on the matter.

When he found out that Elisha was in the town of Dothan, the Syrian king sent his army to surround the city and capture Elisha. When he saw the threatening army surround the city, a servant of Elisha was greatly perplexed until he prayed that the servant's eyes would be opened to see God's surrounding armies.

After praying that the Syrian army be blinded, Elisha went out and volunteered to lead them to the one they were seeking—himself. Once he had them inside the city of Samaria, Elisha prayed again that their eyes would be opened. Instead of killing his prisoners of war, however, Elisha fed them and sent them on their way.

As a result, there was a temporary end of hostilities between the two countries.

Elisha's dealing with the Syrian army are an example for us today; trust in God to defend you and show mercy and goodness to your enemies.

—*Martin R. Dahlquist.*

made sense to me. The Cenozoic era was the most recent, so obviously the fossils in that layer would not be as old as, say, the Paleozoic era.

But this question nagged at my thought processes: "If you date the fossil by the layer it is in, how do you date the layer?" I found this answer on the next page: "The layer is dated by the fossil that is in it." I was confused.

You date the fossil by the layer that it is in, but you date the layer by the fossil that is in it? I remember quietly closing the book and thinking, "I am not that stupid."

That experience forced me to set out on an educational quest that allowed me to discover that science is not as objective as I had once believed. Scientists can be just as biased in their observation and interpretation of the facts as can anyone. Remember, it was the scientific community that opposed Galileo. Scientists were skeptical of Louis Pasteur's explanation of microorganisms called bacteria. Science usually opposes those who turn against its prevailing standard of truth.

Those who study the Bible are often described as people who accept Scripture by faith as though facts were not important. However, faith is only as good as the facts on which it stands. One may have faith that he or she can fly, but the facts deny it.

Facts are not the enemy of Bible believers. If the Bible is the Word of God, which it is, then it can stand up to any line of questioning. Sixty-six books written over a period of fifteen hundred years by over forty different authors can be trusted. The Bible not only claims to be God's love letter to the world, but it also can be examined and authenticated scientifically, historically, and philosophically. It has withstood every test.

While it is true that God's Word must be accepted by faith, it does not mean that faith is accepting tenets without facts.

In Need of Grace

JOE FALKNER

Think about it. There are so many words that Christians regularly use to describe various aspects of their faith, yet many times they are not able to define the concept behind those words. Those words include "love," "faith," "hope," "mercy," and "grace."

Let us look at the word "grace." Genesis 6 describes a time in human history when the depraved notions and actions of men were so great that God decided to destroy the entire world. Although there are differences of opinion as to what kind of sin is being described in Genesis 6, the main point is hard to miss. Sin had so permeated the human race that every thought of men's hearts was to do evil continually. Justice demanded the outpouring of God's wrath upon the entire world. However, grace kept the human race alive through one family.

"But Noah found grace in the eyes of the Lord" (Gen. 6:8). The question is simple: what did Noah find? Yes, he found grace; but what is grace? What does the concept mean? How significant is grace to the program of God for this sinful world?

Perhaps it is best to contrast grace with mercy. They are two sides of the same coin. Mercy means that God does not give us what we deserve. Grace, on the other hand, means that God gives us what we do not deserve. It is apparent from those first chapters of Genesis that the only thing mankind really deserved was harsh judgment. However, in the midst of judgment, God's grace shone most brightly.

Some theologians of liberal persuasion contend that there are two Gods presented in the Bible. There is a God of wrath in the Old Testament and a God of mercy, grace, and love in the New Testament.

One can certainly observe God's wrath throughout the Old Testament. Nowhere does it seem more obvious than in Genesis 6, where God decided to destroy the world because of the infiltration of sin. But in the very decision to show wrath, God chose to show grace to a man of faith. "And the Lord said, I will destroy man whom I have created from the face of the earth; both man, and beast, and the creeping thing, and the fowls of the air; for it repenteth me that I have made them" (vs. 7).

Noah, like all those before him and after him, was a sinner who fell short of the glory of God (cf. Rom. 3:23). Yet God observed his faith in the midst of a perverse generation. He demonstrated His grace to Noah and his family because of Noah's faith. Yes, He is a God of wrath, but He is also a God of unconditional love.

The New Testament certainly emphasizes the love of God, but it also describes His wrath in judgment against sin.

The Apostle Paul highlighted God's judgment in Ephesians 5:6: "Let no man deceive you with vain words: for because of these things cometh the wrath of God upon the children of dis-

obedience." Of course, the wrath of God is greatly evident in the book of Revelation, where the Apostle John describes the end of human history with the outpouring of God's judgment.

The problem is that many doctrinal errors have arisen from the attempt to emphasize one of God's attributes over others. Throughout the history of the church, false teachers have emphasized God's judgment over His grace. Such teaching leads to legalism and a life of dos and don'ts. Human beings become human doings, and the security of the believer in his relationship with God is denied. No one can measure up. False teachers use such teaching as a way to control people.

They might highlight the "nasty nine," the "filthy five," and the "terrible ten" things that a Christian cannot do if he wants to continue to be a Christian. The password of such systems is "don't."

The opposite doctrinal error highlights the teaching of other false teachers. There are many who place a great emphasis on God's love with no regard for His holiness. Grace morphs into licentiousness, and God becomes a lenient grandfather in the sky stroking a long white beard and murmuring, "Oh, well, boys will be boys."

In our present world that seems to be racing toward destruction with it fingers in its ears, it is easy for Christians to grow despondent and to miss the impact of grace on their daily lives. While we are grateful to have found grace in the eyes of the Lord as did Noah, we sometimes forget that the same grace that saved him and his family also sustained him as he prepared the ark and preached righteousness (cf. II Pet. 2:5). Grace not only saved Paul on the road to Damascus, but it also strengthened him as he wrestled with his "thorn in the flesh" (II Cor. 12:7). The Lord told Paul, "My grace is sufficient for thee: for my strength is made perfect in weakness. Most gladly therefore will I rather glory in my infirmities, that the power of Christ may rest upon me" (vs. 9).

We must not relegate grace to the dusty corners of a theological library shelf or the pages of a wornout book on doctrine. We should consider grace as a necessity for our existence. It not only offers a "get out of jail free" card for the future, but it also provides a menu for daily living. Are you feeling weak? God's grace has the strength you need. Have you fallen short of wisdom lately? His grace provides that too. Are you running on empty in the perseverance category? God's grace can provide the second wind to get you back into the race and running to the end. It has been several thousand years since the days of Noah, and God has freely dispensed grace to those who were in need. However, realize that His supply of grace has not yet run dry.

TOPICS FOR NEXT QUARTER

PARAGRAPHS ON PLACES AND PEOPLE

GARDEN OF EDEN

The Garden of Eden was the lush, beautiful area that God created as the home for the first man and woman, Adam and Eve. While the Genesis narrative regarding Eden's creation and mankind's expulsion from that paradise is well known, the garden's precise location is still a mystery.

Genesis 2:8 mentions the garden being "eastward," representing the general area of Mesopotamia. Perhaps the best clue is the mention of the Tigris (Hiddekel) and Euphrates rivers in Genesis 2:14. The Pishon (Pison) and Gihon Rivers, however, have not been identified. It is likely, then, that the Garden of Eden was either near the headwaters of the Tigris and Euphrates or near the mouth of the Euphrates. The cherubim, flaming sword, and tree of life have since vacated the area.

NOD

"The land of Nod" (Gen. 4:16) is where Cain lived after murdering his brother Abel and leaving the Lord's presence. Nod was "east of Eden," but its location is otherwise difficult to identify.

Some claim that the location of this ancient refuge for Cain rests in southwest Iran near the Persian Gulf. "Nod" means "wandering," or "exile," and thus perfectly represents Cain's life subsequent to committing mankind's first murder and separating himself from the Lord and sacrifices that pleased Him. May Nod remind us of such separation and compel us toward God's presence.

ADAM

Adam is the first man ever created. His name means "ruddy," or "earth," and reflects the special kind of creation God employed for him, forming him carefully from dust and breathing "into his nostrils the breath of life" (Gen. 2:7).

While the Old Testament describes in detail Adam's sin and the Fall of man through narrative, the New Testament bears important gospel lessons that develop a comparison and contrast between Adam and Jesus. Jesus is the new and better Adam insomuch that, though they were both human, Jesus was both human *and* divine. Adam brought death into the world through sin, but Jesus brought life through His death. We inherit through Adam a sin nature, but we inherit through Christ new birth and new life through the Holy Spirit by faith (cf. Rom. 5).

EVE

Eve is the second human being God created and the first woman. Her name means "living" and represents her position as the first mother.

Eve's sin is referenced several times negatively in the New Testament. In II Corinthians 11:3, Paul warned the Corinthian church that they might be led astray as Eve was when she was seduced by the serpent's temptations (cf. Gen. 3). Moreover, her sin was referred to in Paul's instructions to Timothy that women should not hold authority over men in the church (I Tim. 2:13-14). However, in verse 15, Paul reflected on Edenic qualities of spiritual purity. One of the possible ways to view this verse is to see that Paul encouraged women to focus on living out biblical character qualities and enjoying the blessings of motherhood, which reflect what God purposed for Eve before her sin.

—J.A. Littler.

Daily Bible Readings for Home Study and Worship

(Readings are for the week previous to the lesson topics.)

1. September 2. The First Days of Creation

M — Laying the Earth's Foundation. Job 38:1-11.
T — The Mysteries of Creation. Job 38:12-21.
W — Wisdom at the Beginning. Prov. 8:22-31.
T — The Outer Fringes of His Work. Job 26:7-14.
F — Nothing Created Without Him. John 1:1-10.
S — All Things Created by Him. Col. 1:15-20.
S — In the Beginning God. Gen. 1:1-13.

2. September 9. Creations in Sky, Sea, and Land

M — The Heavens Declare His Glory. Ps. 19:1-6.
T — Praise from the Heavens and Earth. Ps. 148:1-12.
W — How Vast Are His Works. Ps. 104:24-30.
T — Leviathan the Unparalleled. Job 41:1-11.
F — The Power of Behemoth. Job 40:15-24.
S — All Creatures Cared For by the Creator. Ps. 104:10-22.
S — All Life Created by God. Gen. 1:14-25.

3. September 16. The First Man

M — Crowned with Glory and Honor. Ps. 8:1-9.
T — From the Dust of the Earth. I Cor. 15:45-50.
W — In Him We Have Our Being. Acts 17:24-28.
T — Be Fruitful and Increase. Gen. 9:1-7.
F — Turn to the Creator of All. Isa. 45:18-22.
S — Creation Finished in Six Days. Exod. 20:8-11.
S — God's Work Completed. Gen. 1:26—2:3.

4. September 23. Man's First Home

M — God's Storehouses of Snow. Job 38:22-30.
T — The Lord Who Gives Water. Ps. 65:9-13.
W — Deserts to Be Made like Eden. Isa. 51:1-6.
T — An Abundantly Watered Land. Gen. 13:5-13.
F — Water and Trees for Healing. Ezek. 47:6-12.
S — The Eternal Home of the Redeemed. Rev. 22:1-6.
S — Adam's Home in Eden. Gen. 2:4-14.

5. September 30. A Suitable Helper for Adam

M — Strength in Union. Eccles. 4:7-12.
T — A Noble Wife. Prov. 31:10-22.
W — A Woman Worthy of Praise. Prov. 31:23-31.
T — God's Design for Marriage. Matt. 19:3-9.
F — The Glory of the Woman. I Cor. 11:3-12.
S — A Picture of Christ and the Church. Eph. 5:22-33.
S — The First Marriage. Gen. 2:15-25.

6. October 7. A Reckless Choice

M — The Father of Lies. John 8:42-47.
T — A Deceiving Angel. II Cor. 11:1-15.
W — The Source of Temptation. Jas. 1:13-18.
T — The Lust of the World. I John 2:12-17.
F — No Place to Hide from God. Ps. 139:1-12.
S — Jesus' Victory over the Tempter. Matt. 4:1-11.
S — Mankind's First Sin. Gen. 3:1-13.

7. October 14. Dreadful Consequences

M — Sin Is of the Devil. I John 3:7-10.
T — The Earth Defiled. Isa. 24:1-13.
W — Death Came by Sin. Rom. 5:12-19.

T — Creation in Bondage. Rom. 8:18-25.
F — The Woman and the Dragon. Rev. 12:1-9.
S — Satan Crushed Underfoot. Rom. 16:17-20.
S — Sin's Curse. Gen. 3:14-24.

8. October 21. The First Murder

M — The Grain Offering. Lev. 2:1-10.
T — The Fellowship Offering. Lev. 3:1-11.
W — Unacceptable Offerings. Isa. 1:10-17.
T — The Hatred of the World. John 15:19-25.
F — Shedding the Blood of the Righteous. Matt. 23:29-36.
S — The Person God Accepts. Acts 10:34-43.
S — The Curse on Cain. Gen. 4:1-16.

9. October 28. Worldwide Wickedness

M — Descent into Wickedness. Rom. 1:21-32.
T — None Righteous. Rom. 3:9-18.
W — The Land Made Desolate. Jer. 4:23-28.
T — Sweeping Judgment. Zeph. 1:4-13.
F — Deliverance amid Destruction. Ps. 37:34-40.
S — The Grace That Brings Salvation. Titus 2:11-15.
S — Wickedness, Judgment, and Grace. Gen. 6:1-10.

10. November 4. Preparation for Deliverance

M — All Are Corrupt. Ps. 14:1-6.
T — The End Has Come. Ezek. 7:1-14.
W — Vessels of Wrath. Rom. 9:18-26.
T — In the Days of Noah. I Pet. 3:15-22.
F — Our Help and Shield. Ps. 33:13-22.
S — Faith in God's Promises. Heb. 11:7-16.
S — Instructions for the Ark. Gen. 6:11-22.

11. November 11. Safety in the Ark

M — The Shelter of the Most High. Ps. 91:1-10.
T — Protected from Death. Exod. 12:21-30.
W — God's Mark of Protection. Ezek. 9:3-10.
T — Those Who Heed His Words. Matt. 7:21-27.
F — Few That Are Saved. Luke 13:22-30.
S — The Lord Knows How to Deliver. II Pet. 2:4-9.
S — Entering the Ark. Gen. 7:1-10.

12. November 18. The Great Flood

M — Overthrown in the Sea. Exod. 14:26-31.
T — Overflown in a Flood. Job 22:12-16.
W — Moses' Forty Days with God. Deut. 9:8-19.
T — Deliver Me from Deep Waters. Ps. 69:13-18.
F — So Shall His Coming Be. Matt. 24:34-42.
S — Judgments by Water and Fire. II Pet. 3:2-7.
S — The Earth Covered by Water. Gen. 7:11-24.

13. November 25. Thanksgiving and a Promise

M — He Holds the Clouds. Job 36:26-33.
T — A Boundary Set for the Water. Ps. 104:5-9.
W — Wrath Followed by Mercy. Isa. 54:6-10.
T — Blessing After Affliction. Ps. 107:38-43.
F — A Sweet Savour to the Lord. Phil. 4:14-19.
S — A Covenant with Day and Night. Jer. 33:19-26.
S — A New Start on the Earth. Gen. 8:15-22.

REVIEW

What have you learned this quarter?

Can you answer these questions?

Beginnings

UNIT I: The Beginning of the World

September 2

The First Days of Creation

1. In the summary statement of Genesis 1:1, what does the "beginning" refer to?
2. What does the initial mention of God teach us about Him?
3. What was the earth like when God first created it?
4. What does God's naming of the things in creation show us?
5. What important truth do we see in the creation of seed-bearing vegetation?

September 9

Creations in Sky, Sea, and Land

1. How does the fourth day of Creation parallel the first?
2. What are the four purposes in creating the luminaries?
3. What are the two primary luminaries, and what specifically were they created to do?
4. What was created on day six?
5. What three categories of animals were created that day?

September 16

The First Man

1. In what way are we created in the image of God, and what position does this put us in?
2. In blessing mankind, what command did God give?
3. What was the perfect animal world like, and when will we see this again?
4. How did God evaluate His completed work?
5. Why did God rest?

UNIT II: The Beginning of Human History

September 23

Man's First Home

1. What two reasons are given for there being no plant life?
2. Where did the necessary moisture come from for the plants?
3. What does the repeated use of the words "LORD God" indicate about our relationship with Him?
4. What does Genesis 2 add about how God created Adam?

September 30

A Suitable Helper for Adam

1. What responsibilities did God give Adam in the garden?
2. What did God mean by the statement "it is not good" (Gen. 2:18)?
3. How did God meet Adam's need, and how did Adam respond afterward?
4. What guidelines do we find for marriage in the relationship between Adam and Eve?

October 7

A Reckless Choice

1. On what did Satan concentrate his efforts in attempting to get Eve to fall into sin?
2. What did Satan say that was a direct lie about God's words?
3. What changed for Adam and Eve after they ate the fruit?
4. How do we know Adam and Eve felt alienated from God?

October 14
Dreadful Consequences

1. Why is a purely human perspective insufficient in speaking of God's plans for His creation?
2. Why was the serpent uniquely cursed among all creation? What happened to it?
3. What prophetic significance is found in Genesis 3:15?
4. What was now in store for the woman in the area of childbearing and marriage?

October 21
The First Murder

1. What do Eve's names for her sons indicate about her understanding of God?
2. What are some explanations for why God rejected Cain and his offering?
3. Despite His rejection of the sacrifice, what did God graciously make clear to Cain?
4. What warning did God give Cain about sin that we also need to hear?

UNIT III: Cataclysm and a New Beginning

October 28
Worldwide Wickedness

1. Why would the multiplication of people happen so easily before and during Noah's day?
2. What did God say about His Spirit in those days?
3. How did God describe the depth of wickedness on earth then?
4. What did God decide He had to do to deal with this?

November 4
Preparation for Deliverance

1. What cause-and-effect relationship is presented to us in this text?
2. What did God tell Noah that He was about to do?
3. In what way is the ark a type of Jesus Christ?
4. What did God finally explain He was going to do, and what would this accomplish?

November 11
Safety in the Ark

1. How is Noah a prime example of a person who lives by faith?
2. What does Genesis 7:1 say about Noah that led to God's protection of him through the Flood?
3. What is the stated purpose for sparing the animals?
4. Why would rain have been an unknown concept to Noah and the people of that time?

November 18
The Great Flood

1. What two sources of water brought about the Flood?
2. What categories of animals were included in the ark, and how did they get there?
3. What happened to the ark as the waters began to rise?
4. How are the waters portrayed in the word "prevailed" (Gen. 7:19)?

November 25
Thanksgiving and a Promise

1. How long had Noah and his companions been in the ark?
2. Why did Noah build an altar, and what did he do with it?
3. What did Noah offer to God on his altar?
4. How did God respond to Noah's offerings?